HISTORY OF BROADCASTING: Radio to Television

World Broadcast Advertising

Four Reports

ARNO PRESS and THE NEW YORK TIMES

New York • 1971

Reprint Edition 1971 by Arno Press Inc.

Reprinted from a copy in The State Historical Society of Wisconsin Library

LC# 72-161183
ISBN 0-405-03586-1

HISTORY OF BROADCASTING: RADIO TO TELEVISION
ISBN for complete set: 0-405-03555-1
See last pages of this volume for titles.

Manufactured in the United States of America

CONTENTS

U. S. DEPARTMENT OF COMMERCE

R. P. LAMONT, Secretary

BUREAU OF FOREIGN AND DOMESTIC COMMERCE

WILLIAM L. COOPER, Director

Trade Promotion Series—No. 109

RADIO MARKETS OF THE WORLD, 1930

BY

LAWRENCE D. BATSON

Electrical Equipment Division

UNITED STATES

GOVERNMENT PRINTING OFFICE

WASHINGTON : 1930

CONTENTS

FOREWORD

For 10 years radio broadcasting has been developing throughout the world, and as yet no evidence of abatement in its progress has become apparent. In few sections do the people remain ignorant of the uses of radio, and many policies which have prohibited or seriously restricted its use in the past have practically disappeared. The United States has played an outstanding part in the preliminary " missionary " work, and followed it up by satisfying the demands of foreign markets for both broadcasting and receiving equipment as rapidly as the demands appeared.

The world investment in radio broadcasting and receiving was calculated as of November, 1929, at $1,502,019,720, of which $1,473 - 279,344 represented the listeners' outlay, or approximately 98 per cent of the total investment. Ninety per cent of the operating expenses are borne by listeners. Broadcasting and reception expenses total $743,324,380 annually, of which $671,898,523 is spent in the upkeep and operation of receiving sets, and $71,425,857 for broadcasting stations. Prorated according to the number of receivers, the cost of broadcasting per set per year is thus fixed at $2.96, compared with $27.84 annual operating cost of the receiver itself.

During the past nine years United States exports of radio equipment have amounted to nearly $60,000,000. The number of receiving sets in use has increased to more than 24,000,000. The first broadcasting station is now supplemented by some 1,300 others. Where 10 years ago a small group of scientists and experimenters labored to develop the radiophone to a stage where music could be broadcast and received with moderate satisfaction, to-day millions of people are engaged in work based upon broadcasting. Newly created positions include the many involved in the design, manufacture, and sale of broadcasting and receiving equipment, in service and repair work, in the management and operation of broadcasting stations, in performing before the microphone, in publishing radio magazines or work in radio departments of other periodicals, the preparation of radio advertising material, and many other employments. Nor are these the only jobs broadcasting has made, because it has brought about expansion in innumerable secondary industries.

The amount of money invested to accomplish this development can not be estimated with even reasonable accuracy. Outside the United States statistics are not generally collected, and even when they are the results are seldom made available for publication. Conditions vary, and while they may be easily described, they do not lend themselves to " yardstick " applications.

The purpose of this publication is to present accurate information as to the development of radio broadcasting in foreign countries, for the guidance of American exporters of radio apparatus in entering and maintaining sales in such countries. The data cover

various subjects, including the characteristics of the population, the
laws governing the use of receiving sets, the physical characteristics of the various countries, and the present status of radio development in each. These data have been obtained from all available
sources. In addition to reports from consular officers of the Department of State and representatives of the Department of Commerce
stationed abroad, official reports of various foreign governments,
private publications, trade journals, and encyclopedic works were
consulted. Questions asked by exporters in the past have been
analyzed, and so far as possible have been answered herein, this
work involving much additional research. Similarly, criticisms of
three previous bulletins on this subject have been given full consideration. These findings have been analyzed and compared with reported market conditions. From the results, this publication has
been prepared.

WILLIAM L. COOPER, *Director*,
Bureau of Foreign and Domestic Commerce.

NOVEMBER, 1930.

RADIO MARKETS OF THE WORLD

INTRODUCTION

The radio broadcast is universally recognized as an efficient and economical means of communication, of entertainment, of education, and withal a notable public service. The operation of a receiver is extremely simple. Radio shares with the telephone, automobile, airplane, electric light, and bathtub recognition as a symbol of the universally high standard of living that marks the present age. It has so many angles of popular appeal that there are few people, indeed, who do not have one or more " weaknesses " that radio will satisfy.

In its service radio enters into the foundation of civilization. It is an important adjunct to the government, the press, wire communications, transportation, commerce, and the postal system in the assured exchange of benefits among peoples.

While it is giving the people a great moral foundation for international peace and good will, radio continues to develop a catholicity of tastes in the phonic arts. The classification of music as good or bad solely according to whether it might be classical or popular at its inception has been broken down. The person who is technically interested in music has lost caste as the sole arbiter and court of final appeal as to what constitutes good music, for the great public has taken over that function. Music is now more universally considered good if it is fitting in theme to its sphere, well written, and well played or sung.

The popularization and development of wide appreciation of tonal rather than rhythmic compositions has been a characteristic service of radio. Music is also indebted to radio in the matter of instruments. The intensive search for new effects, that programs might be more varied, has resulted in the rediscovery of many old and forgotten instruments, particularly the harpsichord and lute. There is every possibility that future efforts will bring to light more such discoveries. Only one new instrument—the theremin—can as yet be credited to radio; but this, too, is expected to be joined in time by a growing list of musical devices.

RECENT RADIO ADVANCES

The outstanding development in radio during 1929 appears to have been the beginning of scheduled transatlantic broadcasts. The feat had been accomplished occasionally during a period of several years, but the stage was at last finally attained where regular and frequent exchanges of programs could be made and satisfactory reception for chain rebroadcasting could be assured in most cases.

1

Short waves have brought out-of-the-way parts of the world into touch with world centers of entertainment and affairs. It is but a matter of time before the necessary transmitters can be provided to complete 2-way communication with phone, as radiotelegraphy has already been established, with even the more distant areas. Much in this respect remains to be accomplished, but improvements are rapidly being made. The results are as strikingly apparent as they have been in the case of equipment for home reception. The sound quality of short-wave broadcasts depends upon further research in the same direction as that which has resulted in improved tonal characteristics of short-span long-wave reception.

The future of television remains an enigma, but that progress is being made in experiment is evidenced by the frequent press notices devoted to this subject. The apparatus for transmitting and for satisfactory reception of still pictures and images of moving objects is already available. Even that designed for highly detailed transmissions of the motion-picture type having been successfully demonstrated during the past year. The difficulties to be solved seem to be only those necessary to bring the cost within the reach of the buying public. This is itself somewhat of a problem, and experimenters are not inclined to make definite promises as to the immediate future. The needed discoveries, however, may be made at any time, and it is not improbable that thoroughly reliable and satisfactory television apparatus faithfully transmitting and receiving moving images will be available within a short time.

Legislation and regulation have undergone little change. Countries appear to have settled policies as to the major regulations. Any alterations made have been in the matter of details and have little effect on the use of radio by the public generally. A very few countries have yet to recognize broadcasting with special legislation, and in each of these the appropriate State officer is administering all questions in accordance with existing laws as interpreted by some definite policy. Subsequent legislation is not apt to seriously change the status of broadcasting or reception.

Programs have taken more definite form. Novelties have become rare, and those that have proved adaptable to broadcasting have found place in permanent program practice. The hours of the day and the days of the week have been analyzed by broadcasters to allocate each variety of program to those times when the class of people most likely to be interested will be listening in the greatest numbers. This has been done in many countries even to the point of extreme standardization. Improvement, however, is the universal object and continues wherever broadcasting is done.

While a number of new broadcasting stations were opened during 1929, few were designed to serve new areas. Those regions where local broadcasting is not yet provided are subject to conditions or restrictions which can not readily be overcome, usually because of sparse population and restricted purchasing power. Adverse climatic conditions have stimulated rather than retarded broadcasting development, except in the extreme tropical areas.

The number of receiving sets in use has continued to increase. A few countries show decreases, but most have had moderate advancement. The change from battery to socket-power sets is progressing, but nearly one-half of the number in use are battery sets. Lack of central-station electric service or only part-time service is responsible for most of the sales of battery sets now being made. Crystal sets are also sold and used in surprising numbers, particularly in Europe, where about 50 per cent of the continental total is of this class.

Though the Washington Conference agreement (1927) was to have been effective January 1, 1929, and changes made within one year thereafter to accord with it, broadcasting has been affected very little. Call letters were to have been changed to three-letter combinations for land stations, but this has been impracticable since the number of such combinations available was too few for the purpose. Changes in call-letter allocations have necessitated general reassignments of calls in some countries. In Europe where wave lengths up to 3,000 meters were formerly used for broadcasting, reallocations of long-wave stations to new channels were made, the new lengths being from 1,340 to 1,875 meters and from 200 to 545 meters.

PROGRAMS

The purchaser of a receiving set is not motivated in his choice by the same considerations as the purchaser of other commodities. The sole motives for buying radio are amusement and service, principally amusement. Radio "tinkering" as a pastime is still to be found, though it is by no means as prevalent as in former years.

To retain interest, pleasing radio programs have had to be provided. Broadcasters found that but a small percentage of the listeners are completely pleased with any individual program. A wide variety of features necessary to maintain interest among the whole listening public can be accomplished only by making available simultaneously a number of programs within the receiving range of each set. The basing of broadcast policies on a prevalence of modern or highly sensitive receivers has not been found an effective practice. Instead of stimulating the market for new sets it has tended to annihilate interest on the part of those whose still serviceable sets have been rendered obsolete.

Radio programs have been drawn from all fields where there is reason to believe suitable material may be found. Some of these fields have received greater attention than others, but the efforts of the broadcasters, wherever the listener interest has been recognized as the principal factor in broadcasting success, have been expended in the direction of improving program balance. This effort is common to all parts of the world, regardless of the method employed for radio control. Music of all types, narrative, and the play are three fields susceptible to wide variety within themselves, and they are being constantly explored in the search for something new. Even vaudeville has been successfully presented. The news bulletin, an exclusively European development for several years, is now a well-established part of American programs. The broadcast of public and sporting events is now developed in almost every country where there is broadcasting. There is little expectation, however, that the sport broadcasts of other countries will be as successful as in the United States. The major American games—baseball and football—are sufficiently dramatic that broadcast descriptions are of interest even to people who are not followers of these sports. This characteristic is probably not as common to the national pastimes of other countries.

Upon this general skeleton has been developed what may be called the " universal program." The arrangement in every case is similar, and the interest maintained in each type of program is about the same in all countries. There is extreme variation in the method of presentation; our own familiarity with the Spanish broadcasts from stations in Cuba and Mexico may be cited as exemplifying this. There is the further difference that lies in the availability of artists, which varies from country to country and city to city throughout the world, as in the United States.

In developing the receiving-set market abroad it is necessary for manufacturers to take an interest in broadcasting. Even though direct advertising may not be permitted, the nature of the general market for radio sets depends directly on the quality of the broadcasts, and its development may well be expected to warrant a certain amount of assistance in the preparation of programs. Voluntary acknowledgements through the press of such assistance may on occasion prove even more beneficial than if made over the air. The widest variety possible within the bounds of taste, and the most complete elimination of the mediocre must be maintained if the demand for radio equipment is to spread further.

Though the field of radio presentation is the greatest ever offered by any medium, it has been rigidly restricted to aural transmissions, and the types of programs restricted to a few general classes. Each of these classes is such as to appeal to a single person, who may enjoy one or more of them, remain unaffected by others, and have a strongly adverse reaction to the remainder. The more apparent of these classes are:

Music, instrumental:
    Solo.
    Duet, trio, and quartet, etc.
    Orchestra.
    Band.

      { Classical, including symphony,
         opera, sacred, etc.
       Popular, including dance.
      { Novelty.

Music, vocal:

                    { Opera.
                     Balads, pastorals.
    In all combinations of voice.{ Popular novelties.
                     Religious.
                    { Characteristic, racial and national.

Performances:
    Dialogue.
    Narrative.
    Plays.
Speech:
    Prepared speeches, propaganda, etc.
    Public events, descriptive.
    Public service, weather, markets, news, time, etc.
Religious services.

The 1930 British Broadcasting Corporation Yearbook concisely outlines the basic considerations in program construction as follows:

Experience has shown that the problem of building programs for broadcasting falls quite naturally into two parts. On the one hand there is the actual quality of each individual program, and on the other, the general balance and layout of the whole field of programs. Taking the week as a unit, the program builder must so balance one type of program with another that the final scheme reflects what he takes to be the choice of the majority of the listening audience, without leaving unsatisfied the demands of certain minorities, and without refusing anything which is of particular interest and value in its own field, whatever that field may be.

Though this quotation somewhat reflects the individual policies of the British Broadcasting Corporation, the basis is one upon which any provision for foreign broadcasts must be constructed if the ultimate service in increased sales of sets is to be attained.

The program cycle, ordinarily the week, is also universal in general arrangement. There are four groups of programs in this respect—daily, weekly, intermittent, and special. Daily features are ordinarily relegated to the morning hours and are of a service nature; weekly programs are usually of entertainment, presented on a more extensive scale, being either special performances of musical organizations or public events. Experience, the cost of presentation, and the effort to carry interest from broadcast to broadcast without " wearing out " the interest of the listening public, combine to dictate the frequency of presentation, though each program manager interprets the comparative values of these factors in a different way.

RADIO ADVERTISING

The matter of advertising, which has been discussed in the United States to a considerable extent, is found to be treated variously abroad. There is a definite indication of a trend toward the adoption of the American sponsored-program system in some quarters, but as yet many countries cling to the policy of listeners' licenses. One objection raised in the licensing countries is based on the belief that listeners would be subjected to extended advertising talk. Articles descriptive of American broadcasting, advanced as the outstanding example of this system of financing, frequently appear in foreign publications. These are sometimes colored as arguments against the American method, from which the reader gathers that most American programs consist of direct advertising speeches only. As presented, this argument favoring the retention of license fees seems unanswerable. However, familiarity with actual conditions obtaining here would do much to dispel this impression.

Another difficulty confronting the authorities in the licensing countries is the problem of maintaining a reasonable control of the actual contact of paid radio programs.

DISTANCE RECEPTION

That the reception of distant programs is an important part of the listener's desires is shown by the almost complete disappearance from the market of receivers restricted to local reception. Local receivers, with high reception qualities, could be constructed for sale at a low cost, but the demand to warrant their production would be so limited, even in localities where broadcasting facilities are ideal, as to raise the price level of such receivers above those of sets capable of long-range reception. Selectivity, in countries where a number of stations are within receiving range, is a prime selling point for individual instruments. Where there is no present indication of listener interest in distant reception, the reason is usually found to be that the arrangement of broadcast wave lengths or the climatic conditions are such as to preclude satisfactory reception from distances.

In some areas throughout the world there are only isolated stations of local power, usually operating only a few hours each day. In all such places distant reception is a necessity if radio broadcasting is to be successful. In the United States the demand for distance is largely latent, but if the means can be found of satisfying it once more, with programs not available on intermediate stations of high power, demand for distant reception will become as popular as it is in foreign countries.

The extent to which selectivity in the receiving set is demanded is entirely dependent upon local broadcasting conditions. Sets capable of sharp tuning have an additional selling feature in such areas as Europe and Australia, where congestion is general, and in countries where stations are principally grouped about the largest cities, as in Mexico and Argentina. Sets of less selectivity are not suited to such places, but might through other advantages be of better service in localities where interference is less and reception from distant stations necessary to have a satisfactorily varied program.

CHAIN AND RELAY BROADCASTS·

Two methods have been developed for broadcasting a single program from several stations simultaneously—the chain or American, and the relay or European system. The chief difference depends upon whether the secondary stations operate continuously with the originating stations (the relay system) or only part of the time (chain). During the earlier years relay stations were designed solely for relaying, with a total lack or only a minimum of studio facilities. Chain practice developed from occasional interconnection of stations originally constructed as complete broadcasting units. Both systems have undergone considerable modification, and their operation is now very similar.

The chain system has few variations, but the methods employed in relay systems are sufficiently distinct to have some interest. In Sweden there are two major groups of stations, one owned by the broadcasting monopoly, and the other made up of smaller stations operated by radio clubs. The small stations are of a modified relay classification, broadcasting programs from the monopoly stations three or four days a week and originating their own programs the remaining days. The Swedish method, therefore, may be classified as a chain system. In Germany each main station is assigned a definite territory, with connected relay stations situated where necessary to guarantee proper reception in all parts of the designated area, this being the perfect example of the relay method. The British system, now being abandoned in favor of a more promising arrangement, designated several relay stations over the country, these rebroadcasting the London program, while the remaining stations normally operated independently.

PERSONAL CHARACTERISTICS AFFECTING THE MARKET

Study of the personal factor is one of considerable importance in the marketing of all commodities. The radio market is probably affected by individual characteristics in more ways than other commodity markets. In some parts of the world religion constitutes a retarding influence, but elsewhere religious organizations have adopted radio as a potent aid to the furtherance of their purposes, with results that have proved mutually advantageous. In similar cases various other so-called national characteristics will be found to operate with opposite effect, under varying conditions.

In addition to these more peculiar factors of the radio market, and their effects, there are also several other personal characteristics which apply to the demand for all commodities. These include, among others, individual purchasing power, the standard of living, the existence or absence of competitive desires as concerns the living standards, and the inclination toward frugality in matters beyond strictly necessary comforts.

There is no method by which these personal factors may be exactly measured. Their effects change from year to year. Efforts have been made to express this market element mathematically, but with no exceptional success. The human element is most elusive; similar conditions unexpectedly and sometimes inexplicably reverse their effects. Certain races have been known as free spenders when money was available. Among these, radio sets could not be sold because money is spent as quickly as it is received, and a radio purchase would involve saving for some period beforehand, or credit which dealers could not wisely extend.

CLIMATIC CONDITIONS AND SEASONAL CYCLES

The effect of climate on reception is a most important market factor. Much has been done to eliminate the disadvantages arising in reception from adverse climate, but up to the present time those countries where poor results are obtained find even the improved devices of little use.

The growth of short-wave broadcasting, however, has provided the means of circumventing a large part of this difficulty. It has been found that the short waves carry signals satisfactorily through even the most troublesome atmosphere. The countries bordering the southwestern part of the Caribbean Sea have long been recognized as having the most difficult conditions in the world in this respect. Short-wave broadcasts in a few of these countries are noticeably increasing the interest in radio. Such territory is almost untouched, providing virgin markets for future development. Though the per capita demand may not be large, these markets should be watched closely.

The following table shows the principal climatic characteristics of various areas throughout the world, and the seasons of best radio reception.

WORLD CLIMATE AND RADIO SEASONS

Countries	Summer	Winter	Range of mean temperatures [1]		Mean annual rain-fall	Radio reception	
			Monthly	Annual		Possible	Best
NORTH AMERICA			° F.	° F.	Inches		
Alaska	Cool	Cold	10- 60	0-50	0- 80	Continuous	Sept.-May.
Canada: South	Warm	do	0- 80	40-70	10- 80	do	Oct.-May.
Central America	Hot	Hot	60-100	80-90	20-120	Sept.-Mar	Dec.-Jan.
Mexico	do	Cool	30- 90	50-80	0- 80	do	Nov.-Feb.
United States:							
North	Hot and warm.	Cold	20- 90	50-70	20- 60	Continuous	Oct.-May.
South	Hot	Cool	30- 90	50-80	0- 80	do	Nov.-May.
West Indies	do	Hot	70-100	70-90	20- 80	Oct.-Mar.	Nov.-Jan.
SOUTH AMERICA							
Argentina	Hot	Cool	30- 90	40-90	0- 60	Continuous	Apr.-Sept.
Bolivia	(2)	(2)	70- 80	0-60		do	Do.
Brazil	Hot	{Hot and warm.}	60- 90	70-90	0- 80	{May-Oct / Continuous}	Do. / Do.
Chile	(2)	(2)	30- 70	40-70	0- 80	do	Do.
Colombia	Hot	Hot	70-100	80-90	80-120	Jan.-Mar	Do.
Ecuador	do	Warm	70- 90	70-90	0- 80	Apr.-Oct	
Paraguay	do	do	60- 90	70-80	10- 40	Continuous	May-Sept.
Peru	(2)	(2)	60- 80	60-80	0- 80	May-Oct	July-Sept.
Uruguay	Hot	Warm	50- 90	60-90	20- 60	Continuous	Apr.-Oct.
Venezuela	do	Hot	70-100	80-90	40-100	Jan.-Mar	
EUROPE							
Balkan States	Hot and warm.	Cool and cold.	30- 90	50-70	40- 80	Sept.-May	Nov.-Feb.
Baltic States	Warm	Cold	10- 70	30-50	10- 40	Continuous	Sept.-May
British Isles	do	Cool	30- 7C	40-60	40- 60	do	Do.
Central States	do	do	20- 80	40-60	10- 60	do	Do.
Latin Europe	Hot	do	30- 90	50-70	10- 60	Sept.-Jan	Oct.-Apr
Scandinavia	Warm	Cold	10- 70	10-50	10- 60	Continuous	Sept.-May
Russia	(3)	(3)	0- 80	20-60	0- 40	Sept.-May	
ASIA							
China	Hot	Cool	10- 90	30-90	0- 80	Sept.-May	Nov.-Feb.
Malay Peninsula	do	Warm	70- 90	70-90	80-120	Oct.-May	Dec.-Feb.
OCEANIA							
Australia (except arid regions of north).	Hot	Warm	40- 90	50-70	10- 80	Continuous	Apr.-Sept.
AFRICA							
Algeria	Hot	Warm	50-100	60-80	10- 30	Sept.-May	Nov.-Apr.
Sahara	do	do	50-100	70-90	0- 20		
Sudan	do	Hot	60- 90	70-90	0-160		
South Africa	do	Warm	50- 90	60-90	20- 80	Continuous	Apr.-Oct.

[1] Temperature zones of 10° variation were used in making up this table. The extremes of the zones encountered in each country are taken for the ranges. Thus, a point at which the monthly mean ranges from 43° to 68° is given as having a range of from 40° to 70°. Rainfall is similarly measured in 10-inch zones.

[2] Climatic variations are due mainly to altitudes along the tropical west coast of South America, the difference between seasons not being great. The very narrow coastal strip is hot throughout the year but includes only a very small percentage of the territory of these countries.

[3] Varies widely.

SHIPPING SEASONS

The appropriate season for shipping radio to foreign countries is indicated by the results of an analysis made of United States exports as reported by months. The findings are shown in the following table, which considers receiving-set and vacuum-tube shipments. These commodities were selected as representing, respectively, the growth of the radio market and the maintenance of equipment in use. Statistics for 1928 and 1929 were combined for the study and treated as a single year. The 2-month figures for the period indicated as January-February are based on the sum of the figures for

January and February, 1928, and the same months in 1929. The world is divided into four climatic zones, each country being considered as totally within the zone in which the preponderance of its population is to be found.

The zoning is based on mean annual temperature ranges, since the purpose of this analysis is to determine the time of year at which each market is at its best (midwinter) and the relation of the actual shipping periods to such seasons. The north and south zones have definite contrasts of summer and winter seasons, regardless of the actual range of climate in other respects, while the torrid division for the greater part has less sharply defined seasons and a generally higher temperature range.

From the radio standpoint, the north zone has constant reception with noticeably better results between October and March. The north Torrid Zone has satisfactory reception during longer or shorter periods extending more or less equally before and after the middle of December. The south zone experiences best reception from April to September, with constant reception possible. The south torrid is similar to the north torrid with the season generally reaching its middle in June or July. In the torrid divisions, the quality of reception is dependent upon the effects of the rainy season, the time of which varies between different regions with little apparent regard for the solar season.

The countries included in each zone are:

NORTH ZONE

North America: Canada, Greenland, Miquelon and St. Pierre Islands, Newfoundland and Labrador, Bermuda, Barbados.
Europe: All countries.
Asia: China, Japan, Kwantung, Palestine, Persia, Siam, Russia in Asia, Syria, Turkey.

NORTH TORRID ZONE

North America: Mexico, Central America, West Indies, except Bermuda and Barbados.
South America: Ecuador, Colombia, Venezuela, British Guiana, Surinam, French Guiana.
Asia: Aden, Arabia, India, British Malaya, Ceylon, French Indo-China, Hong Kong, Philippine Islands.
Africa: Egypt, Algeria, Tunisia, Morocco, Canary Islands.

SOUTH TORRID ZONE

South America: Bolivia, Brazil, Paraguay, Peru.
Asia: Netherland East Indies.
Oceania: All except Australia and New Zealand.
Africa: All except Egypt, Algeria, Tunisia, Morocco, Canary Islands.

SOUTH ZONE

South America: Argentina, Chile, Falkland Islands, Uruguay.
Oceania: Australia, New Zealand.

In the following table the " per cent of period total " refers to that portion of the total shipments during the 2-month periods that were allocated to each zone, and the " per cent of zone total " to that portion of the year's total shipments to the zone represented by each period.

Thus, of the total set shipments during the January-February period, 64 per cent went to the north, 10 per cent to the north torrid, 3 per cent to the south torrid, and 23 per cent to the south zone. Of the total set shipments to the north zone, 10 per cent were shipped during the first, 5 per cent during the second, 6 per cent during the third, 17 per cent during the fourth, 33 per cent during the fifth, and 29 per cent during the sixth period. Of the total year's shipments of sets, 64 per cent went to the north, 12 per cent to the north torrid, 3 per cent to the south torrid, and 20 per cent to the south zone.

The table shows that the peak shipments to the north zone occur in early fall, to the north torrid in late fall, to the south torrid and south in late spring. Not much period variation is noted in respect to the torrid divisions.

RADIO SHIPPING SEASONS

[Based on United States exports for 1928-1929]

Item	Jan.–Feb.	Mar.–Apr.	May–June	July–Aug.	Sept.–Oct.	Nov.–Dec.	Total
NORTH ZONE							
Sets:							
Per cent of period total	64	37	40	64	77	70	64
Per cent of zone total	10	5	6	17	33	29	100
Tubes:							
Per cent of period total	49	35	33	29	40	44	38
Per cent of zone total	17	14	14	12	18	25	100
NORTH TORRID ZONE							
Sets:							
Per cent of period total	10	13	13	11	10	15	12
Per cent of zone total	9	10	11	15	23	32	100
Tubes:							
Per cent of period total	10	9	12	9	19	20	14
Per cent of zone total	10	10	14	10	24	32	100
SOUTH TORRID ZONE							
Sets:							
Per cent of period total	3	4	5	3	2	2	3
Per cent of zone total	10	14	16	18	20	22	100
Tubes:							
Per cent of period total	5	7	8	25	8	6	10
Per cent of zone total	7	11	13	41	15	13	100
SOUTH ZONE							
Sets:							
Per cent of period total	23	41	43	22	12	12	20
Per cent of zone total	11	21	21	17	14	16	100
Tubes:							
Per cent of period total	36	49	47	37	33	30	38
Per cent of zone total	13	19	20	16	15	17	100

RECEIVING-SET STATISTICS

One and one-half billion people live within constant receiving distance of broadcasting stations, based on the League of Nations estimate of the world population at 1,906,000,000. The number of receiving sets in use is over 24,000,000, practically all of them being within the areas where reception of at least one station is certain. With an average of five members to each family, 120,000,000 people are equipped with receiving facilities, or 6.3 per cent of the total population in these zones. To put radios in all their homes, 320,-000,000 sets would be required. With broadcasting facilities provided throughout the world, over 380,000,000 sets would be required. These figures, of course, must be greatly modified by factors representing purchasing power, personal desires, and many other considerations before they give any indication of the potential markets.

The number of receiving sets in any country is a matter of conjecture. In countries where registration for a receiver or a license for its ownership or operation is required, statistics are sometimes published; these provide a basic figure which may be employed in making estimates. There are several countries which do not publish returns, though registration or license is required, and others which do not require registration or license. In general, trade estimates are frequently far more reliable than license counts.

One of the major questions in regard to licensing is the enforcement of the law. The percentage of unlicensed sets in any country where licenses are required is admittedly large. Sets may be easily concealed, and so may be the necessary traffic to provide sets for those desiring to conceal them after the purchase. These conditions arise in direct ratio to the cost of licenses and the rigor of the restrictions imposed. Hence licensing statistics do not give a complete total of the sets in use. Another qualifying factor is that the licenses generally cover sets and not their owners; additional licenses are required for successive sets used during the year, though in some countries steps have been taken to eliminate the worst features of this requirement.

Estimates of the numbers of sets illegally operated appear to be made with a paucity of facts. Where the attempts to enforce the law are carried on with less energy, it is entirely possible that authoritative estimates of the number of such sets may be made, inasmuch as the traffic and operation are not so carefully hidden. When such estimates are made they are generally based on parallel but unrelated statistics. In the absence of anything more reliable they are of some service.

Where registration or licensing is not required, there are no official statistics to which to refer. Estimates, however, are more likely to be authoritative, but much depends upon their source. Those which have been accepted are in each case the ones which are believed to be from the most reliable of the sources considered. The British electrical press has provided several of the figures used, but since the origin of many of these is obscure, they have been accepted only in the absence of estimates made in the country under consideration. Consular officers of the United States Department of State and representatives of the Department of Commerce in various countries provided most of the local estimates used. Members of the radio trades have proved another fruitful source.

There has been no lack of estimates, so far as the United States is concerned, in past years. Most of those considered appear to have been based on conditions in a small portion of the country. Where the New York area was considered as being representative of the entire country, for instance, estimates have run from 12,000,000 to 15,000,000. Estimates as a whole, however, average considerably lower, 10,500,000 being the average of the most probable estimates for the beginning of the 1929–30 winter season. Statistics on the number of families owning radio sets (not the number of sets in use) are to be made available by the United States Bureau of the Census, compiled from returns on this question in the 1930 decennial census. This will be the first actual count ever attempted in this country and will be the basis for future estimates.

In one or two cases the number of sets exported from the United States during one or more of the last few years will show incongruity when compared with the number of sets estimated to be in use. No attempt has been made to adjust the estimates to agree in this connection, since it is not improbable that the sets imported have not been put into service; they might remain on the dealers' shelves, delivery might have been refused, they might have been reexported, they might have been destroyed, or other diversion might have followed their importation, none of which would show in the United States export statistics.

The following statement shows the number of receiving sets in use, according to the most reliable figures as defined above:

North America:

Alaska	1, 250
Bahamas	300
Barbados	250
Bermuda	700
British Honduras	75
Canada	423, 557
Canal Zone	160
Costa Rica	250
Cuba	28, 875
Dominican Republic	1, 250
French West Indies	100
Greenland	25
Guatemala	250
Haiti	750
Honduras	78
Jamaica	250
Mexico	100, 000
Miquelon and St. Pierre	25
Netherland West Indies	50
Newfoundland and Labrador	1, 250
Nicaragua	45
Panama, Republic of	300
Porto Rico	5, 000
Salvador	51
Trinidad and Tobago	35
United States	10, 500, 000
Virgin Islands	50
Continent	11, 064, 926

South America:

Argentina	400, 000
Bolivia	65
Brazil	175, 000
British Guiana	15
Chile	35, 000
Colombia	350
Ecuador	150
Falkland Islands	15
French Guiana	8
Paraguay	150
Peru	70, 000
Surinam	18
Uruguay	17, 150
Venezuela	2, 000
Continent	699, 921

Europe:

Albania	12
Austria	371, 011
Azores	200
Belgium	63, 125
Bulgaria	1, 612
Czechoslovakia	300, 000
Danzig	155
Denmark	343, 000
Estonia	14, 426
Finland	90, 232
France	1, 500, 000
Germany	3, 066, 682
Gibraltar	150
Greece	1, 000
Hungary	240, 000
Iceland	50
Irish Free State	26, 000
Italy	250, 000
Latvia	33, 000
Lithuania	12, 000
Luxemburg	2, 000
Madeira	180
Malta	250
Netherlands	152, 000
Norway	75, 000
Poland	202, 586
Portugal	2, 500
Rumania	25, 000
Spain	500, 000
Sweden	450, 000
Switzerland	77, 959
United Kingdom	3, 093, 000
Yugoslavia	40, 000
Continent	10, 933, 130

Europe-Asia:

Russia	500, 000
Turkey	5, 200
Total [1]	505, 200

Asia:

Aden	5
Arabia	12
Ceylon	1, 500
China	10, 000

[1] Not included in total for Europe or Asia

Asia—Continued.		Africa :	
Chosen	12, 000	Algeria	9, 500
French India	50	Angola	50
French Indo-China	25	Basutoland	10
Hong Kong	700	Bechuanaland	15
India	3, 600	Belgian Congo	6
Iraq	24	British Somaliland	5
Japan	641, 774	British West Africa	50
Kwantung	3, 910	Canary Islands	200
Macao	40	Egypt	4, 000
Netherland East Indies	106	Ethiopia	2
Palestine	150	French Equatorial Af-	
Persia	300	rica	500
Philippine Islands	1, 300	French Morocco	2, 500
Siam	25	Italian Africa	250
Straits Settlements	500	Kenya	250
Syria	150	Liberia	5
		Madagascar	150
Continent	676, 171	Mozambique	75
		Northern Rhodesia	25
Oceania :		Southern Rhodesia	150
American Samoa	12	Southwest Africa	50
Australia	311, 322	Swaziland	5
British Oceania	250	Tanganyika	10
French Oceania	30	Tunisia	1, 000
Guam	12	Union of South Africa	20, 000
Hawaii	15, 000	Zanzibar	5
New Zealand	52, 124		
		Continent	38, 963
Total	379, 250		
		World	24, 297, 561

THE RADIO INVESTMENT

There has been much interest in the question of the direct and indirect investment in radio, so far as broadcasting is concerned. Statistics are nonexistent and authoritative estimates are also lacking. There is, however, an estimate of the world total investment in receiving sets in use and broadcasting stations in operation, which is given here as the only one available. The calculations were made as of the month of November, 1929.

BROADCASTING-STATION INVESTMENT

The investment in broadcasting stations totaled $28,740,376, with 1,250 stations operating, of which approximately half were in the United States. This valuation was built up from reports submitted to the Federal Radio Commission by American broadcasters, giving a total valuation for each station. Two items enter into this valuation, the studio and the transmitter.

In the matter of studios it was observed that these tended decidedly toward fixed amounts. Small stations—up to and including 100 watts—often reported no studio investment beyond bare microphone and control equipment, while others of this class have more pretentious fully equipped studios which equal those of stations of higher power. The sum of their several studio investments averaged approximately $1,000, and this figure was therefore taken as representing the average of all world stations in this power class.

Complete studio arrangements showed an unusual similarity in value, $4,000 being reported in most cases, and only a very few were at much variance. Stations between 100 and 1,000 watts in general reported a single studio, those up to 10,000, two studios, and the higher powered group, three, as an average. In this, too, there was wide divergence, but these averages were maintained.

The per watt transmitter values are dependent upon the power of the station according to logarithmic recession, as shown by these reports. The equipment was usually given a valuation somewhat lower than manufacturer's quotations.

The 1,250 stations operating at the time of this calculation were divided among the seven major divisions of the world, according to their power rating as shown in the following table. Subsequent changes in the broadcasting structures have not been exceptional and would probably not affect the total valuation more than 2 to 5 per cent.

NUMBER OF BROADCASTING STATIONS THROUGHOUT THE WORLD, BY CONTINENTS AND POWER RATING

Power rating in watts	North America	South America	Europe	Russia and Turkey	Asia	Oceania	Africa	Total
2½						1		1
5	4					1		5
7						1		1
7½	2					2		4
8		2						2
10	18	4				1		23
12		2						2
15	19					2		21
17						1	1	1
20	10	1	1	2		5		19
22½	1							1
25	2		1				1	4
30	8		1					9
35		1				1		2
40		1			1			2
45				1				1
50	80	14	3		6	2		105
60	1	1						2
65		1						1
70	1							1
75	2							2
100	178	14	12		1	5	2	212
110	1							1
120		1						1
130			8					8
150	1		3	1		1		6
160						1		1
180			1	1				2
200	7	3	17	2	1		1	31
240					1			1
250	75	3	16	1	3	2		100
300	3	1	2	1				7
320						1		1
350	3	1	2	1				7
400	1	1	2					4
500	164	10	17	3	6	5	1	206
550		2						2
600			5					5
630			1					1
700			7	1				8
750	7		7					14
800				1				1
1,000	99	13	16	5	5	4	2	144
1,200			1	14				15
1,250	1	1						2
1,500	2	7	16	1	2	2	1	30
1,650	1							1
1,800				1				1
2,000	7	3	3	2	1	1	2	19
2,200			1					1
2,500	8		2		1			11
3,000		1	3		2	1		7
3,500	2							2
3,600			1					1
4,000	1		9	5				15

NUMBER OF BROADCASTING STATIONS THROUGHOUT THE WORLD, BY CONTINENTS AND POWER RATING—Continued

Power rating in watts	North America	South America	Europe	Russia and Turkey	Asia	Oecania	Africa	Totol
5,000	41	1	4	2	2	1	--------	51
6,200	--------	--------	1	--------	--------	--------	--------	1
7,000	--------	--------	4	--------	--------	--------	--------	4
7,500	2	--------	2	--------	--------	--------	--------	4
8,000	--------	--------	1	--------	--------	--------	--------	1
10,000	11	--------	8	1	7	--------	--------	27
12,000	--------	--------	3	--------	--------	--------	--------	3
12,500	1	--------	--------	--------	--------	--------	--------	1
15,000	1	--------	1	--------	--------	--------	1	3
20,000	1	--------	1	--------	--------	--------	--------	2
25,000	1	--------	2	--------	--------	--------	--------	3
30,000	1	--------	2	--------	--------	--------	--------	3
40,000	--------	--------	2	1	--------	--------	--------	3
50,000	7	--------	--------	--------	--------	--------	--------	7
60,000	--------	--------	1	--------	--------	--------	--------	1
Not reported [1]	6	7	26	--------	7	8	5	59
Total	781	96	216	47	46	49	15	1,250

[1] Considered hereafter as 1,690 watts.

The valuation of individual stations, and the total for each power group, accords with the following table, allowing 10 per cent above the transmitter and studio values as defined for remote-broadcast equipment, office furniture, extra transmitters, and other miscellaneous investment. Care should be exercised that the allowances for studio and for miscellaneous equipment are not accepted as correct for each individual station or power group, inasmuch as they represent averages. Real-estate investment is not included, but rental value is allowed under annual expenses.

VALUATION OF WORLD BROADCASTING STATION EQUIPMENT, BY POWER RATING

Power rating in watts	Studio valuation	Transmitter valuation	Miscellaneous investment	Total invested per station	Number of stations	Grand total
2½	$1,000	$220	$122	$1,320	1	$1,320
5	1,000	360	136	1,496	5	7,480
7	1,000	450	145	1,595	1	1,595
7½	1,000	475	148	1,625	4	6,500
8	1,000	500	150	1,650	2	3,300
10	1,000	600	160	1,760	23	40,480
12	1,000	660	166	1,726	2	3,452
15	1,000	780	178	1,858	21	39,018
17	1,000	850	185	2,035	1	2,035
20	1,000	950	195	2,045	19	38,855
22½	1,000	1,000	200	2,200	1	2,200
25	1,000	1,150	215	2,365	4	9,460
30	1,000	1,300	230	2,530	9	22,770
35	1,000	1,450	245	2,695	2	5,390
40	1,000	1,600	260	2,860	2	5,720
45	1,000	1,700	270	2,970	1	2,970
50	1,000	1,900	290	3,190	105	334,955
60	1,000	2,100	310	3,410	2	6,820
65	1,000	2,250	325	3,575	1	3,575
70	1,000	2,350	335	3,686	1	3,686
75	1,000	2,500	350	3,850	2	7,700
100	1,000	3,100	410	4,510	212	956,120
110	4,000	3,300	730	8,130	1	8,130
120	4,000	3,500	750	8,250	1	8,250
130	4,000	3,800	780	8,580	8	86,640
150	4,000	4,200	820	9,020	6	54,120
160	4,000	4,400	840	9,240	1	9,240
180	4,000	4,700	870	9,570	2	19,140
200	4,000	5,000	900	9,900	31	128,700
240	4,000	5,800	980	10,780	1	10,780
250	4,000	6,000	1,000	11,000	100	1,100,000

VALUATION OF WORLD BROADCASTING-STATION EQUIPMENT, BY POWER
RATING—Continued

Power rating in watts	Studio valuation	Transmitter valuation	Miscellaneous investment	Total invested per station	Number of stations	Grand total
300	4,000	6,750	1,075	11,825	7	82,775
320	4,000	7,000	1,100	12,100	1	12,100
350	4,000	7,500	1,150	12,650	7	88,550
400	4,000	8,250	1,225	13,475	4	53,900
500	4,000	10,000	1,400	15,400	206	3,172,400
550	4,000	10,500	1,450	15,950	2	31,900
600	4,000	11,000	1,500	16,500	5	82,500
630	4,000	12,000	1,600	17,600	1	17,600
700	4,000	12,500	1,650	18,150	8	145,200
750	4,000	13,000	1,700	18,700	14	261,800
800	4,000	13,500	1,750	19,250	1	19,250
1,000	4,000	16,000	2,000	22,000	144	3,168,000
1,200	8,000	18,000	2,600	28,600	15	429,000
1,250	8,000	18,500	2,650	29,150	2	58,300
1,500	8,000	21,000	2,900	31,900	30	957,000
1,650	8,000	22,500	3,050	33,550	1	33,550
1,800	8,000	24,000	3,200	35,200	1	35,200
2,000	8,000	26,000	3,400	37,400	19	710,600
2,200	8,000	28,000	3,600	39,600	1	39,600
2,500	8,000	31,000	3,900	42,900	11	471,900
3,000	8,000	35,000	4,300	47,300	7	331,100
3,500	8,000	39,000	4,700	51,700	2	103,400
3,600	8,000	40,000	4,800	52,800	1	52,800
4,000	8,000	42,500	5,050	55,550	15	833,250
5,000	8,000	50,000	5,800	63,800	51	3,253,800
6,200	8,000	60,000	6,800	74,800	1	74,800
7,000	8,000	62,000	7,000	77,000	4	308,000
7,500	8,000	66,000	7,400	91,400	4	365,600
8,000	8,000	70,000	7,800	85,800	1	85,800
10,000	8,000	82,500	9,050	99,550	27	2,687,850
12,000	12,000	96,000	10,800	118,800	3	356,400
12,500	12,000	100,000	11,200	123,200	1	123,200
15,000	12,000	115,000	12,700	139,700	3	419,100
20,000	12,000	140,000	15,200	167,200	2	334,400
25,000	12,000	165,000	17,700	194,700	3	584,100
30,000	12,000	180,000	19,200	211,200	3	633,600
40,000	12,000	230,000	24,200	266,200	3	798,600
50,000	12,000	280,000	29,200	321,200	7	2,248,400
60,000	12,000	320,000	33,200	365,200	1	365,200
1,690 [1]	8,000	22,500	3,050	33,550	59	1,979,450
Total						28,740,376

[1] This power rating represents the estimated average for stations not reported.

THE RECEIVING-SET INVESTMENT

The investment in receiving sets, as of November, 1929, amounted
to $1,473,279,344. To determine this valuation, the number of receiving sets in use was divided by the apparent ratio maintaining in
each major area into crystal, battery, and socket-power categories.
Only scattered statistics were available, but a study of these and
general information, evolved the following data:

PER CENT OF RECEIVING SETS IN WORLD USE, BY CATEGORIES, 1929

Major area	Per cent crystal sets	Per cent battery sets	Per cent socket-power sets	Total
North America	1	47	52	100
South America	2	73	25	100
Europe	10	40	50	100
Russia and Turkey	20	45	35	100
Asia	5	75	20	100
Oceania	2	70	28	100
Africa	2	78	20	100

Derived from these constants, the number of sets in each category and area was found to be as follows:

NUMBER OF RECEIVING SETS IN WORLD USE, BY CATEGORIES, 1929

Major area	Crystal	Battery	Socket power	Total sets
North America	110, 649	5, 200, 515	5, 753, 762	11, 064, 926
South America	10, 698	390, 493	133, 730	534, 921
Europe	1, 093, 313	4, 373, 252	5, 466, 565	10, 933, 130
Russia and Turkey	101, 040	227, 340	176, 820	505, 200
Asia	33, 809	507, 128	135, 234	676, 171
Oceania	7, 585	265, 475	106, 190	379, 250
Africa	779	30, 391	7, 793	38, 963
Totals	1, 357, 873	10, 994, 594	11, 780, 094	24, 132, 561

Crystal sets were valued at $5, including head set, aerial, and ground, and considered as having had one year's (average) use at 40 per cent depreciation, or a current value of $3, or a total value of $4,073,619.

Of the battery sets, 50 per cent were considered as using storage batteries for A power and 30 per cent employed B battery eliminators. To dispense with unnecessary operations 50 per cent of the allowance for a storage A battery and 30 per cent of the allowance for a B battery eliminator were added to the valuation of each battery set. The sets were valued at $50 each, storage batteries at $10, and B battery eliminators at $25. A–B eliminators are accounted at $35 and absorbed in the allowances for separate A storage batteries and B battery eliminators. The allowances per set were, respectively, $5 and $7.50, giving each set a total value of $62.50, from which is deducted depreciation for four years' average service at 10 per cent per year, or 40 per cent, $25. The current value of battery sets is thus placed at $37.50. This is higher than the markets in some sections, but in such places the prices have been driven down by " distressed " merchandise, both new and used. The 10,994,594 battery sets at this price represent an investment of $408,997.265.

Socket-power sets were valued at $100, with an average of one year's use, at 10 per cent depreciation, or $10, making a current value of $90 each, or a total value of $1,060,208,460, represented by 11,780,094 sets.

The grand total receiving investment of $1,473,279,344 thus shown includes in all cases the necessary accessories of an investment character, such as loud-speaker, aerial and ground, lightning arrester, and similar devices. Furniture, however, often of extremely expensive character, is not considered. Cabinets costing of themselves from $50 to $500 are frequently purchased but do not add to the quality or efficiency of reception; therefore all sets are considered as being installed in the popular-price cabinets which are of minor importance in the fixing of prices.

CONCLUSIONS

The total broadcasting investment is $28,740,376, or the equivalent of $1.19 per set of the 24,132,561 receivers in use. The receiving set investment is $1,473,279,344, or over fifty times that in broadcasting stations. By allowing one-half, the United States broadcasting investment is $14,370,188. It is estimated that 105,000 crystal, 4,935,000 battery, and 5,460,000 socket-power sets are in use in this country, with a total value of $676,777,500, or approximately 45 per cent of the world total.

ANNUAL EXPENSES

RECEIVING

The expenses involved in broadcasting and reception total $743,324,380 annually, of which $671,898,523 is spent in the upkeep and operation of receiving sets. Receiving license fees and repairs are not included.

The annual depreciation of receiving sets is considered at 10 per cent, and interest on investment at 6 per cent of the receiver investment, or $147,327,934 and $88,396,760, respectively, these items totaling $235,724,695.

Power supply is an important item of expense. Dry-cell purchases for 7,696,216 sets using dry B batteries and for 5,497,297 sets using dry A batteries, are averaged at $10 per year per set of either A or B cells. Dry A batteries cost $54,972,970 and B battery blocks $76,-962,160 per year. C batteries are included in these allowances. Storage A battery recharging is also averaged at $10 per year, which averages between home and commercial charging costs; 5,492,970 sets use storage A batteries and that item totals $54,972,970. The average cost of current used through B battery eliminators, numbering 3,298,378, is $12 per year, or $39,580,536. The meter charge for socket-power sets averages $6 per year for each of the 11,780,094 sets, or $70,680,564. The total power supply expense is $297,169,200.

Vacuum-tube replacements are averaged at 3 per set per year for the 10,994,594 battery sets, making 32,983,782 tubes at $1, or $32,-983,782. An average of six tubes are required for socket-power sets, or 70,680,564 tubes for 11,780,094 sets, at $1.50 per tube, or $106,-020,846. Tube replacements cost $139,004,628.

In recapitulation, interest and depreciation are entered at $235,-724,695, power supply at $297,169,200, and tubes at $139,004,628. The total receiving cost, less repairs and license fees comes to $671,898,523, or $27.84 as the average annual cost per set. The expense of operating battery receivers amounts to $324,911,980, or $29.55 per average set; socket-power receivers $346,334,763, or $35.40 per set, and of crystal sets, interest and depreciation only, comes to $651,779, or $0.48 per set.

BROADCASTING EXPENSE

The annual cost of broadcasting was fixed at $71,425,857. Interest at 6 per cent on the $28,740,376 investment totals $1,724,422. Because of the necessity of maintaining more nearly perfect operation, the life of a broadcasting station is much shorter than of a receiving set, though replacement is necessarily made piecemeal in most cases. Depreciation was figured at 25 per cent per year, or $7,185,094, a total for interest and depreciation of $8,909,516.

Operating costs, as reported to the Federal Radio Commission, were in unusual agreement, and averaged $14.95 per watt per year, with little variation between stations of different power groups. The total wattage used in broadcasting was 1,986.879; the cost of operating broadcasting stations during the year was therefore $29,703,841. This figure included pay roll, rent, heat, light, power, taxes, and repairs, other than those included under normal depreciation.

Wire charges for chain operation can not be so accurately determined from existing statistics, but expenditures reported in the United States warrant the fixing of the world cost at $10,000,000.

Talent is yet more difficult of accounting. Individual stations seldom pay high rates for talent, and may have no expenditures of this kind. Fabulous fees are reputed to be paid to certain artists for chain features, but these sums must be divided among many stations in an accounting of this character. The majority of the stations are of 500 watts or less, few of which involve any expenditure for talent. Whether this cost devolves upon a sponsor or upon the broadcasting station is of no moment in this respect, since the sponsor merely assumes this part of the broadcasting cost. No satisfactory figure has been evolved for this cost, but the preponderance of small stations undoubtedly brings the per station cost to a very low figure. Allowing $50 per night per station, which is estimated to be a liberal allowance, the world total is $22,812,500 per year.

The annual cost of broadcasting thus is set at:

Interest	$1,724,422
Depreciation	7,185,094
Operation	29,703,841
Wire charges	10,000,000
Talent	22,812,500
Total	71,425,857

Prorated according to the number of receivers, the cost of broadcasting per set per year is thus fixed at $2.96, compared with $27.84 annual operating cost of the receiver itself.

THE REGULATION OF RADIO

Recognizing radio's many advantages, with little attendant disadvantage to existing rights and privileges, most of the governments of the world have bent unusual efforts toward encouraging the development of radio broadcasting and reception. There remain very few governments which deny the public the privilege of using it. In only a few countries is political influence used to exploit radio for personal advantage; wherever censorship operates it almost universally secures the use of radio to the best advantage of the listener.

The extent to which restrictive laws—as are all laws governing radio—are enforced and affect the market can not be ascertained. There is perhaps no such thing as an informed, disinterested observer from whom a definite and unbiased opinion can be obtained.

Two classes of radio regulations exist, those adopted nationally and those provided by international convention. International regulations are designed to promote the efficiency of all kinds of radio communications by avoiding interference between stations of different countries and by promoting uniformity of practice to facilitate the use of radio in general.

Interference is eliminated by providing for the use of various wave bands for dissimilar purposes; thus much ship-to-shore and commercial code which might interfere on the broadcasting band through lack of international uniformity is allocated to noninterfering channels, while a ship passing through foreign waters is assured of the same wave lengths for its communications which it would have in its home port. Contact is also possible in communications through wave-length control, since it is known that all stations of certain categories will be listening on certain wave lengths, whatever might be their nationality.

The control exercised over call letters is effective in avoiding confusion, for the identity of a station becomes positive when there is no duplication of call letters between countries. International regulation specifies call groups to serve this purpose.

The types of apparatus to be used in various services are often affected, particularly since obsolete types have created considerable interference in the past. Under present arrangements these will be withdrawn entirely from use.

The field covered by these laws is being constantly expanded as new conditions arise, and late developments give them wider latitude in such requirements. These purposes are made effective through national legislation in the signatory countries, usually forming the central structure of the national system of regulation.

Effective January 1, 1929, the regulations of the Washington Radio Conference of 1927 make provision for international relations in the use of radio. They specify that the choice of apparatus and devices to be used by a station shall be unrestricted except by national regulations, provided the waves emitted comply with the international agreements; that each country shall have entire freedom in the assignment of wave lengths and wave types if no interference with stations in another country will result, but where such interference is to be expected frequencies and wave types shall be assigned in accordance with the provisions of the regulations, that the wave lengths to be used for broadcasting shall be from 200 to 545 meters and from 1,340 to 1,875 meters, and that the call letters of all land stations shall be changed to three-letter combinations. Four-letter calls are reserved for ship, and five-letter calls for aircraft stations.

The degree to which radio broadcasting is regulated in various countries is widely divergent. Absolute prohibition is maintained in a few countries, while at the opposite extreme utter freedom within the bounds of public convenience, interest, and necessity prevails.

In countries where monopolies have not been declared, any person or firm showing satisfactory general qualifications will usually be given permission to broadcast at its own expense. Licenses may be required for receiving sets in such countries, but the fees revert entirely to the Government.

The monopoly system of broadcasting has been growing in popularity in countries where licenses in any form are required. Austria, Czechoslovakia, Germany, the Irish Free State, Italy, Poland, Sweden, the United Kingdom, Yugoslavia, Japan, Australia, New Zealand, and other countries are under the monopoly system, as well as Latvia and several other countries where the demand for broadcasting permits is so limited that there has been no opposition to the monopoly system.

It is a peculiarity of broadcasting that it is subject to all of the regulations provided for other kinds of radio transmission and reception, in addition to many other specific regulations that govern broadcasting alone. Thus, broadcasting may be prohibited—and the number of reasons why it is prohibited is equal to the number of countries where these prohibitions maintain—or it may be permitted under monopoly, held either by the Government or by one or more private concessionaires, or it may be permitted to any number of citizens showing the proper qualifications, which themselves vary without limitation.

Reception may be prohibited, and this has been done in some countries in the past, though such rigid limitations are disappearing. It may be necessary to secure permission to receive, or at least to deliver a proper notification to a designated Government agency that the set is installed. The unrestricted use of receiving sets is permitted in only a few countries, and one or two others add only such requirements as are outlined above.

Most countries require the listener to pay some fee for the privilege. Installation fees, annual license fees, and subscription fees are common; these may be collected by the Government or by the broadcaster, and in either case may be shared with the other agency. They vary from a few cents to several dollars a year, and may or may not be expected to pay the costs of broadcasting.

The following data show the outstanding characteristics of radio regulation of the different countries.

Broadcasting unrestricted (subject only to general license and laws for safeguarding of radio services and national interests in general, no monopoly or prohibition maintaining) ; receiving unrestricted (not subject to payment of any license or subscription fees, nor prohibited to residents generally) ; importing and merchandising unrestricted (subject only to general laws governing all commodities, no monopoly being granted) :

Barbados.	Paraguay.	Italian Africa.
Cuba.	Surinam.	Kenya.
Dominican Republic.	Uruguay.	Liberia.
Greenland.	Portugal.	Mozambique.
Honduras.	Macao.	Northern Rhodesia.
Netherland West Indies.	Netherland East Indies.	Southern Rhodesia.
United States.	Persia.	Spanish Africa.
British Guiana.	Angola.	Swaziland.
Falkland Islands.	British Somaliland.	Tanganyika.
French Guiana.	British West Africa.	Zanzibar.

Broadcasting and receiving unrestricted; importing or merchandising subject to restrictions: China ; importing subject to permit.

Broadcasting, importing, and merchandising unrestricted; receiving restricted :
    Bermuda, license required.
    British Honduras, annual license $5.
    Canada, annual license $1.
    French West Indies, annual license $0.40.
    Guatemala, installation permit $5.
    Jamaica, annual license.
    Mexico, registration, no fee.
    Miquelon and St. Pierre, annual license $0.40.
    Nicaragua, annual license.
    Trinidad and Tobago, annual license $2.83 to $4.87.
    Argentina, registration, no fee.
    Bolivia, installation fee $1.70, annual license $12.25.
    Brazil, installation fee $2.40.
    Chile, registration, no fee.
    Belgium, installation fee, annual license.
    Estonia, annual license $2.41 to $4.02.
    Finland, annual license $2.50.
    France, annual license, $0.40.

Netherlands, registration, no fee.
Spain, annual license $0.75.
Hong Kong, annual license $2.20.
Iraq, annual license.
Palestine, annual license.
New Zealand, annual license $7.29.
Algeria, annual license $0.40.
Canary Islands, annual license $1.08 to $10.80.
French Equatorial Africa, annual license $0.40.
French Morocco, annual license $0.40.
Madagascar, annual license $0.40.
South West Africa, annual license $3.55 to $9.75.
Tunisia, annual license $0.80.
Importing and merchandising unrestricted; broadcasting and receiving restricted:
Bahamas, broadcasting prohibited, annual receiving license $1.22.
Panama, broadcasting prohibited, installation fee $2.50.
Peru, broadcasting Government monopoly, annual receiving license $4.
Austria, broadcasting monopoly, annual receiving license $3.36 to $10.08.
Bulgaria, broadcasting concessions, annual receiving license $1.44.
Czechoslovakia, broadcasting monopoly, annual receiving license $3.60.
Danzig, broadcasting prohibited,[1] annual receiving license $3.37.
Denmark, Government broadcasting monopoly, annual receiving license $2.68.
Germany, broadcasting limited to corporations using Government stations. annual receiving license $5.71.
Gibraltar, broadcasting prohibited, annual receiving license $2.43.
Greece, broadcasting prohibited, annual receiving license $6.50.
Italy, broadcasting monopoly, receiving license $3.95.
Latvia, broadcasting monopoly, annual license $0.46.
Lithuania, broadcasting monopoly, annual license $10.
Malta, broadcasting prohibited, annual license $2.43 to $5.20.
Norway, broadcasting concessions, annual license $5.36.
Poland, broadcasting monopoly, annual license $3.36.
Rumania, broadcasting monopoly, annual license $3.60.
Sweden, modified broadcasting monopoly, installation fee $10.72, annual license $2.68.
United Kingdom, broadcasting monopoly, annual license $2.43.
Turkey. broadcasting monopoly, annual license $44.
Hong Kong. broadcasting monopoly, annual license $2.20.
India, broadcasting monopoly, annual license $3.65.
Japan, broadcasting monopoly, annual license $5.98.
Australia, modified broadcasting monopoly, annual license $4.15 and $5.83.
New Zealand, modified broadcasting monopoly, annual license $7.29.
Union of South Africa, broadcasting monopoly, annual license $4 87 to $8.50.

INTERNATIONAL CALL LETTERS OF STATIONS

The service regulations of the international telegraphic conventions of 1912 and 1927 provide that call letters of stations in the international system must when feasible be formed of a group of three letters for land stations. This regulation was adopted at Washington in 1927, with the specification that it should be made effective in all cases by the end of the year 1929. The initial letters of the calls are to designate the nationality of the station, these being assigned according to the following statement. There is considerable variation from the assignments existing previous to the Washington conference.

CAA–CEZ_____	Chile.	CPA–CPZ_____	Bolivia.
CFA–CKZ_____	Canada.	CRA–CRZ_____	Portuguese colonies.
CLZ–CMZ_____	Cuba.	CSA–CUZ_____	Portugal.
CNA–CNZ_____	Morocco.	CVA–CVZ_____	Rumania.

[1] Station of German system operating near Danzig.

CWA–CXZ	Uruguay.	RAA–RQZ	Russia.
CZA–CZZ	Monaco.	RVA–RVZ	Persia.
D	Germany.	RXA–RXZ	Panama.
EAA–EHZ	Spain.	RYA–RYZ	Lithuania.
EIA–EIZ	Ireland.	SAA–SMZ	Sweden.
ELA–ELZ	Liberia.	SPA–SRZ	Poland.
ESA–ESZ	Estonia.	SUA–SUZ	Egypt.
ETA–ETZ	Ethiopia.	SVA–SZZ	Greece.
F	France, colonies, etc.	TAA–TCZ	Turkey.
G	United Kingdom.	TFA–TFZ	Iceland.
HAA–HAZ	Hungary.	TGA–TGZ	Guatemala.
HBA–HBZ	Switzerland.	TIA–TIZ	Costa Rica.
HCA–HCZ	Ecuador.	TSA–TSZ	Saar Basin.
HHA–HHZ	Haiti.	UHA–UHZ	Hedjaz.
HIA–HIZ	Dominican Republic.	UIA–UKZ	Netherland East Indies.
HJA–HKZ	Colombia.	ULA–ULZ	Luxemburg.
HRA–HRZ	Honduras.	UNA–UNZ	Yugoslavia.
HSA–HSZ	Siam.	UOA–UOZ	Austria.
I	Italy and colonies.	VAA–VGZ	Canada.
J	Japan.	VHA–VMZ	Australia.
K	United States.	VOA–VOZ	Newfoundland.
LAA–LNZ	Norway.	VPA–VSZ	British colonies, etc.
LOA–LVZ	Argentina.	VTA–VWZ	British India.
LZA–LZZ	Bulgaria.	W	United States.
M	United Kingdom.	XAA–XFZ	Mexico.
N	United States.	XGA–XUZ	China.
OAA–OBZ	Peru.	YAA–YAZ	Afghanistan.
OHA–OHZ	Finland.	YHA–YHZ	New Hebrides.
OKA–OKZ	Czechoslovakia.	YIA–YIZ	Iraq.
ONA–OTZ	Belgium and colonies.	YLA–YLZ	Latvia.
		YMA–YMZ	Danzig.
OUA–OZZ	Denmark.	YNA–YNZ	Nicaragua.
PAA–PIZ	Netherlands.	YSA–YSZ	Salvador.
PJA–PJZ	Curacao.	YVA–YVZ	Venezuela.
PKA–POZ	Netherland East Indies.	ZAA–ZAZ	Albania.
		ZKA–ZMZ	New Zealand.
PPA–PYZ	Brazil.	ZPA–ZPZ	Paraguay.
PZA–PZZ	Surinam.	ZSA–ZUZ	Union of South Africa.
Q	(Abbreviations).		

In addition to these assignments each country has available a full series of calls made up of letters and numbers, initial letters indicating the nationality being prefixed. Most countries have used calls out of this group for broadcasting stations. A few countries, notably Germany, do not assign call letters to broadcasting stations.

BROADCASTING SERVICE

Broadcasting service, with few exceptions, is available in every inhabited region of the world. One can now hear the latest news, popular music, as well as the opera and sports from such widely separated cities as Berlin, Tokyo, Johannesburg, Par:s, Sydney, Pittsburgh, and many others, as easily as though such cities were but a few hundred miles distant. World-wide broadcasting is now a fact, developed beyond the point generally imagined by Americans and Europeans. Short-wave stations in these two continents are received throughout the world, though our own reception of the other—particularly southern—continents awaits the construction of appropriate transm:tters.

The following list of foreign radio broadcasting stations includes all stations outside the United States and its possessions which transmit programs for popular reception on either broadcast or short-wave lengths. This list is as complete as is possible to be obtained by the Bureau of Foreign and Domestic Commerce.

FOREIGN RADIO BROADCASTING STATIONS

NORTH AMERICA

City	Call	Wave length, in meters	Frequency, in kilo-cycles	Power, in watts
CANADA				
Bowmanville, Ontario	OKGW	435	690	5,000
Brandon, Manitoba	CKX	556	540	500
Calgary, Alberta	CFAC-CNRC	435	690	500
Do	CFCN-CNRC	435	690	500
Do	CJCJ-CHCA	435	690	500
Charlottetown, Prince Edward Island	CFCY	313	960	250
Do	CHCK	313	960	30
Chatham, Ontario	CFCO	248	1,210	50
Chilliwack, British Columbia	CHWK	248	1,210	5
Cobalt, Ontario	CKMC	248	1,210	15
Edmonton, Alberta	CHMA	517	580	250
Do	CJCA-CNRE	517	580	500
Do	CKUA	517	580	500
Fleming, Saskatchewan	CJRW	500	600	500
Fredericton, New Brunswick	CFNB	248	1,210	50
Halifax, Nova Scotia	CHNS	323	930	500
Hamilton, Ontario	CHML	341	880	50
Do	CKOC	341	880	50
Do	CHCS	341	880	10
Iroquois Falls, Ontario	CFCH	500	600	250
Kamloops, British Columbia	CFJC	268	1,120	15
King, York County, Ontario	CFRB-CJBC	313	960	4,000
Kingston, Ontario	CFRC	268	1,120	500
Lethbridge, Alberta	CJOC	268	1,120	50
London, Ontario	CJGC-CNRL	330	910	500
Middlechurch, Manitoba	CJRX	25.6	11,711	2,000
Midland, Ontario	CKPR	268	1,120	50
Moncton, New Brunswick	CNRA	476	630	500
Montreal, Quebec	CFCF	291	1,030	1,650
Do	CHYC	411	730	500
Montreal, Quebec (St. Hyacinthe)	CKSH	297	1,010	50
Do	CKAC-CNRM	411	730	5,000
Moose Jaw, Saskatchewan	CJRM	500	600	500
Ottawa, Ontario	CKCO	337	890	100
Do	CNRO	500	600	500
Pilot Butte, Saskatchewan	CHWC-CFRC	313	960	500
Prescott, Ontario	CFLC	297	1,010	50
Preston, Ontario	CKPC	248	1,210	50
Quebec, Quebec	CHRC	341	880	100
Do	CKCI	341	880	22.5
Do	CKCV-CNRQ	341	880	50
Red Deer, Alberta	CKLC-CHCT	357	840	1,000
Do	CNRD	357	840	----------
Regina, Saskatchewan	CKCK-CNRR-CJBR	313	960	500
St. John, New Burnswick	CFBO	337	890	50
Saskatoon, Saskatchewan	CFQC-CNRS	330	910	500
Do	CJHS	330	910	250
Sea Island, British Columbia	CJOR	291	1,030	50
Summerside, Prince Edward Island	CHGS	268	1,120	25
Sydney, Nova Scotia	CJCB	341	880	50
Toronto, Ontario	CFCA-CKOW-CNRT	357	840	500
Do	CKCL - CFCL - CJBC - CJSC	517	580	500
Do	CKNC-CJBC	517	580	500
Vancouver, British Columbia	CKCD-CHLS	411	730	50
Do	CKFC	411	730	50
Do	CKMO	411	730	50
Do	CKWX	411	730	100
Do	CNRV	291	1,030	500
Victoria, British Columbia	CFCT	476	630	500
Waterloo, Ontario	CKCR	297	1,010	50
Winnipeg, Manitoba	CJRX	25.6	11,710	2,000
Do	CKY-CNRW	385	780	5,000
Wolfville, Nova Scotia	CKIC	323	930	50
Yorkton, Saskatchewan	CJGX	476	630	500
COSTA RICA				
Heredia		30.8	9,734	7.5
San Jose	TIC	340	882	15

FOREIGN RADIO BROADCASTING STATIONS—Continued

NORTH AMERICA—Continued

City	Call	Wave length, in meters	Frequency, in kilo-cycles	Power, in watts
CUBA				
Camagüey	CMJA	225	1,332	50
Do	CMJC	227	1,321	15
Camajuani	CMHF	200	1,500	20
Cárdenas	CMGE	218	1,375	30
Ciego de Avila	CMJB	225	1,332	10
Do	CMJD	192	1,561	15
Cienfuegos	CMHA	260	1,154	200
Do	CM6DW	224	1,335	10
Cifuentes	CMHH	345	870	10
Colon	CMGA	360	834	300
Guanabacoa	CMCG	245	1,225	30
Do	CMCT	202	1,487	5
Guanajay	CMAA	275	1,090	30
Habana	CMBA	223	1,345	50
Do	CMBC	265	1,130	150
Do	CMBD	314	955	150
Do	CMBE	213	1,405	15
Do	CMBF	223	1,345	7.5
Do	CMBH	202	1,487	30
Do	CMBI	213	1,405	30
Do	CMBJ	233	1,285	15
Do	CMBL	202	1,487	15
Do	CMBN	213	1,405	30
Do	CMBP	202	1,487	15
Do	CMBR	213	1,405	15
Do	CMBS	380	790	150
Do	CMBT	280	1,070	150
Do	CMBX	245	1,225	15
Do	CMBZ	297	1,010	150
Do	CMC	355	845	500
Do	CMCA	245	1,225	100
Do	CMCC	280	1,070	150
Do	CMCD	223	1,345	15
Do	CMCE	233	1,285	100
Do	CMCF	333	900	250
Do	CMCN	345	1,225	100
Do	CMCQ	314	955	1,000
Do	CMCR	233	1,285	20
Do	CMCU	223	1,345	50
Do	CMCY	223	1,345	----------
Do	CMK	411	730	2,000
Do	CMQ	265	1,130	250
Do	CMW	500	600	1,000
Do	CMX	333	900	250
Marianao	CMBK	245	1,225	15
Do	CMBM	233	1,285	15
Do	CMBQ	233	1,285	50
Do	CMBW	297	1,010	150
Do	CMBY	213	1,405	100
Do	CMCM	202	1,497	15
Do	CMCO	454	660	50
Matanzas	CMGB	253	1,185	7.5
Do	CMGC	282	1,315	30
Do	CMGD	263	1,140	5
Do	CMGF	286	1,050	10
Pinar del Rio	CMAB	240	1,250	20
Sagua la Grande	CMHB	200	1,500	10
Santa Clara	CMHE	210	1,429	20
Do	CMHI	270	1,110	15
Santiago de Cuba	CMKA	205	1,450	20
Do	CMKB	250	1,200	15
Do	CMKC	230	1,364	150
Do	CMKD	273	1,100	40
Do	CM8AZ	240	1,250	50
Santiago de las Vegas	CMBG	280	1,070	150
Tuinucu	CMHC	379	790	500
DOMINICAN REPUBLIC				
Santo Domingo	HIX	448	669	1,000
GUATEMALA				
Guatemala	TGW	525	571	50
HAITI				
Port au Prince	HHK	326	290	1,080

FOREIGN RADIO BROADCASTING STATIONS—Continued

NORTH AMERICA—Continued

City	Call	Wave length, in meters	Frequency, in kilocycles	Power, in watts
HONDURAS				
Tegucigalpa	HRB	49.95	6,005	2,300
MEXICO				
Chihuahua	XFF	325	926	250
Ciudad Juarez	XEJ	350	857	100
Guadalajara	XEA	250	1,200	100
Jalapa	XFC	475	631	350
Merida	XEY	549	547	100
Mexico City	XEB	335	895	1,000
Do	XEK	300	1,000	100
Do	XEN	411	730	1,000
Do	XEO	305	984	100
Do	XER	280	1,071	100
Do	XEX	326	920	500
Do	XEW	385	780	5,000
Do	XEZ	510	588	500
Do	XFA	0–14 / 42–43 / 500–600		50
Do	XFD	33 / 27	9,086 / 11,100	50
Do	XFG	470	638	2,000
Do	XFX	342	880	500
Do	XFY	507	591	1,000
Do	XC51	44	6,814	
Monterrey	XEH	311	947	100
Do	XET			1,500
Morelia	XEI	300	1,000	100
Oaxaca	XEF	265	1,132	100
Puebla	XEE	312	961	
Reynosa	XED	312	961	10,000
Saltillo	XEL	275	1,090	10
Tampico	XEM	357	840	500
Do	XES	337	890	1,500
Toluca	XEC	225	1,333	50
Vera Cruz	XEU	375	800	50
NEWFOUNDLAND				
St. John's	8WMC	415	723	500
SALVADOR				
Salvador	RUS	452	663	500

SOUTH AMERICA

City	Call	Wave length, in meters	Frequency, in kilocycles	Power, in watts
ARGENTINA				
Azul	E4	340	882	350
Bahia Blanca	D5	286	1,050	
Buenos Aires	B2	215	1,395	50
Do	C1	229	1,315	100
Do	C4	222	1,350	100
Do	LR1	380	789	500
Do	LR2	345	870	3,000
Do	LR3	316	949	1,000
Do	LR4	303	990	2,000
Do	LR5	362	828	2,000
Do	LR6	330	909	1,000
Do	LR7	400	750	1,250
Do	LR8	261	1,149	1,500
Do	LR9	291	1,030	2,000
Do	LS1	425	706	5,000
Do	LS2	252	1,190	1,000
Do	LS3	236	1,270	1,000
Do	LS4	270	1,112	1,000
Do	LS5	281	1,076	1,000
Do	LS6	210	1,428	1,000
Do	LS7	222	1,351	1,000
Do	LS8	244	1,230	100
Concordia	J2	226	1,330	400
Cordoba	H7	319	940	100
Do	I4	326	920	120

Foreign Radio Broadcasting Stations—Continued

SOUTH AMERICA—Continued

City	Call	Wave length, in meters	Frequency, in kilo-cycles	Power, in watts
ARGENTINA—continued				
La Plata	LT2	438	685	1,000
Mar del Plata	D4	213	1,410	100
Mendoza	LT4	395	760	500
Do	M4	282	1,052	10
Do	M5	242	1,239	40
Do	M6	348	862	10
Parana	J1	240	1,249	50
Rafaela	G4	233	1,287	560
Rosario	F5	219	1,369	100
Do	LT3	275	1,090	1,500
San Francisco	H8	217	1,381	35
San Luis	Q4	205	1,463	60
Santa Fe	F1	297	1,009	100
Do	F3	256	1,168	100
Tucuman	K4	313	956	250
Venado Tuerto	G5	357	840	250
Villaguay	J5	263	1,138	65
Villa Maria	I1	246	1,219	50
BOLIVIA				
La Paz	CPX	300	1,000	1,000
BRAZIL				
Amparo	PRAM			50
Bahia	PRAH	600	500	50
Do	SQBE	24	12,490	
Curityba	PRAN	380	789	8
Franca	PRAZ			50
Juiz de Fora	PRAJ	380	789	200
Manaos		100	2,998	1,500
Mogy das Cruzes	PRAY	298	1,006	50
Para		34	8,818	
Pelotas	PRAD			
Pernambuco	PRAP	310	967	300
Porto Alegre	PRAG	250	1,199	500
Ribeirao Preto	PRAI	350	857	50
Rio de Janeiro	PRAA	400	750	1,000
Do	PRAB	320	937	500
Do	PRAC	260	1,153	500
Do	PRAD	350	857	500
Santos	PRAS	420	714	50
Sao Paulo	PRAE	360	833	1,000
Do	PRAL	400	750	100
Do	PRAO	225	1,330	1,000
Do	PRAR	280	1,071	500
Sorocaba		425	706	
BRITISH GUIANA				
Georgetown	VRY	43.86	6,832	8
CHILE				
Santiago	CMAB	480	625	1,000
Do	CMAC	373	804	1,000
Do	CMAK	225	1,333	100
Do	CMAO	295	1,016	250
Do	CMAQ	245	1,224	100
Valparaiso	CMAJ	290	1,034	100
COLOMBIA				
Bogota	HJN	425	706	550
Do	HKF	39	7,688	50
PARAGUAY				
Asuncion				12
PERU				
Arequipa	OA6U	170	1,764	20
Lima	OAX	380	789	1,500
Do	OA4M	210	1,428	12

FOREIGN RADIO BROADCASTING STATIONS—Continued

SOUTH AMERICA—Continued

City	Call	Wave length, in meters	Frequency, in kilo- cycles	Power, in watts
URUGUAY				
Montevideo	CX6	462	650	1,000
Do	CX10	411	730	1,000
Do	CX12	390	770	500
Do	CX14	370	810	1,000
Do	CX18	337	890	250
Do	CX20	323	930	2,000
Do	CX22	309	970	250
Do	CX24	297	1,010	1,000
Do	CX26	286	1,050	2,000
Do	CX30	266	1,130	250
Do	CX32	256	1,170	200
Do	CX36	240	1,250	250
Do	CX38	233	1,290	100
Do	CX40	226	1,330	100
Do	CX42	219	1,370	500
Do	CX44	213	1,410	20
Do	CX46	207	1,450	100
Do	CX48	201	1,490	50
Do	CX34	248	1,210	500
Salto	CW32	254	1,180	50
Do	CW34	246	1,220	50
Do	CW36	238	1,260	30
Do		231	1,300	30
Paysandu	CW40	224	1,340	30
Do	CW44	211	1,420	30
Tucuarembo	CW46	206	1,460	20

EUROPE

City	Call	Wave length, in meters	Frequency, in kilo- cycles	Power, in watts
ALBANIA				
Tirana				300
AUSTRIA				
Graz		353	851	7,000
Innsbruck		284	1,058	500
Klagenfurt		453	662	500
Linz		246	1,220	500
Vienna	UON2	49.4	6,073	20
Do		516	581	15,000
BELGIUM				
Andritmont	ON4EX	216	1,388	100
Antwerp	ON4ED	206	1,455	50
Brussels	ON4GT	219	1,372	100
Do	ON4RB	509	5,894	1,500
Do	ON4RC	207	1,448	100
Do	ON4FO	246	1,219	100
Chatelineau	ON4CE	216	1,388	200
Dampremy	ON4FG	206	1,459	25
Ghent	ON4RG	246	1,219	400
Liege	ON4RW	246	1,219	200
Verviers	ON4CF	206	1,459	100
CZECHOSLOVAKIA				
Bratislava	OKR	279	1,075	12,500
Brunn	OKB	342	877	2,500
Kosice	OKK	293	1,023	2,500
Prague	OKP	487	616	5,000
Do	OK1MP1	58	5,169	5,000
DANZIG				
Danzig	PTB	453	662	250
DENMARK				
Copenhagen		281	1,067	1,000
Kalundborg		1,153	260	7,500
Lyngby		19.6 / 31.6	15,300 / 9,488	500
Soro		49.5 / 971	6,057 / 3,088	

FOREIGN RADIO BROADCASTING STATIONS—Continued

EUROPE—Continued

City	Call	Wave length, in meters	Frequency, in kilo-cycles	Power, in watts
ESTONIA				
Tallinn		296	1,013	10,000
Do		1,200	250	100
Tartu (Dorpat)		408	735	2,200
FINLAND				
Abo		246	1,220	
Bjorneborg (Pori)		246	1,220	1,500
Helsingfors (Helsinki)		221	1,355	10,000
Jakobstad (Pietarsaari)		246	1,220	750
Lahtis		1,796	167	40,000
Tammerfors (Tampere)				700
Viborg (Vipuri)		291	1,030	750
FRANCE				
Agen	F2BD	{ 312	961	} 480
		30.75	9,761	
Angers		275	1,091	250
Beziers		220	1,364	1,500
Biarritz		198	1,515	250
Bordeaux		250	1,200	5,000
Do		304	986	1,500
Caen		278	1,080	200
Grenoble		328	914	1,500
Juan-les-Pins		248	1,219	250
Lille		265	1,132	500
Limoges		293	1,022	500
Lyon	YN	466	643	3,000
Do	YR	{ 291	1,029	} 500
		40.2	7,463	
Marsan		400	750	250
Marseille		316	949	500
Montpellier		286	1,049	200
Nancy		15.5	19,355	
Nimes		240	1,250	500
Nogent-sur-Seine	F8AV	80	3,750	
Paris	FL	{ 32	9,375	} 15,000
		1,446	207	
		2,650	113	
Do	FPTT	448	671	1,000
Do	F8GC	{ 368	815	} 1,500
		61	4,915	
Do		331	905	500
Do		1,725	174	13,500
Do		{ 310	968	} 2,000
		41	7,317	
Rennes		272	1,103	1,500
Rheims		386	777	500
St. Etienne		220	1,364	250
Toulon		250	1,200	500
Toulouse	MRD	225	1,175	1,500
Do		381	770	8,000
GERMANY				
Aachen		227	1,319	300
Augsburg		559	536	300
Berlin		419	716	1,700
Do		1,635	184	35,000
Do		284	1,058	600
Bremen		316	950	300
Breslau		325	923	1,700
Cologne		227	1,319	1,700
Dresden		319	941	300
Flensburg		219	1,373	600
Frankfort on the Main		390	770	1,700
Freiburg		569	527	300
Gleiwitz		259	1,157	5,600
Hamburg		372	806	1,700
Hanover		566	530	300
Kaiserslautern		270	1,112	300
Kassel		246	1,220	300
Kiel		232	1,292	300
Konigsberg		277	1,085	1,700
Langenberg		473	635	17,000
Leipzig		253	1,184	2,300

FOREIGN RADIO BROADCASTING STATIONS—Continued

EUROPE—Continued

City	Call	Wave length, in meters	Frequency, in kilo-cycles	Power, in watts
GERMANY—continued				
Magdeburg		284	1,058	600
Muenster		227	1,319	600
Munich		533	563	1,700
Nuremberg		239	1,256	2,300
Stettin		284	1,058	600
Stuttgart		360	833	1,700
Zeesen		31.38	9,560	30,000
HUNGARY				
Budapest		550	545	20,000
ICELAND				
Akureyri	G2SH	192	1,560	
Reykjavik		333	8,995	500
IRISH FREE STATE				
Cork	6CK	224	1,337	1,000
Dublin	2RN	413	726	1,500
ITALY				
Bolzano	IBZ	453	662	200
Genoa (Genova)	IGE	385	779	1,200
Milan (Milano)	IMI	50	599	7,000
Naples (Napoli)	INA	331	905	1,500
Rome (Roma)	IRO	441	680	3,000
Do	IIAX	45	6,663	
Turin (Torino)	ITO	272	1,031	7,000
LATVIA				
Riga	YLZ	525	571	10,000
LITHUANIA				
Kovno	RYK	1,935	155	7,000
LUXEMBURG				
Luxemburg	LOAA	223	1,344	10,000
NETHERLANDS				
Hilversum	PBF1	1,071	280	7,000
Huizen	PH1	16.9	17,778	40,000
Do	PH9	298	1,006	6,200
		1,875	160	
Scheveningen	PCF	1,071	280	1,500
NORWAY				
Aalesund	LKA	447	671	350
Bergen	LKB	364	824	1,000
Do	LGN	30	9,994	
Fredrikstad	LKF	385	779	700
Hamar	LKH	570	526	700
Notodden	LKN	447	671	50
Oslo	LKO	493	608	60,000
Porsgrund	LKP	453	662	700
Rjukan	LKR	447	671	
Tromsoe	LKM	453	662	100
Trondhjem		244	1,229	1,000
POLAND				
Katowice		409	734	10,000
Krakow		313	959	1,500
Poznan		335	896	1,500
Warsaw		1,412	203	12,000
Wilna		385	779	500
PORTUGAL				
Lisbon	CT1AA	319	942	1,000
RUMANIA				
Bucharest		394	759	12,000

Foreign Radio Broadcasting Stations—Continued

EUROPE—Continued

City	Call	Wave length in meters	Frequency, in kilocycles	Power, in watts
SPAIN				
Almeria	EAJ18	261	1,195	200
Barcelona	EAJ1	349	855	7,500
Do	EAJ13	268	1,119	10,000
Cartagena	EAJ15	246	1,219	100
Madrid	EAJ2	400	750	750
Do	EAJ7	424	708	1,500
Do	EAM	30.7	9.772	
Oviedo	EAJ19	368	815	30
San Sebastian	EAJ5	368	809	1,000
Seville		368	809	
SWEDEN				
Boden	SBE	1,200	250	600
Boras	SCA	229	1,309	1,500
Eskilstuna	SCB	246	1,219	200
Falun	SCC	322	931	500
Gavle	SCD	204	1,470	200
Goteborg	SBB	322	931	10,000
Halmstad	SCE	216	1,390	200
Helsingborg	SCG	231	1,298	200
Horby	SBH	257	1,167	10,000
Hudiksvall	SCF	270	1,110	150
Jonkoping	SCH	202	1,484	250
Kalmar	SCI	246	1,219	200
Karlsborg	SAS	25.5	11,760	
Karlskrona	SCJ	196	1,530	250
Karlstad	SCK	218	1,375	250
Kiruna	SCL	246	1,219	200
Kristinhamn	SCM	203	1,481	250
Malmberget	SCN	436	6,877	250
Malmo	SBC	231	1,298	600
Motala	SBG	1,348	222	30,000
Norrkoping	SCO	270	1,110	260
Orebro	SCV	237	1,265	200
Ormskoeldsvik	SCW	218	1,375	200
Ostersund	SBF	770	400	600
Saffle	SCP	246	1,219	400
Stockholm	SBA	436	688	1,000
Sundsvall	SBD	542	553	600
Trollhattan	SCQ	266	1,129	250
Uddevalla	SCR	286	1,050	50
Umea	SCS	231	1,298	200
Uppsala	SCT	453	662	150
Varberg	SCU	283	1,059	300
SWITZERLAND				
Basel		1,010	297	250
Berne		403 / 32	743 / 9,375	1,000
Geneva		760	395	250
Lausanne		680	441	600
Zurich	H9XD	85 / 32	3,529 / 9,375	
Do		459	653	630
UNITED KINGDOM				
Aberdeen	2BD	302	994	1,000
Belfast	2BE	242	124	1,000
Bournemouth	6BM	289	1,039	1,000
Cardiff	5WA	310	967	1,000
Caterham	2NM	32.5	9,225	
Daventry	5XX	1,554	193	25,000
Do	5GB	479	626	25,000
Dundee	2DE	289	1,039	130
Edinburgh	2EH	289	1,039	330
Glasgow	5SC	399	751	1,000
Hull	6KH	289	1,039	130
Leeds and Bradford	2LS	200 / 289	1,499 / 1,039	130
Liverpool	6LV	289	1,039	130
London	2LO	356 / 261	841 / 1,149	30,000
Manchester	2ZY	376	816	1,000
Newcastle	5NO	261	1,147	1,000

FOREIGN RADIO BROADCASTING STATIONS—Continued

EUROPE—Continued

City	Call	Wave length, in meters	Frequency, in kilo-cycles	Power, in watts
UNITED KINGDOM—continued				
Plymouth	5PY	289	1,039	130
Sheffield	6FL	289	1,039	130
Stoke-on-Trent	6ST	289	1,0˙˙	130
Swansea	5SX	289	1	130
YUGOSLAVIA				
Belgrade		432	695	2,500
Ljubljana		569	527	3,000
Zagreb		307	977	700
SOVIET RUSSIA				
Armavir	RA47	720	416	200
Artemovsk	RA56	790	380	1,200
Astrakhan	RA26	700	428	1,000
Baku	RA45	750	400	4,000
Bogorodsk	RA8	750	400	700
Dneipropetrovsk	RA30	525	571	1,000
Erivan	RA49	1,050	286	1,200
Gomel	RA39	925	324	1,200
Irkutsk	RA57	1,100	273	500
Ivanovo-Vosnessensk	RA7	800	375	180
Kharkov	RA43	{ 477 1,700	629 176	} 4,000
Kiev	RA5	755	397	1,200
Koursk	RA34	575	521	1,000
Krasnodar	RA38	513	584	1,000
Leningrad	RA42	1,000	300	10,000
Do	RA51	150	1,999	350
Minsk	RA18	860	349	1,200
Moscow	RA1	1,450	207	40,000
Do	RA2	450	666	500
Do	RA4	450	666	300
Nalchik	RA67	1,075	279	1,200
Nizhni-Novgorod	RA13	840	357	1,800
Novorossisk	RA33	1,117	268	4,000
Odessa	RA40	975	308	1,200
Orenburg	RA25	640	469	1,000
Petrapavlovsk	RA64	350	857	45
Petrozavodsk	RA46	765	392	2,000
Rostov-on-Don	RA14	820	366	4,000
Samara	RA22	900	333	1,200
Saratov	RA32	420	714	200
Sevastopol	RA9	800	375	250
Smolensk	RA68	330	909	20
Do	RA72	150	1,999	800
Stalino	RA77	730	411	1,200
Stavropol	RA20	550	545	1,200
Sverdlovsk	RA15	1,050	286	500
Tashkent	RA27	715	419	2,000
Tiflis	RA11	870	345	4,000
Tomsk	RA21	300	999	150
Tver	RA44	690	435	1,200
Ulyanovsk	RA51	500	600	20
Vel Ustjuk	RA16	650	461	1,200
Vladivostock	RA17	480	625	1,500
Vologda	RA41	875	343	1,200
Voronezh	RA12	950	316	1,200

ASIA

City	Call	Wave length, in meters	Frequency, in kilo-cycles	Power, in watts
TURKEY				
Angora		1,600	187	5,000
Osmanie		1,200	250	6,000
BRITISH MALAYA				
Singapore	VS1AB	41.3	7,260	----------
Johore	VS3AB	42.5	7,055	----------
CEYLON				
Colombo		800	375	1,750

FOREIGN RADIO BROADCASTING STATIONS—Continued

ASIA—Continued

City	Call	Wave length, in meters	Frequency, in kilo-cycles	Power, in watts
CHINA				
Canton	CAB	435	689	1,000
Hangchow	XGY	335	895	250
Harbin	COHB	445	674	1,000
Mukden	COMK	420	714	2,000
Nanking	XGZ	485	606	500
Peking	COPK	320	937	1,000
Shanghai	NKS	310	967	50
Do	KRC	338	887	250
Do	KSMS	277	1,082	50
Do	RSC	235	1,276	50
Do	SSC	280	1,071	50
Do	XAH	240	1,240	50
Tientsin	CRC	280	1,071	500
Do	COTN	480	625	500
CHOSEN				
Seoul	JODK	435	690	1,000
FRENCH INDO-CHINA				
Haiphong		87	3,446	2,500
HONG KONG				
Victoria Peak	ZBW	350	857	1,500
INDIA				
Bombay	VUB	357	840	3,000
Calcutta	VUC	370	810	3,000
JAPAN				
Hirasio	JHBB	37.5	7,995	----------
Hiroshima	JOFK	353	849	10,000
Kumamoto	JOGK	380	789	10,000
Nagoya	JOCK	370	810	10,000
Osaka	JOBK	400	750	10,000
Sapporo	JOIK	361	831	10,000
Sendai	JOHK	390	769	10,000
Taihoku	JFAK	850	353	1,000
Taipeh	JFAB	39.5	7,590	----------
Tokyo	JOAK	345	869	10,000
KWANTUNG				
Dairen	JQAK	395	759	500
NETHERLAND EAST INDIES				
Bandoeng	PLE	{ 15.93 / 31.86	18,860 } / 9,410 }	30
Do	IBR	58	5,170	1,000
Batavia	PK1AA	75	3,998	500
Djokjakarta	PK2AF	50	5,996	500
Macassar	PK6KZ	41	7,313	500
Malabar	PLF	17	17,640	
Palembang	PK4PA	5	59,964	240
Semarang	PK2AG	----------	----------	
Surabaya	PK3CH	45	6,662	250
Do		140	2,142	500
AUSTRALIA				
Adelaide	5CL	409	733	2,500
Do	5DN	313	958	250
Do	5KA	250	1,199	500
Do	5AD	----------	----------	----------
Ballarat	3BA	----------	----------	----------
Bathurst	2MK	260	1,153	125
Brisbane	4QG	385	779	2,500
Hobart	7ZL	516	581	1,500
Melbourne	3AR	484	620	2,500
Do	3DB	255	1,176	250
Do	3LO	{ 32 / 371	9,369 } / 808 }	2,500
Do	3UZ	319	940	50
Newcastle	2HD	288	1,041	50
Perth	6WF	435	689	2,500

FOREIGN RADIO BROADCASTING STATIONS—Continued

ASIA—Continued

City	Call	Wave length, in meters	Frequency, in kilocycles	Power, in watts
AUSTRALIA—continued				
Sydney	2BL	{ 32.5 / 353	9,225 / 849	} 2,500
Do	2FC	{ 28.5 / 451	10,520 / 665	} 2,500
Do	2GB	316	949	1,500
Do	2KY	280	1,071	750
Do	2ME	28.5	10,520	
Do	2UE	293	1,023	125
Do	2UW	267	1,123	250
FIJI ISLANDS				
Suva		Short.	High.	
NEW ZEALAND				
Auckland	1YA	333	900	500
Do	1ZB	275	1,089	15
Do	1ZQ	252	1,188	
Christchurch	3YA	306	980	500
Do	3ZC	{ 50 / 250	5,996 / 1,199	} 250
Dunedin	4YA	462	648	500
Do	4ZH	278	1,078	20
Do	4ZL	246	1,219	35
Do	4ZM	278	1,078	17
Do	4ZO	278	1,078	7
Eketahuna	2ZE	248	1,209	5
Gisborne	2ZM	261	1,147	160
Masterton	2ZD	254	1,180	2.5
Do	2ZQ	254	1,180	10
Napier	2ZH	238	1,260	15
New Plymouth	2YB	244	1,229	100
Palmerston	2ZF	286	1,049	150
Wanganui	2ZG	500	600	7.5
Do	2ZK	500	600	7.5
Wellington	2YA	417	718	5,000

AFRICA

City	Call	Wave length, in meters	Frequency, in kilocycles	Power, in watts
ALGERIA				
Algiers		364	824	2,400
CANARY ISLANDS				
Las Palmas	EAR5	280	1,071	500
EGYPT				
Cairo		342	869	
Do		330	909	
KENYA				
Nairobi	7LO	{ 31.1 / 400	9,600 / 750	} 2,000
MOROCCO				
Casablanca	AIN	51	5,879	
Do	CNO	305	983	25
Rabat		{ 43.6 / 414	6,877 / 724	} 2,500
TUNISIA				
Carthage	TNU	1,850	162	
Copstantine	8KR	42.8	7,005	
Tunis	TUA	1,250	240	500
UNION OF SOUTH AFRICA				
Cape Town	ZTC	375	800	1,000
Durban	ZTD	407	789	1,000
Johannesburg	ZTJ	{ 32 / 444	9,369 / 676	} 15,000

Revised lists of foreign broadcasting stations are issued by the electrical equipment division of the Bureau of Foreign and Domestic Commerce in mimeographed form whenever changes and additions warrant the revision. There is no charge for such lists, which will be sent to any American firm or individual requesting them.

THE FINANCING OF BROADCASTING

The cost of broadcasting may be borne by the broadcaster who uses radio as a good-will adjunct to another business or operates radio as an avocation; it may be borne by an advertiser or advertisers through fees for direct advertisements; it may be paid by the listeners through any of the multifarious systems previously indicated; or it may be provided through some form of government subsidy. The methods of radio financing, while of prime importance in understanding the character of the market, do not in themselves have more than a superficial effect on the volume of sales. The question of paying the costs of broadcasting requires early attention in setting up a broadcasting system. The importance of this question is readily recognized when it is remembered that a system once adopted can not be discarded without trouble.

Where the costs fall upon the broadcaster, as return for his efforts and expense, he is granted the limited use of a given channel for broadcasting commercial publicity in connection with programs, either for himself or for a paying clientele. Few countries permit advertising of a commercial nature; in those which do not, the cost is placed on the government or the listener.

Radio administration divides advertising into two classes. These have been termed " direct " and " indirect," although the terms are no longer descriptive of the methods. Direct advertising is arranged by the sale of a limited amount of the station's time, usually 5 minutes out of each hour, during which period there is no restraint upon the advertising broadcast. The remaining 55 minutes are devoted to program material designed to entertain the listener. Under the alternative method the station sells the entire hour, the advertiser furnishing the program. Between numbers, advertising matter is given, to whatever extent the advertiser believes most effective. (To offset lengthy advertising talks a recently announced device will silence a set for whatever period a beam of light is directed upon a photoelectric cell, a flashlight being suggested.)

Another source of revenue is the government. The methods by which it may be interested in broadcast financing are numerous. It may be and often is the owner of one or more, or all, of the broadcasting stations in a country. If there is no provision for receiving licenses, these stations are operated entirely on public funds. If there is a licensing system, some income accrues to the stations, deficits or surpluses usually being liquidated from the general treasury. Few governments contribute toward the support of broadcasting stations not owned by them.

Receiving licenses have been adopted by most countries as a means of financing broadcasting. The licensing idea takes many different forms, and the fees are collected in many ways.

In several instances licenses are required only for statistical purposes, the revenue being utilized to defray a part of the cost of issuing licenses and apprehending operators of unlicensed sets.

The license fee is usually an annual charge but may be collected monthly, quarterly, or semiannually, either by the government or by the broadcaster. Subscription fees differ from license fees only in that the collection is invariably made by the broadcaster. In most countries the governments retain or collect appreciable portions of license fees to defray the cost of their connected activities and of necessary police expenses, the broadcasters receiving the remainder. An installation fee is sometimes collected. This fee is ordinarily a strictly government collection and is the only charge made in several countries.

The following table shows the license and other fees charged in various countries for receiving sets.

LICENSE AND OTHER RECEIVING-SET FEES

[Amounts converted to United States dollars at current exchange]

Country	Inspection and installation fees	Annual license fee	Annual broadcasting subscription	Total	
				First year	Subsequent years
Bahamas		$1.22		$1.22	$1.22
Barbados		(1)			
Bermudas		(1)			
British Honduras		5.00		5.00	5.00
Canada		1.00		1.00	1.00
Guatemala	$5.00			5.00	
Trinidad and Tobago		2 2.43–4.87		2.43–4.87	2 2.43–4.87
Bolivia	1.70	12.28		13.98	12.28
Brazil	2.40			2.40	
Peru		4.00		4.00	4.00
Venezuela		11.58		11.58	11.58
Austria		3 3.39–10.16		3.39–10.16	3.39–10.16
Belgium	(1)	(1) (2)			
Bulgaria		1.44		1.44	1.44
Czechoslovakia			$3.60	4 3.30	3.60
Danzig		3.37		3.37	3.37
Denmark		2.68		2.68	2.68
Estonia		2 2.40–4.00		2.40–4.00	2.40–4.00
Finland		2.00		2.00	2.00
France		.39		.39	.39
Germany		5.71		5.71	5.71
Gibraltar		2.43		2.43	2.43
Greece		6.50		6.50	6.50
Hungary		5.40		5.40	5.40
Irish Free State		2.43		2.43	2.43
Italy		.15	3.80	3.95	3.95
Latvia		4.83		4.83	4.83
Lithuania		10.00	1.20–6.00	11.20–16.00	11.20–16.00
Malta	2.67	2.43		5.10	2.43
Norway		5.36		5.36	5.36
Poland		3.36		3.36	3.36
Rumania			3.60	3.60	3.60
Spain		.97		.97	.97
Sweden	10.72	2.68		13.40	2.68
Switzerland	.60	3.00		3.60	3.00
United Kingdom		2.43		2.43	2.43
Yugoslavia		3.96		3.96	3.96
Turkey		44.00		44.00	44.00
Hong Kong		2.20		2.20	2.20
India		3.65		3.65	3.65
Japan (including Chosen and Kwantung)		.50	5.97	6.47	6.47
Syria	.96			.96	
Australia		5 4.25–5.84		4.25–5.84	5 4.25–5.84
New Zealand		7.29		7.29	7.29
Canary Islands		.97		.97	.97
Tunisia		.78		.78	.78
Union of South Africa		5 4.87–8.52	5 4.87–8.52	5 4.87–8.52	5 4.87–8.52

1 Required; no data as to cost.
2 Depending on number of tubes.
3 Depending on income of owner.
4 No charge for first 30 days to permit demonstration without penalty.
5 Depending on distance from main station.

WORLD MARKET CONDITIONS

GEOGRAPHIC FACTORS IN RADIO MARKETING

Among most important factors to be considered in judging the world radio markets are geography, geology, and climate. Of little importance in general marketing, except as transportation may be affected, these factors are of exceptional interest in determining the possibilities of radio reception.

There may be such spottiness in reception that a major degree of difference results in the moving of a set, even to another house in the same neighborhood. Where only a few sets are in operation, the experience in operating them can not give a good basis for judging reception unless the particular situations are identically balanced at the average point for the entire area they are intended to represent. On the other hand, experience is the only guide to the quality of reception. Radio engineering has not yet reached the point where it is possible to state with certainty what results a given type of broadcasting station will give on a particular power or wave length in a chosen place until it has been tried. Thorough and precise analysis of climatic, geological, and other natural factors is impossible because of the lack of sufficient detailed basic information as to how each character might affect the transmission of radio waves. But general data may be accepted as having a reasonable amount of value in making a broad judgment.

The natural conditions as given in this publication are for the most part taken from encyclopedic works privately published, which have been checked with such official information as is available.

Climatic conditions have a deteriorating effect on many radio parts. This is particularly true as regards metals and insulating materials. Certain types of batteries are also prone to develop faults quickly in some climates. Exporters should make a study of the materials employed in their products with a view to determining their suitability for use in the countries where such difficulties are experienced. In some instances changes in receivers would probably increase their marketability. In hot countries with high humidity, insulation and plates for condensers must be of particular qualities to avoid early and inevitable failure.

WAVE LENGTHS USED ABROAD

Sets limited to reception only within the 200–545 meter wave band are completely satisfactory for any part of the Western Hemisphere, but those to be employed elsewhere, particularly Europe, must be capable of receiving on the higher wave lengths in use there. A large number of stations employ waves between 1,340 and 1,875 meters, the higher of the two bands approved by the Washington conference. Sets not capable of covering both these bands are not in demand in such places. The limitation is actually a disability, even greater than that which would maintain in the United States toward a set that received only on wave lengths of from 200 to 300 meters. The stations on this higher band are almost without exception selected stations of high power, broadcasting the highest type of programs.

Short waves continue to show a significant advance in popularity. With modern short-wave sets and adapters for broadcast receivers distant reception has become more important. Evidence of this fact is presented by the demand for long-range sets and the almost total disappearance of demand for strictly local receivers.

CHANGES IN MARKET CONDITIONS

Radio markets are constantly changing, and radio apparatus is one of the first commodities to respond to any important change in economic conditions. The wide range of initial costs brings appropriate radio equipment within the reach of nearly everyone, and any change in the purchasing power of any class is soon reflected in change in the demand for radio sets. An attempt has been made to indicate in this publication, so far as possible, the character of each market under a normal condition of prosperity, eliminating consideration of transitory developments.

The market conditions are being reported constantly by consular officers of the Department of State and representatives of the Department of Commerce stationed in foreign countries, and these reports are published in various ways. This information is highly " perishable" and will be found in Commerce Reports, the weekly foreign trade journal of the Department of Commerce, and in Electrical Foreign Trade Notes, a mimeographed circular issued weekly.

COMPARISON OF MARKETS

Radio markets are as yet incapable of accurate measurement. The diversity of the conditions affecting the demand and variations of the importance of each condition are responsible for this. Such matters include climate, tastes and desires of the people, religion, the form of government, educational opportunities and standards, business methods, wealth, density of population, races, standards of living, availability of broadcasting, language, recreational activities, and other such factors. Few of these conditions can be precisely defined, much less mathematically evaluated, but any one or a combination of them may determine the position of the decimal point in transacting radio business. Statistics covering a few of these factors are available for only a few countries. Where they agree between countries as to the matters covered they are seldom to be found parallel in regard to important definitions.

United States export figures, though not entering into any precise definition of market absorption, have proved a valuable guide for judging this elusive factor. Estimates comparing markets, when based on these statistics are for all practical purposes a correct valuation for market analyses.

Requests are often made for foreign import and export statistics, to be used in conjunction with American figures. While all countries collect and publish them, the matter of classification often precludes their use. Only the United States divides radio equipment into several classes. Two or three other countries have radio accounted separately, while all others group these goods with other kinds so broadly that all statistical value is lost, sometimes as " scientific instruments," sometimes as " electrotechnical goods," sometimes in a single group for " electrical equipment," sometimes with " telephone and telegraph equipment," and in a few cases, with other electrical goods as " machinery." From such data nothing of value to the radio exporter can be abstracted.

AMERICAN EXPORTS OF RADIO EQUIPMENT

Comparing the last two calendar years (1928–1929) with 1925, the previous peak year in radio exporting, 12 markets stand out as being consistently best, appearing among the first 15 in all three years. Canada ranks first, with notable yearly increases; Japan was second in 1925, eighth in 1928 with a considerable loss in value, and fifteenth in 1929 with a small increase. Argentina, fifth in 1925, almost quadrupled its purchases in 1928 to attain second place, and with a further slight increase maintained that position in 1929. Australia with consistent increases, held third place all three years. The United Kingdom, in fourth, fourth, and eighth places, respectively, dropped off about one-fifth in 1928, but in 1929 nearly equalled the 1928 total.

Italy has increased its purchases spectacularly, not appearing among the first fifteen in 1925, but ranking sixth in 1928, and fourth in 1929 by tripling the 1928 purchases. Brazil ranked sixth, fifth, and ninth with moderate increases, and Mexico seventh and tenth in 1925 and 1928 with a slight loss, but fifth in 1929 with more than four times the 1928 figure. New Zealand, thirteenth, seventh, and sixth, shows large increases, as does Cuba, fourteenth, eleventh, and seventh. Spain eighth, thirteenth, and twelfth, shows erratic tendencies, with an appreciable decrease followed by a large increase. The Netherlands, ninth in 1925, dropped to twelfth and thirteenth, but the money value increased each year. The Philippine Islands dropped from twelfth to fifteenth in 1928, was fourteenth in 1929. but increased purchases considerably both years. A tabulation of these markets showing the years considered follows:

UNITED STATES EXPORTS OF RADIO EQUIPMENT TO LEADING COUNTRIES IN 1928 AND 1929, COMPARED WITH 1925

Rank	1925		1928		1929	
	Country	Value	Country	Value	Country	Value
1	Canada	$3,682,929	Canada	$5,264,642	Canada	$10,784,156
2	Japan	2,216,535	Argentina	1,513,693	Argentina	1,775,531
3	Australia	675,483	Australia	1,179,450	Australia	1,541,876
4	United Kingdom	644,916	United Kingdom	460,003	Italy	1,145,376
5	Argentina	408,593	Brazil	432,524	Mexico	1,041,288
6	Brazil	358,156	Italy	337,285	New Zealand	699,736
7	Mexico	272,135	New Zealand	286,771	Cuba	658,038
8	Spain	230,265	Japan	267,253	United Kingdom	631,186
9	Netherlands	138,695	Uruguay	244,309	Brazil	550,037
10	Sweden	122,451	Mexico	224,255	Russia in Europe	414,762
11	Chile	113,671	Cuba	222,391	China	412,694
12	Philippine Islands	109,030	Netherlands	209,199	Spain	366,763
13	New Zealand	98,265	Spain	171,325	Netherlands	307,452
14	Cuba	84,087	China	127,913	Philippine Islands	297,107
15	Czechoslovakia	71,813	Philippine Islands	120,337	Japan	282,175

During the last four years, during which United States radio exports have been divided into five classes, our exports to foreign countries have been as follows:

VALUE OF UNITED STATES EXPORTS OF RADIO APPARATUS

Country of destination	1926	1927	1928	1929
TRANSMITTING SETS AND PARTS				
Austria				$2,412
Belgium	$9,222	$317		399
Bulgaria				66
Czechoslovakia		475	$807	5,198
Denmark	33			7,806
Estonia				122
France	1,902	329	287	2,451
Germany	1,144	8,932	32,238	12,553
Greece				18
Hungary				68
Italy	50,152	3,119	8,087	154,481
Latvia				327
Netherlands	423	220	1,618	6,447
Norway	59			350
Poland and Danzig		1,744	5,896	4,720
Portugal		70		539
Rumania				34
Russia in Europe	9,429	5,745	1,318	355,751
Spain	156	4,349	1,098	41,010
Sweden	260	106	381	
United Kingdom	8,647	34,499	26,403	8,097
Canada	15,263	30,141	255,434	380,396
British Honduras	38	500	12	
Costa Rica		411	4,337	3,202
Guatemala	26		75	2,913
Honduras	21,220	21,545	34	5,204
Nicaragua	250	196	281	1,820
Panama	520	1,825	3,195	18,220
Salvador	60		15	1,457
Mexico	21,293	3,523	8,377	21,218
Newfoundland and Labrador	480	174	360	2,097
Barbados		13		93
Jamaica	50		159	
Trinidad and Tobago	124			180
Other British West Indies		568	676	1,275
Cuba	3,277	21,877	13,825	28,685
Dominican Republic	896	29,011	25,426	1,794
Netherland West Indies		853	117	650
Haiti	22,427			6,298
Virgin Islands				120
Argentina	75,826	51,014	99,454	208,372
Bolivia			4,660	316
Brazil	11,405	18,271	101,420	86,143
Chile	13,136	2,172	216	10,628
Colombia		14,060	24,100	8,667
Ecuador		39	1,000	
Peru		100	38	2,271
Uruguay	15,203	26,131	1,108	3,646
Venezuela	13,368	2,932	8,945	22,382
British India	365		19	
British Malaya	15	23		81
Ceylon			78	
China	2,459	34,262	47,239	235,063
Netherland East Indies			5,845	60,553
Hong Kong	84		2,174	626
Japan	163,317	55,874	41,053	43,359
Kwantung				186
Philippine Islands	7,609	15,142	24,859	168,345
Siam			8,975	50
Russia in Asia	60,657			
Australia	5,608	3,995	6,244	9,616
British Oceania			22	
French Oceania	259	72		7
New Zealand	18,975	2,496	700	1,461
British South Africa		67		21
Egypt				73
Liberia		3,905		157
Mozambique			33	
Total	555,640	401,109	768,728	1,940,483
RECEIVING SETS				
Austria	1,786	209	817	2,128
Azores and Madeira Islands	75	52	51	788
Belgium	1,995	1,103	2,015	5,079
Bulgaria		1,285	464	948
Czechoslovakia	1,524	2,802	8,177	10,671
Denmark	15,818	13,872	8,466	1,475
Estonia	180	1,471	485	254
Finland	4,046	5,232	6,095	1,168

VALUE OF UNITED STATES EXPORTS OF RADIO APPARATUS—Continued

Country of destination	1926	1927	1928	1929
RECEIVING SETS—continued				
France	$6,158	$4,841	$4,990	$23,250
Germany	5,892	6,833	7,147	8,330
Gibraltar			45	50
Greece	785	3,064	1,177	1,184
Hungary	170		543	217
Iceland	165		78	107
Irish Free State	307	626	709	398
Italy	39,887	65,489	171,555	574,069
Latvia	78	44		
Lithuania	50	33		
Malta, Gozo, and Cyprus	510	45	51	
Netherlands	6,832	1,001	7,083	3,096
Norway	11,195	3,604	961	2,493
Poland and Danzig	1,614	580	460	
Portugal	4,845	4,333	5,302	14,831
Rumania	2,142	3,292	2,145	19,056
Russia in Europe	268	5,133	345	5,001
Spain	76,191	71,659	100,051	169,680
Sweden	17,933	9,653	3,534	4,049
Switzerland	3,026	24,441	10,647	45,529
Turkey in Europe	100	296		
United Kingdom	55,375	34,256	21,150	20,801
Yugoslavia and Albania	130	323	190	246
Canada	1,237,960	1,128,893	2,449,666	5,406,233
British Honduras	549	760	482	264
Costa Rica	1,306	1,348	4,370	2,948
Guatemala	5,302	1,941	4,007	7,881
Honduras	2,334	1,393	2,465	4,107
Nicaragua	1,024	195	2,146	1,097
Panama	4,032	2,855	2,328	5,343
Salvador	17,202	3,385	6,781	3,436
Mexico	73,170	63,013	147,513	747,657
Miquelon and St. Pierre Islands		25	48	149
Newfoundland and Labrador	7,157	15,637	12,575	46,751
Bermudas	2,948	1,666	6,164	10,777
Barbados	153	128	248	365
Jamaica	3,275	3,162	3,826	6,226
Trinidad and Tobago	1,673	349	1,370	1,549
Other British West Indies	2,515	3,468	7,548	10,314
Cuba	41,813	17,452	110,325	381,980
Dominican Republic	3,304	3,310	12,390	9,844
Netherland West Indies		802	1,209	633
Haiti	2,851	4,335	1,217	2,538
Virgin Islands	446		137	301
Argentina	293,202	453,475	482,371	669,484
Bolivia	701	2,129	2,799	3,314
Brazil	86,061	91,540	99,026	171,973
Chile	16,718	15,005	33,197	101,335
Colombia	5,095	2,441	12,689	29,992
Ecuador	1,332	267	3,171	478
British Guiana	40	260	132	
Surinam				34
French Guiana				310
Paraguay	147	62	196	
Peru	2,995	3,416	3,341	4,742
Uruguay	26,403	111,830	148,385	130,050
Venezuela	29,928	1,309	1,879	2,800
British India	6,632	22,574	8,654	7,011
British Malaya	398	185	485	959
Ceylon	542	630	223	470
China	15,257	20,976	34,279	51,902
Java and Madura	414	214	657	585
Other Netherland East Indies	60	613	188	2,264
Hong Kong	2,058	690	440	8,522
Iraq		164		
Japan	82,502	15,478	29,540	16,551
Kwantung	391	435		2,020
Palestine	350	86	150	125
Persia				226
Philippine Islands	27,817	20,093	52,808	46,620
Siam		55	2,154	639
Russia in Asia		95		
Syria	60	10		100
Turkey in Asia	164	32		
Australia	266,617	429,831	349,414	489,989
British Oceania	1,151	1,191	396	2,511
French Oceania	200	852	1,180	2,572
New Zealand	319,272	229,313	112,519	378,768
Belgian Congo				208
British East Africa				317
British South Africa	16,425	15,667	25,147	77,569

VALUE OF UNITED STATES EXPORTS OF RADIO APPARATUS—Continued

Country of destination	1926	1927	1928	1929
RECEIVING SETS—continued				
Egypt	$800	$403	$163	$2,059
Algeria and Tunisia			40	158
Liberia	164	164	115	
Morocco		78	618	2,174
Mozambique	28		651	166
Other Portuguese Africa		89		
Canary Islands	1,601	392	95	
Other Spanish Africa		163	231	1,627
Total	2,873,676	2,961,301	4,549,825	9,775,655
TUBES				
Austria	526	1,235	2,237	8,017
Azores and Madeira Islands			175	
Belgium	5,447	9,267	23,918	5,100
Bulgaria		125	357	426
Czechoslovakia	1,276	4,285	2,838	4,589
Denmark	1,621	7,569	10,859	33,348
Estonia	203		1,727	90
Finland	287	278	833	264
France	3,890	4,420	8,551	26,562
Germany	4,885	2,967	1,576	6,510
Gibraltar				35
Greece	76	430		198
Hungary	128	874	1,257	687
Iceland			33	
Irish Free State		185		
Italy	7,529	11,528	38,179	117,624
Latvia			172	36
Malta, Gozo, and Cyprus			229	
Netherlands	2,199	970	1,532	2,133
Norway	2,809	1,234	785	630
Poland and Danzig	162	633	739	84
Portugal	68	1,324	1,938	4,527
Rumania	196	412	592	6,397
Russia in Europe	143	1,329	520	1,807
Spain	11,763	18,229	21,705	50,609
Sweden	3,167	1,137	1,980	1,060
Switzerland	312	8,081	10,211	15,760
United Kingdom	34,089	11,056	22,256	69,536
Yogoslavia and Albania		47		99
Canada	114,068	145,051	173,843	317,217
British Honduras	56	82	222	151
Costa Rica	164	1,795	1,836	3,674
Guatemala	695	306	1,268	2,729
Honduras	668	1,094	925	1,063
Nicaragua	574	215	1,171	3,540
Panama	2,328	5,629	5,218	5,366
Salvador	1,822	472	759	1,250
Mexico	8,297	7,880	17,787	108,406
Miquelon and St. Pierre Islands		12		20
Newfoundland and Labrador	1,308	1,509	1,864	9,475
Bermudas	512	193	657	1,484
Barbados			171	206
Jamaica	52	743	443	1,694
Trinidad and Tobago	36	110	254	838
Other British West Indies	77	199	1,260	1,586
Cuba	18,045	19,651	23,959	101,907
Dominican Republic	5,049	225	4,455	1,686
Netherland West Indies		309	497	922
French West Indies			30	
Haiti	822	1,017	262	1,247
Virgin Islands	27			73
Argentina	79,659	117,257	123,515	213,023
Bolivia	14	304	279	1,488
Brazil	33,150	56,012	69,142	90,248
Chile	8,961	11,898	17,200	31,577
Colombia	361	10,249	16,055	18,324
Ecuador	33	139	563	1,901
British Guiana		33	19	65
Surinam				25
Paraguay	43	68		
Peru	684	1,849	1,890	6,006
Uruguay	7,007	19,734	25,904	35,581
Venezuela	3,693	3,781	3,286	7,842
British India	913	554	1,366	2,487
British Malaya	12	275	306	1,136
Ceylon	37	29		712
China	5,811	22,927	33,178	46,021
Java and Madura	1,125	1,050	145	4,627

Value of United States Exports of Radio Apparatus—Continued

Country of destination	1926	1927	1928	1929
TUBES—continued				
Other Netherland East Indies			$124	$38
French Indo-China				62
Hong Kong	$597	$167	128	9,186
Japan	194,951	95,283	74,918	89,263
Kwantung				181
Palestine				2,524
Philippine Islands	14,573	39,039	18,708	31,454
Russia in Asia			3,445	
Siam			1,423	621
Syria		21		
Australia	221,608	267,093	178,534	329,745
British Oceania	73	239	11	2,953
French Oceania		139	198	
New Zealand	53,955	76,166	46,937	125,857
British East Africa		315		
British South Africa	4,649	3,930	3,575	18,475
British West Africa			58	20
Egypt	20	15		372
Algeria and Tunisia				28
Liberia		1,600		473
Morocco			49	700
Mozambique			62	13
Canary Islands	203	44	110	148
Other Spanish Africa		10	51	661
Total	867,631	1,004,337	1,017,560	1,997,409
RECEIVING-SET COMPONENTS				
Austria	1,002	1,771	1,674	1,559
Azores and Madeira Islands		49		40
Belgium	3,111	4,184	24,286	41,982
Bulgaria			106	
Czechoslovakia	9,415	8,816	3,904	8,019
Denmark	35,565	36,601	22,942	27,368
Estonia		32	60	5
Finland	1,978	5,035	8,742	832
France	8,175	3,653	17,388	54,776
Germany	7,794	5,321	14,506	15,494
Greece	22	1,786	819	
Hungary	87	351	143	1,906
Iceland	199			
Irish Free State	4,081	2,403	1,038	
Italy	8,752	26,240	58,483	117,132
Latvia	163		473	774
Lithuania		33		
Malta, Gozo, and Cyprus	322		37	
Netherlands	85,979	71,306	148,412	216,459
Norway	5,714	2,789	627	870
Poland and Danzig	1,177	15,015		1,237
Portugal	2,074	2,202	2,456	8,037
Rumania	5,614	3,460	593	11,126
Russia in Europe	341	607	799	2,653
Spain	37,304	43,854	32,393	63,418
Sweden	17,055	7,801	5,157	3,484
Switzerland	1,593	3,686	9,499	52,885
Turkey in Europe	27	26		
United Kingdom	238,055	120,907	165,523	205,362
Yugoslavia and Albania		20		100
Canada	500,427	635,671	1,280,602	2,213,762
British Honduras	203	54	61	163
Costa Rica	920	624	1,054	4,488
Guatemala	1,147	1,072	725	2,886
Honduras	2,223	829	1,407	1,923
Nicaragua	799	444	1,188	2,360
Panama	4,939	6,994	6,216	15,121
Salvador	3,857	563	944	698
Mexico	25,861	29,771	14,655	61,256
Miquelon and St. Pierre Islands				80
Newfoundland and Labrador	2,149	1,443	2,911	7,765
Bermudas	337	1,063	2,531	2,417
Barbados	131	621	773	841
Jamaica	322	1,209	1,941	3,877
Trinidad and Tobago	143	889	1,899	2,989
Other British West Indies	670	970	1,794	1,692
Cuba	12,510	14,261	36,412	46,373
Dominican Republic	1,337	2,236	3,318	5,147
Netherland West Indies	43	1,115	1,994	3,068
French West Indies			87	50
Haiti	670	1,535	1,136	877

Value of United States Exports of Radio Apparatus—Continued

Country of destination	1926	1927	1928	1929
RECEIVING-SET COMPONENTS—continued				
Virgin Islands		$99	$138	$189
Argentina	$194, 295	481, 852	583, 335	416, 129
Bolivia	843	364	1, 565	3, 592
Brazil	102, 947	134, 224	89, 456	128, 422
Chile	5, 097	10, 542	11, 614	19, 879
Colombia	2, 564	8, 958	12, 021	16, 106
Ecuador	237	562	432	2, 081
British Guiana	130	224	1, 630	1, 311
Surinam		69	88	29
Paraguay	166	218	254	546
Peru	2, 071	5, 088	6, 325	6, 650
Uruguay	15, 268	33, 541	37, 674	41, 692
Venezuela	3, 611	10, 899	2, 575	10, 653
Arabia			360	
British India	2, 168	5, 038	3, 747	2, 873
British Malaya	462		733	1, 013
Ceylon	356	319	5, 237	147
China	9, 734	2, 572	14, 725	50, 232
Java and Madura	3, 254	2, 095	1, 705	19, 446
Other Netherland East Indies	668	696	724	396
French Indo-China				297
Hong Kong	1, 572	6, 650	4, 801	26, 108
Japan	107, 306	53, 368	55, 549	33, 882
Kwantung	832		777	1, 075
Palestine			125	
Philippine Islands	5, 890	10, 089	8, 657	25, 972
Russia in Asia	500	2, 025		1, 149
Siam		76	640	3, 590
Turkey in Asia		13	99	
Australia	391, 668	343, 119	239, 992	273, 382
British Oceania	3, 574	2, 368	348	450
French Oceania	144	89	289	
New Zealand	122, 296	126, 330	77, 799	92, 406
British East Africa				15
British South Agrica	4, 250	4, 466	6, 986	19, 685
British West Africa				210
Egypt	683	209	547	3, 761
Liberia	115	20	78	34
Morocco				713
Mozambique			1, 616	243
Canary Islands	428	168	211	1, 311
Other Spanish Africa				361
Total	2, 016, 466	2, 305, 721	3, 054, 310	4, 419, 381
RECEIVING-SET ACCESSORIES [1]				
Austria	616	450	867	1, 678
Azores and Madeira Islands		31		107
Belgium	5, 509	2, 595	4, 847	3, 733
Bulgaria		291	233	
Czechoslovakia	14, 346	6, 611	3, 034	1, 665
Denmark	60, 338	24, 786	31, 317	11, 885
Estonia	650		119	24
Finland	2, 189	3, 212	4, 827	973
France	11, 870	17, 326	31, 674	41, 769
Germany	17, 743	11, 954	49, 871	73, 850
Gibraltar			22	5
Greece	1, 491	1, 375	239	71
Hungary	735	338	2, 106	865
Iceland			74	
Irish Free State	94	220	26	26
Italy	10, 866	24, 423	60, 981	40, 980
Latvia	210	17		
Malta, Gozo, and Cyprus		326	385	224
Netherlands	59, 674	55, 692	50, 554	38, 485
Norway	7, 597	1, 735	1, 944	104
Poland and Danzig	150	1, 011	184	1, 786
Portugal	1, 056	1, 352	1, 938	1, 101
Rumania	684	746	488	2, 442
Russia in Europe	454	410	106	49, 514
Spain	29, 909	14, 610	16, 082	11, 273
Sweden	18, 063	16, 903	8, 182	7, 649
Switzerland	2, 756	4, 838	11, 878	12, 277
Turkey in Europe		188		
United Kingdom	125, 313	64, 780	224, 671	118, 946
Yugoslavia and Albania	28	57	42	
Canada	1, 019, 957	1, 224, 147	1, 105, 097	1, 732, 195

[1] 1926–1928 included loud-speakers.

VALUE OF UNITED STATES EXPORTS OF RADIO APPARATUS—Continued

Country of destination	1926	1927	1928	1929
RECEIVING-SET ACCESSORIES [1]—continued				
British Honduras	$767	$349	$171	$174
Costa Rica	1,999	1,927	3,067	9,723
Guatemala	3,452	2,239	3,316	2,609
Honduras	4,288	7,547	1,484	1,735
Nicaragua	1,208	1,601	2,097	1,248
Panama	6,585	6,191	6,471	3,554
Salvador	4,199	802	1,477	1,144
Mexico	51,092	33,978	35,923	48,038
Miquelon and St. Pierre Islands		8	61	944
Newfoundland and Labrador	2,221	4,401	7,954	5,932
Bermudas	302	787	2,060	473
Barbados	239	120	349	69
Jamaica	341	875	2,279	2,128
Trinidad and Tobago	127	681	1,555	435
Other British West Indies	2,205	533	1,248	4,010
Cuba	24,696	26,599	37,870	26,121
Dominican Republic	10,254	907	3,736	1,227
Netherland West Indies	15	496	573	799
French West Indies			95	
Haiti	1,528	1,783	827	2,091
Virgin Islands	16			14
Argentina	113,542	135,956	225,218	73,738
Bolivia	572	186	812	4,829
Brazil	57,071	66,207	73,480	29,815
Chile	10,723	10,799	15,377	23,126
Colombia	1,706	2,577	9,157	17,334
Ecuador	1,460	77	1,017	992
British Guiana	37	33	228	66
Surinam		104	10	102
Paraguay	248	117	319	
Peru	2,350	1,705	2,320	6,566
Uruguay	7,685	29,839	31,238	11,500
Venezuela	13,185	4,418	1,041	2,269
British India	1,994	1,075	1,654	1,527
British Malaya	220	4	471	141
Ceylon	259	35	60	61
China	23,330	11,964	22,766	19,420
Java and Madura	1,538	4,239	2,239	2,827
Other Netherland East Indies	215	2,090	1,089	606
Hong Kong	3,149	897	3,786	11,688
Iraq	53	19		
Japan	168,765	84,705	61,693	42,416
Kwantung	670	112	120	65
Philippine Islands	12,990	9,846	15,305	14,951
Russia in Asia		34	100	18
Siam			127	1,338
Syria		3		75
Turkey in Asia		191		
Other Asia		79		
Australia	419,444	457,949	405,266	109,960
British Oceania	12,801	904	458	745
French Oceania	227	1,003	549	917
New Zealand	112,724	100,215	48,756	42,403
British East Africa			36	
British South Africa	5,043	7,417	19,573	10,520
British West Africa	15	30	65	1,430
Egypt	667	235	45	309
Algeria and Tunisia			10	
Liberia		2,478	1,581	1,544
Morocco	55	49	404	135
Mozambique	42		42	58
Other Portuguese Africa		33		
Canary Islands	488	55	174	
Other Spanish Africa		19		143
Total	2,481,040	2,539,946	2,670,987	2,699,728

[1] 1926–1928 included loud-speakers.

The value of loud-speakers exported in 1929 and the total value of all radio equipment sent to each country during that year are shown in the following table:

VALUE OF LOUD-SPEAKERS AND TOTAL VALUE OF ALL RADIO EQUIPMENT EXPORTED
FROM THE UNITED STATES IN 1929

Country	Loud-speakers	Grand total	Country	Loud-speakers	Grand total
Austria	$1,279	$17,073	Haiti	$178	$13,229
Azores and Madeira Islands	70	1,005	Virgin Islands	15	712
Belgium	20,381	76,663	Argentina	194,785	1,775,531
Bulgaria		1,440	Bolivia	716	14,255
Czechoslovakia	3,278	33,420	Brazil	43,436	550,037
Denmark	5,213	87,094	Chile	31,387	217,932
Fstonia	16	511	Colombia	8,673	99,096
Finland	691	3,928	Ecuador	457	5,909
France	54,708	203,516	British Guiana	180	1,622
Germany	74,353	191,090	Surinam	13	203
Gibraltar	10	100	Paraguay		546
Greece	316	1,787	Peru	1,685	27,893
Hungary	479	4,222	Uruguay	28,116	253,585
Iceland	5	112	Venezuela	2,822	48,768
Irish Free State	32	456	British India	846	14,744
Italy	141,090	1,145,376	British Malaya	407	3,737
Latvia		1,137	Ceylon	31	1,421
Malta, Gozo, and Cyprus	48	272	China	10,056	412,694
Netherlands	40,832	307,452	Java and Madura	921	85,216
Norway	597	5,044	Other Netherland East Indies	47	7,094
Poland and Danzig	327	8,154	French Indo-China		359
Portugal	2,091	31,126	Hong Kong	3,426	59,556
Rumania	5,599	44,654	Japan	56,704	282,175
Soviet Russia in Europe	36	414,762	Kwantung	459	3,986
Spain	30,773	366,763	Palestine		2,699
Sweden	2,887	19,129	Persia	18	244
Switzerland	17,155	143,516	Philippine Islands	9,765	297,107
United Kingdom	208,444	631,186	Siam	265	6,503
Yugoslavia and Albania	78	523	Soviet Russia in Asia		1,167
Canada	734,353	10,784,156	Syria		175
British Honduras	50	802	Australia	329,184	1,541,876
Costa Rica	816	24,851	British Oceania	172	6,831
Guatemala	1,204	20,222	French Oceania	52	3,548
Honduras	394	14,426	New Zealand	58,841	699,736
Nicaragua	228	10,293	Belgian Congo		208
Panama	2,460	50,064	British East Africa		332
Salvador	945	8,930	Union of South Africa	10,336	135,808
Mexico	54,713	1,041,288	Other British South Africa		798
Miquelon and St. Pierre Islands	12	1,205	Gold Coast	146	396
			Other British West Africa		1,410
Newfoundland and Labrador	7,587	79,607	Egypt	447	7,021
Bermudas	1,585	16,736	Algeria and Tunisia	338	524
Barbados	325	1,899	Liberia		2,208
Jamaica	1,800	15,725	Morocco	122	3,844
Trinidad and Tobago	1,808	7,799	Mozambique		480
Other British West Indies	1,760	20,637	Canary Islands	58	1,517
Cuba	72,972	658,038	Other Spanish Africa	137	2,929
Dominican Republic	325	20,023			
Netherland West Indies	152	6,224	Total	2,289,491	23,122,147
French West Indies		50			

THE RADIO MARKETS BY COUNTRIES

Note.—The languages given are those in which broadcasting is done, or, in the absence of local broadcasting, the language in which broadcasting should be most successful. This is not necessarily the commercial language or the mother tongue of the country. This statement is deemed important in view of the fact that a certain amount of confusion has arisen in the past where differentiation has not been made.

NORTH AMERICA

BAHAMAS

Language, English ; area, 4,404 square miles ; population, 54,886

The development of radio in the Bahamas is steadily increasing. The group consists of 29 inhabited islands and numerous cays. The climate is poor for radio, being warm and damp, with hot summers and cool winters. From December to March conditions are said to be good, but during the remainder of the year there is considerable trouble from atmospherics.

Broadcasting is prohibited. Receiving licenses are issued upon payment of a fee of 5 shillings, required annually. No other restrictions are imposed. Some 300 receiving sets are in use, 4, 5, and 6 tube battery sets predominating. Nassau, with 16,000 population, has about 98 per cent of these. Most of the sets are of American origin, though some British sets have been installed. One American 6-tube set is reported to regularly receive stations as far west as Chicago, being powered by storage battery and B eliminator.

Only Nassau has central-station electric service, which is 110 volts, 60-cycle alternating current. A growing number of socket power sets are in use. Because of the climatic difficulties, short-wave sets and adapters are increasing in popularity, though it is reported that reception of short-wave broadcasts from Europe is not entirely satisfactory.

Reception from stations in the United States and Canada is good between the months of October and April, and some reception is to be had all year, though from May to September there is considerable trouble from static.

BARBADOS

Language, English ; area, 166 square miles ; population, 198,336

In common with other English-speaking parts of North America, Barbados presents a radio development of a higher order than the general conditions would indicate. There is evidence that development will continue. The climate is poor for reception; the summers are hot and the winters warm, and static is bad at all seasons. Reception is possible only from December to March.

The law governing radio was adopted on December 3, 1925, placing the controlling authority with the governor in executive committee.

Licenses are required for broadcasting, receiving, and importing, with a penalty of not exceeding £100 for violations. No broadcasting stations are operating in Barbados, the nearest ones being in the United States, Cuba, Haiti, Dominican Republic, and Porto Rico. The number of receiving sets in use is estimated at 250. Very few, if any, alternating-current receivers are in use. The lighting plant at Bridgetown gives service at 110-volt, 50-cycle alternating current. Some short-wave sets have been put into operation.

BERMUDAS

Language, English; area, 19 square miles; population, 21,987

Bermuda is one of the most advanced of the smaller colonial possessions of the British Empire in respect to radio. While conditions in this part of the world are not entirely satisfactory for reception, development has been comparatively rapid, and the number of sets in use is constantly increasing. About one-third of the population is white. Hamilton is the only city; almost the entire population of the colony is included in this urban district. Some 350 small coral islands, only 20 of which are occupied, make up the group. The weather is hot throughout the year, but radio reception is fairly good from October to March. Reception is subject to fading, static, and interference from a Government wireless station at all times.

The only regulations are those specified for communicating stations, under which it has been ruled that receiving-set owners must secure licenses. There is no broadcasting in Bermuda, the nearest stations being those in the United States. Receiving sets are said to number 700. Most of these were purchased from American sources and are of the better quality. The cheaper sets do not meet the requirements of conditions existing in Bermuda. Few alternating current or short-wave sets have been installed. Where central-station electric service is available, 100-volt, 60-cycle alternating current is provided.

CANADA

Language, English; area, 3,684,723 square miles; population, 9,796,800

Only a few countries of the world precede Canada in point of progress in radio development, all being countries of appreciably greater population. The conditions affecting development are almost identical with those in the United States, to which this development is comparable. In some respects, such as climate, Canadian conditions are more advantageous than our own. In the populous southern section broadcast reception is very popular, while in the more sparsely settled northern areas radio has provided a highly valuable means of entertainment and news communication.

Canada has warm summers, winters being cool in the southern areas and cold through the north. Radio reception is good at all times of the year throughout all Provinces, only slight static interference being encountered from heat during the summer. There are no exceptional regulations governing broadcasting, though there has been much recent agitation for a change to a system based on that of the United Kingdom. The use of receiving sets is restricted only by the assessment of an annual license fee of $1. Broadcasting by more than one station in any city at one time is discouraged by assigning identical wave lengths to all stations in or near that city, with particular exceptions made by the Department of Marine and Fisheries, the Government body administering radio matters.

Canada has 64 broadcasting stations, in all populated parts of the country, and nine amateurs who broadcast occasionally, using a wave of 250 meters. Receiving licenses numbered 296,926 on July 1, 1930. Some estimates of the sets not registered run as high as 40 per cent of the total, though it is generally questioned whether, in view of the small license fee, the actual number of evasions is large. Alternating-current sets are popular, and short-wave sets are becoming numerous, especially in the more isolated districts of the north. Central-station electric service is usually at 110-volt, 60-cycle alternating current.

Formerly nearly all of the receiving equipment used in Canada was of American manufacture, but there has been a strong impetus given to Canadian radio manufacturing by the establishment of numerous branch factories in Canada by American firms and by the growth of a considerable independent industry. This overcomes the difficulty arising from the high duty on radio apparatus and the sales tax on imported goods required by Canadian law. This tendency has been apparent in recent years in the trend of American radio exports to Canada. That country, nevertheless, remains the best market for American radio apparatus. In 1928 Canada set a new record in the proportion of American radio exports purchased, and the total itself was considerably higher than in any previous year. In 1929 the statistics were yet more striking, Canada taking nearly $11,000,000 out of slightly over $23,000,000 total radio exports, the Canadian figure barely falling short of the previous world record total.

Because of the tendency that has become particularly apparent during 1928 in all radio-manufacturing countries for the owners of radio patents to exercise more strictly their rights under those patents, the marketing of equipment in Canada should follow only after a study of the situation in regard to patents under which the merchandise is manufactured. Licensing in the United States is not sufficient procedure in most cases. A corporation, Canadian Radio Patents (Ltd.) has secured control of many important radio patents and requires the payment of a minimum fee of $10,000, plus a royalty of 10 per cent, on all radio sets and tubes manufactured or imported into Canada. As a direct result several American manufacturers have withdrawn from the Canadian market.

The Government-controlled Canadian National Railways have developed the use of radio on trains to the extreme. Broadcasting stations throughout the railway's service area are operated as a chain to provide programs primarily for reception on the various transcontinental trains. This development is the subject of considerable interest from an engineering point of view and is the most intensive example of such use of radio in the world.

COSTA RICA

Language, Spanish; area, 23,005 square miles; population, 471,521

Costa Rica has shown considerable interest in broadcasting, and the resulting developments are of a reasonably well-advanced nature, although general conditions are not such as to encourage any expectation of great developments. The experience of Costa Rica should prove of value in advancing radio throughout Central America.

Agriculture is the principal industry. The most important cities are San Jose, Port Limon, and Heredia. The country is mountainous with plains on the coast. The climate, as in the rest of Central America, is poor for radio, being hot at all seasons. Reception is fair from November to March. No reception is possible during the summer months.

Radio regulations adopted by Costa Rica in 1920 and 1921 were of such nature as to have no application beyond wave-length control in broadcasting. In July, 1929, the Government transmitted the recommendations of the Washington Radio Conference to the Constitutional Congress, recommending their acceptance and the provision of a radio law to be enforced by a radio commission.

A Government broadcasting station, the gift of the Mexican Government, is operated in San Jose, and a short-wave station at Heredia. Balboa, Guatemala, and Salvador may be received with more or less success. Estimates of up to 700 sets installed have been made, but it is believed that about 250 is a more nearly accurate figure. Most of these sets are of American manufacture, but a fair number of British and German sets are also in use. Only one or two alternating-current sets have been installed, with about the same number of short-wave sets. Central-station service is preponderantly 110-volt, 60-cycle alternating current, but there is some variation in regard to many of the smaller plants.

CUBA

Language. Spanish ; area, 44,164 square miles ; population, 3,418,033

Cuba, the largest island of the West Indies, has much the greatest degree of radio development, broadcast reception having proved especially popular with Cubans. Although at no time has there been any spectacular development, a steady advance has been maintained. Further increase in the future is clearly indicated by the steady promotion of radio that has maintained in the past. The principal cities of the island are Habana, Camaguey, Cienfuegos, Santiago, and Matanzas. The three topographical regions are the eastern mountain, the central plain, and the western hill areas. The climate is fair for radio except in summer, reception being good from November to March. The mean annual temperature at Habana is 77° F. Both summers and winters are classed as hot, and reception is marred by static at all times.

The local purchasing power depends almost entirely upon the market price for raw sugar, and, to a lesser extent, that for tobacco. When prices are high there is a great influx of money, but when prices are low the number of families having any surplus for luxuries is very few.

Permits are required for broadcasting. Receiving is allowed without restriction.

There are 66 broadcasting stations, 31 being in Habana and the remainder scattered throughout Cuba. Stations in the United

States are received regularly, as well as those in Porto Rico, Haiti, and other Caribbean countries. Since Cuban stations cover the entire dial, international reception is somewhat hampered, while climatic conditions prevent such reception except in winter.

On September 5, 1930, the wave lengths of Cuban broadcasting stations were reassigned on a basis resembling the channel system employed in the United States. A few of the channels coincide with American assignments, the remainder being fixed midway between them.

Recent estimates indicate that some 28,875 receiving sets are in service in Cuba. Most of these are of American origin, while a number have been constructed locally from American parts. Alternating-current sets have proved popular among the classes able to afford the investment necessitated and are now sold almost to the complete exclusion of battery sets. The current supplied by central stations varies widely, with 110-volt, 60-cycle alternating current slowly taking predominance. There is also considerable 220-volt, 60-cycle alternating current. Both these voltages are used in Habana. Short-wave reception is also popular, but among a much smaller class.

DOMINICAN REPUBLIC

Language, Spanish ; area, 19,325 square miles ; population, 897,405

Radio conditions in the Dominican Republic have not warranted any particularly great development. While there has been some advance, it is not comparable with that in Haiti, Cuba, or Porto Rico.

The Republic occupies roughly half the island of San Domingo, or Haiti, the Haitian Republic covering the remainder. The surface consists mainly of plains, bordered along the Atlantic coast by low mountains, with high mountains in the center of the island. The southern coast is arid. The climate is hot, both in summer and winter. Radio reception is fair from October to March, but very poor the rest of the year.

No radio regulations have been reported. There is one broadcasting station at Santo Domingo. Stations at Port-au-Prince (Haiti), San Juan (Porto Rico), and in Cuba and the United States are received. Estimates place the number of receiving sets in use at 1,250, mostly of American manufacture. Short-wave sets have proved particularly popular, and some alternating-current sets are in use. The largest cities have central-station service of 110 volts, 60-cycles.

FRENCH WEST INDIES

Language, French ; area, 1,073 square miles ; population, 474,268

Radio equipment in the French West Indies (Guadeloupe, Martinique, etc.) is practically nonexistent. In common with other parts of the West Indies, the climate is always hot and radio reception accordingly poor.

No radio regulations have been issued, but under the general French law receiving sets are licensed at a cost of 10 francs annually. There is no broadcasting, programs from stations in various Caribbean countries being received with more or less success. About 100 receiving sets are in use, all of French manufacture. While it would be necessary to lay all of the groundwork, it is not improbable that a number of short-wave sets might be sold, particularly in view of the short-wave broadcasts from the Eiffel Tower in Paris. The lighting current in Fort de France and Lamentin is 110 volts direct, but is not well maintained in either place.

GREENLAND

Language, Danish; area, 46,740 square miles; population, 14,355

Very little is known about radio in Greenland. A rumor that a broadcasting station is operating in Greenland has not been authenticated. About 25 receiving sets have been reported in use. Short-wave sets might be sold to a certain extent for the purpose of keeping in touch with Denmark, although sets limited to the broadcast band probably are able to serve this purpose equally well. All sales would be through Danish houses.

GUATEMALA

Language, Spanish; area, 42,353 square miles; population, 2,119,165

Radio has proved particularly popular in Guatemala, even though the field is limited by natural conditions and the concentration of wealth in the hands of a small part of the population. Greater future developments are indicated. About 20 per cent of the people are of the white race. Guatemala, Quezaltenango, Coban, and Totonicapan are the principal cities. The country is mountainous and has a very poor climate for radio. It is hot in the coastal lowlands and warm in the mountains through the year. The mean annual temperature ranges in different sections from 70° to 80° F., and the rainfall is heavy. Static is very bad. There is no reception from April to August, but it is fair from November to early February; during the remainder of the year results are poor.

Owners of receiving sets are required to pay a $5 installation fee, and merchants must notify the Government of all sales of radio apparatus. A broadcasting station is operating in Guatemala City, and stations in Salvador, Costa Rica, Panama Canal Zone, and Mexico may be received with more or less regularity. Installations of receiving sets now number about 250. Practically all are of American manufacture, though a few German sets are in use.

Alternating-current receivers have not been purchased in any number. In Guatemala City the central-station service is provided at 110 volts, 60 cycles, but elsewhere various voltages are used, including 100, 125, 200, 220, and 250, some direct current, and varying frequencies in alternating current. Short-wave sets have been introduced quite successfully.

HAITI

Language, French; area, 10,204 square miles; population, 2,300,200

Haiti, the only French-speaking Republic in North America, has an exceptionally high degree of radio development, considering the general conditions and the limited number of people who could be expected to purchase radio equipment. The Government encourages radio reception, but the market remains somewhat unresponsive.

One-tenth of the population is white. The principle cities are Port au Prince, Cape Haitien, and Gonaives. Almost all of the territory is mountainous, and the climate very poor for radio. Reception is possible only between October and April. Hot weather maintains at all seasons.

Broadcasting is a government monopoly, one station being installed at Port au Prince for educational purposes. There is no restriction on the ownership or operation of receiving sets. Stations in the Dominican Republic, Porto Rico, Cuba, and the southeastern part of the United States are received. It is estimated that 750 receiving sets are in use, but a greater number is not improbable. Almost all are of American manufacture. Alternating-current sets have been introduced, but their success is not yet fully known. Most central-station service is 110 volts, 60 cycles, alternating current. A combination short and long wave receiver is the most popular type. Short-wave reception is commonly demanded, and short-wave adapters are sold.

HONDURAS

Language, Spanish; area, 46,332 square miles; population, 773,408

Honduras does not have any great radio development, although broadcasting is·proving popular among a small class of the population. The principal cities are Tegucigalpa, Comayagua, and La Esperanza. The country consists of a broad central plateau with wide coastal plains. The climate of the coast is hot, but the plateaus are cool. Rainfall is abundant. Static is bad most of the year, reception being possible only during the wet season—from September to March. No radio regulations have been adopted. A short-wave broadcasting station was opened in Tegucigalpa in 1929. Stations in Salvador, Guatemala, and Costa Rica are received with fair success, with intermittent reception from Panaman, Mexican, Cuban, and American stations. Some 78 receiving sets are in use, nearly all of American manufacture. The use of alternating-current and of short-wave sets has not been reported. Lighting current is usually 110 volts, but variations in the case of several communities, some of them important, are noted. The frequency in the case of the 110-volt stations is generally 60 cycles.

JAMAICA

Language, English; area 4,450 square miles; population, 858,188

Jamaica has a greater development than seems warranted by the conditions existing there, which probably may be explained by the fact that the population is English speaking, and reception of American stations is good. Approximately 15,000 of the population are white. The purchasing power is generally low. Kingston, Port Antonio, Spanish Town, and Montego Bay are the principal cities. The surface is generally mountainous, only about one-sixth of the territory being flat. The climate is tropical except in the highlands, where it is more temperate. Because of static, reception is impossible except between October and March, and then is satisfactory only after 10 p. m.

No regulations governing radio have been issued, but a license on each receiving set is required. There is no broadcasting; stations in

Cuba, the United States, and the Caribbean countries are depended upon for programs. About 250 receiving sets are in use, according to a recent report. These are about evenly divided between British and American manufacture. Short-wave sets have practically displaced all others because of static conditions. The best service is obtained from 3, 5, and 7 tube models. Alternating-current sets in use have not proved entirely satisfactory because of static conditions. Central-station service is provided at 110 volts, 25 and 40 cycles, and at other voltages and frequencies in various parts of the island.

MEXICO

Language, Spanish ; area, 760,200 square miles ; population, 14,308,753

Radio in Mexico enjoys an increasing popularity, and development has been steady. The climate and other conditions do not interfere with good reception sufficiently to discourage the purchase of receiving sets by a comparatively large part of the population. Unity of language and nationality gives a greater value to broadcasting in distant parts of the country; in other parts of Latin North America no station has this advantage at any great distance. Mexico City, Guadalajara, and Puebla are among the principal cities. The interior is mainly a high table-land broken by mountains, while the coasts are bordered by plains. The central and northern table-land has a moderate climate, but the coasts and southern areas are tropical. The rainy season extends from May to October, and static is bad in all sections during that season. Reception becomes fair in all parts of the country during November, extending to February in the south and April in the north.

Broadcasting is administered through the Department of Communications and Public Works. Permits to broadcast are required and are granted only to Mexican citizens. The Government reserves the right of censorship. Broadcasting is supported by the owners and operators of the stations. There is no monopoly. While many of the stations are operated by Government departments, the majority are privately owned. Registration of receiving sets is required.

Mexico has 28 broadcasting stations, 12 being in Mexico City. Three of these operate on short waves. Northern Mexico and the Gulf coast receive American stations easily. To the southeast, Central American stations are picked up. More distant stations provide occasional reception.

The number of receiving sets in use is estimated at 100,000. More than 90 per cent are of American origin. Several other countries are represented, and there is a small but growing radio-manufacturing industry in Mexico.

Alternating-current sets are at present most in demand. While 110-volt, 60-cycle, alternating current is general, characteristics vary so greatly that particular information should be secured. Short-wave reception is common among a small part of the population, but in general is popular only with experimenters.

When installment sales are contemplated, it is well to investigate the Mexican law. Suspension of title transfer until payments are completed is not legal, nor are chattel mortgages.

MIQUELON AND ST. PIERRE

Language, French ; area, 93 square miles ; population, 3,918

The development of radio in Miquelon and St. Pierre has been slow since there is no broadcasting in French available, except such as may be received from the French-speaking stations in Quebec. No regulations are in force except such as have been adopted in France for all colonies. Under these regulations, a 10-franc annual license fee is collected from the owner of each receiving set. About 25 receiving installations have been made. Most of these sets are of French origin. No alternating-current sets are yet in use. Short-wave reception has aroused some interest.

NETHERLAND WEST INDIES

Language, Dutch ; area, 403 square miles ; population. 58,931

The Netherland West Indies lie in the poorest part of the Caribbean for radio reception, and the development has been correspondingly small. There is a further disadvantage in the lack of broadcasting in the Dutch language. The weather is hot throughout the year, and radio reception is poor at all times, although some success is attained between October and February.

Through lack of development, there has been no incentive to the drawing up of a code of radio regulations. There is no broadcasting in the island and none sufficiently near to give really satisfactory service. The station at Caracas, Venezuela, and some of those along the northern part of the Caribbean and Gulf of Mexico can be received occasionally during the best seasons. There are no restrictions upon receivers. Some 50 sets are in use. These are various in origin, including American, British, Dutch, French, and German. Short-wave reception should prove popular, since there is a large station in the Netherlands broadcasting on short waves primarily for the benefit of Netherland colonies. No information as to the present status of short-wave reception is available. Alternating-current sets have not been introduced. Curacao has lighting service at 110 volts, 60 cycles, alternating current.

NEWFOUNDLAND AND LABRADOR

Language, English ; area, 165,000 square miles ; population, 267,330

Newfoundland and Labrador show a comparatively high rate of radio development, considering the distance from broadcasting stations. The climate and the availability of programs from Canadian and American stations have made it possible for the people to satisfy their unusual interest in radio. The market is small but active. The principal city is St. Johns, in Newfoundland. The surface is generally flat; the summers are cool and the winters long and cold. Reception is good only during the winter, because of interference from the aurora borealis.

There is one broadcasting station in St. Johns, operating on a 395-meter wave length, opened in 1929. Stations in Canada, the United States, and Europe are easily received. There are some 1,250 receivers in Newfoundland and Labrador. Practically all are of Canadian or American manufacture.

Alternating-current sets have aroused considerable interest, although only a few have been placed in service. Lighting service in Newfoundland is uniformly at 110-volt, 60-cycle alternating current. Short-wave reception (up to 50 meters) has been found good at most times. It should grow in popularity.

NICARAGUA

Language, Spanish; area, 49,200 square miles; population, 638,119

The climate of Nicaragua is generally poor for radio, and static is very bad. The principal cities are Bluefields, Corinto, and Managua. The eastern section is a table-land, the remainder of the country being mountainous. The climate of the table-land, however, is more moderate than that of the coast, and reception is therefore a little better. Reception is possible only from November to March during the dry season.

Receiving licenses are necessary, but there are no other special requirements. The country has no broadcasting stations, depending on San Jose, Guatemala City, and San Salvador for programs. A contract for the provision of broadcasting within the Republic was negotiated, but as it carried a monopoly on the importation and sale of radio equipment, which violated the national constitution, it was later cancelled. There has been no subsequent attempt to revive the question. Receivers number 45. There do not appear to be any alternating-current or short-wave sets in use. Most central stations provide service at 110-volt, 60-cycle alternating current, but there are some important variations.

PANAMA

Language, Spanish; area, 33,667 square miles; population, 442,522

Radio has been retarded in the Republic of Panama by a number of highly important conditions, but it has nevertheless proved popular. There is every indication that the future will show an even greater development. The capital and principal city is Panama. The western portion of the country is flat, the eastern mountainous. The climate of the plains is hot and damp, the mean annual temperatures of various sections averaging 80° F. Static is usually very bad. Reception is possible only from December to April.

Broadcasting is prohibited under a treaty between the United States and Panama dealing with the defense of the canal. Receiving permits, costing $2.50, are required.

Broadcasting from stations in the Canal Zone, Salvador, Guatemala, and Costa Rica is received. The Republic is reported to have same 300 receiving sets installed. Most of them are of American manufacture, with a small percentage of German and other European sets.

A few alternating-current sets are reported to be in use. Lighting current is mostly 110-volt, 60-cycle-alternating, but some variations are noted. Short-wave reception is successfully accomplished by a small part of those interested in radio, but the interest has not yet spread to any great extent.

SALVADOR

Language, Spanish; area, 7,225 square miles; population, 1,610,000

Salvador has a comparatively high degree of radio advancement, since its situation on the west coast of Central America gives it a variety of conditions favorable to reception. Radio is popular, but the ownership of sets is restricted to a small class. The principal cities are San Salvador, Santa Ana, and San Miguel. Plains extend along the coast, the interior being a plateau; the region is volcanic. The climate is hot, and the rainy season extends from May to October. Static is very bad. Reception on broadcast waves is possible only between November and February.

Broadcasting is a monopoly of the Government. Receiving is limited to Salvadorians; foreigners will be issued permits if they renounce their right to present claims through diplomatic channels. The following rates are fixed by decree: Application for permit, 5 colons; installation of receiving set, if made by the Government, 30 colons; monthly payment, 3 colons. Regenerative sets are prohibited. Importing, manufacturing, and merchandising are Government monopolies, but concessions are granted.

There is one broadcasting station at San Salvador. Stations in the United States, Cuba, and Mexico are sometimes received, while the stations in Guatemala, Costa Rica, and the Canal Zone are easily picked up. Estimates place the number of receiving sets installed at 51. Nearly all are American, and most of the rest are German. Alternating-current receivers have not yet been fully tested in this market. Lighting service is mostly 110-volt, 60-cycle, alternating current, but many stations provide 220-volt, direct current, and alternating current is supplied in various combinations of 110 and 220 volts with frequencies of 20 and 60 cycles. Popularity has swung to short waves, since reception on this band is much better than on broadcast waves.

TRINIDAD AND TOBAGO

Language, English; area, 1,976 square miles; population, 381,753

There is no great degree of radio development in the British islands of Trinidad and Tobago as compared with other English-speaking countries, since they are situated in a part of the Caribbean subject to extreme difficulties in reception and at a distance from broadcasting stations using the English language.

The principal cities are Port of Spain and San Fernando. The surface is low and flat, with mountains rimming the north and south coasts of Trinidad. The climate is very poor for radio, static being bad at all times.

License fees are charged, varying according to the number of tubes in the receiver, from 10 shillings to £1 annually. No other regulations are in force.

The only satisfactory reception is from Caracas, Venezuela, with some programs coming from Cuba, Porto Rico, Haiti, and the United States. Some 35 receiving installations have been made. Locally assembled sets of British and American parts are being sold. Alternating-current sets have not yet been introduced, except in possible isolated instances. Short-wave programs are received, but not many people have provided themselves with the proper equipment. The use of long-wave sets has been practically abandoned. Where central-station service is available, the current is alternating, 110 volts, 60 cycles.

SOUTH AMERICA

ARGENTINA

Language, Spanish; area, 1,153,418 square miles; population, 10,904,022

Argentina leads all South American countries in radio develop ments and ranks fourth among the countries of the world. Aside from Chile and Uruguay, no other South American country has the climatic advantages enjoyed by Argentina, while various other characteristics of the country aid in the use of radio. The people, while concentrated in a limited part of the country's area, are scattered through that area to an extent which makes radio as a means of entertainment and news dissemination particularly advantageous. Buenos Aires is the principal city; Rosario and Cordoba have populations in excess of 100,000, and there are several other important municipalities.

The country consists of a great prairie, bounded on the east by the Atlantic coast and on the west by the Andes Mountains. The climate is temperate in the north and cold in the south. At Buenos Aires the mean annual temperature is 63° F. Radio reception is good through the year, especially from April to September.

Radio is controlled by the Government through the Minister of Marine and the Minister of the Interior. Broadcasting is permitted freely, permits costing only a 1-peso stamp tax on the application. Advertising is employed for revenue. Receiving sets may be installed by anyone, the only requirement being that the chief of naval communications be advised of the installation. There are no exceptional restrictions on importing, manufacturing, or merchandising.

There are 43 broadcasting stations in the Republic, of which 20 are in Buenos Aires. At present those stations actually in Buenos Aires are being moved to the outlying sections beyond the city limits. Additional service in the vicinity of Buenos Aires is provided by stations in Uruguay and Brazil to the northeast and Chile to the west. Small areas receive Bolivian and Paraguayan stations.

A true estimate of the number of sets in use is difficult to obtain, but those from the more reliable sources indicate about 400,000. American sets are the most popular and are in the majority, but many Argentine, British, and German sets are also in use. Argentinians insist upon late-model receivers. The demand is for approximately the same types of sets as are most used in the United States. The use of short-wave reception has shown advancement.

Alternating-current sets are finding increased popularity in Argentina. By far the greatest number of towns and cities are provided with 220-volt direct-current service, and the others have various voltages and frequencies. Buenos Aires has 225 volts, 25 and 50 cycles. The standard American voltage of 110 is rare.

BOLIVIA

Language, Spanish ; area, 506,467 square miles ; population, 2,952,139

The development of radio in Bolivia is limited by the small proportion of whites and the general lack of desire on the part of the Indians for any of the advantages of civilization. The principal cities are La Paz, Cochabamba, Potosi, Sucre, and Oruro. The eastern section consists of plains, the western of mountains. The climate is good for radio, the mean annual temperature at various altitudes ranging from 50° to 74° F. The rainy season lasts from December to May, 75 inches of rain falling in the lowlands. The best season for radio reception is from April to September.

Radio broadcasting is under the control of the Director General of Telegraphs of the Ministry of Communications. Licenses are granted, without monopoly, for only the gratuitous broadcasting of entertainment. Five minutes of each hour may be employed for the broadcasting of advertising matter. Stations are licensed to operate certain hours daily.

Receiving licenses will be granted to all applicants. An initial registration fee of 5 bolivianos ($1.70) and an annual license fee of 36 bolivianos ($12.25) are charged.

There is one broadcasting station in La Paz. Some reception from Chilean stations and from Lima, Peru, is accomplished. The number of receiving sets in use in Bolivia is about 65, of various origins. Alternating-current receivers have not yet been introduced, and little headway has been made in the introduction of short-wave sets and adapters. The lighting service in La Paz is 120 volts, 50 cycles, while elsewhere 110 or 220 volts, direct current, and 25, 50, and 60 cycles alternating current are found in various combinations.

BRAZIL

Language, Portuguese ; area, 3,285,319 square miles ; population, 39,163,855

Brazil, because of its size and extent of its coast line, variety of economic activities, and distribution of population. will undoubtedly have great development of radio in the future. The great variance in climate tends to increase advancement in the southern part far beyond the north, in proportion to the population, which itself is largely concentrated in the southern localities. The people are occupied in a number of ways, including agriculture, forestry, and manufacturing, but the concentration of wealth restricts the number of set owners considerably. Broadcasting facilities have developed slowly, this perhaps being the most important factor which has heretofore retarded the growth of the market. Rio de Janeiro, Sao Paulo, Pernambuco, Bahia, and Para, all seaports, are the principal cities.

The radio region of Brazil includes only the coastal strip. The interior is generally heavily forested and sparsely settled. In the list of States in which receiving sets are licensed, only two interior ones are included, and these two are only short distances from the coast. Further references to the " north," " middle," and " south " will mean those sections of the coastal strip.

In the north there are the usual atmospheric disturbances of the Tropics. There is also some interference from marine telegraphs and shore stations. Climatic conditions improve southward, but even the extreme south is subtropical, and there is a prevalence of atmospherics almost always in an annoying degree. Sao Paulo and Rio de Janeiro, the radio centers of Brazil, lie in latitudes comparable to that of Cuba. The average humidity is high throughout the radio regions of Brazil. Sets should be protected against this condition, especially metal parts and transformers. The use of brass and bronze in preference to aluminum and nickel is highly desirable. Only enameled wire should be installed.

Radio is administered by the Department of Public Works and Transportation, the Department of Marine, and the Department of War. Concessions for the establishment of broadcasting stations are required. There is no monopoly. Receiving is permitted on registration, the fee for which is 20 milreis ($2.40 in United States currency). No annual charge is made. Sets are subject to Government inspection.

Brazil has 23 broadcasting stations scattered along the coast from the mouth of the Amazon to the Uruguayan border, the bulk of them being in the south. Two of these are short-wave transmitters. The southern area also receives Uruguayan and Argentine stations. A recent estimate places the number of receiving sets at 175,000, mostly crystal, approximately 4,000 of which are registered. American sets are in the majority and greatly outsell European products, though German, French, British, and Italian sets are popular in certain sections settled by immigrants of those nationalities. Current of 110, 120, and 220 volts, both alternating and direct current, 50 and 60 cycle frequency, are supplied in various combinations. Rio de Janeiro has 110-volt, 50-cycle alternating current for lighting. Short-wave receivers are becoming popular, and it is possible that this class of receivers will prove more popular than long-wave sets.

BRITISH GUIANA

Language, English; area, 89,480 square miles; population, 299,839

Radio has had little development in British Guiana. Only about 15 receiving sets are in use, mostly British. A short-wave broadcasting station was opened in May, 1929, but there is no indication that the market for radio sets has been greatly stimulated by it. All seasons are hot and static is bad. Reception is possible only between November and February. There are no alternating-current sets and not more than one or two short-wave receivers in the colony. The only central station supplies 110-volt, 60-cycle alternating current.

CHILE

Language, Spanish; area, 281,820 square miles; population, 4,364,395

Chile is one of the foremost countries of South America in radio development, but because of the concentration of wealth, promotion has been slow. Particularly in Santiago there is a great amount of cross-interference between broadcasting stations, and throughout the more heavily populated regions considerable difficulty from static has been reported from some localities. Climatically, Chile extends through warm, cool, and cold regions, the latter extending to uninhabited regions of frigid temperatures.

The Republic has an extreme width of less than 120 miles and a length of 2,800 miles. Practically all of the population lives in the northern and central parts. Santiago, Valparaiso, Concepcion, and Antofagasta are the principal cities. The country comprises the western slope of the lower Andes Mountains and the narrow coastal plain. The climate varies considerably, owing to the wide ranges of both altitude and latitude. The mean annual temperature at Iquique is 64° F., at Valparaiso 59°, and at Ancud 53°. The rainfall varies extremely.

FIGURE 1.—A cosmopolitan station in Chile, American and British equipment predominating

Radio is controlled by the Ministry of Marine. The only regulations affecting broadcasting are those requiring registration and the ordinary precautions for the safety of the State and the protection of public morals. Registration of receiving sets is required, but no tax or fee is assessed. Six broadcasting stations are operating in Chile, all being in the twin cities of Santiago and Valparaiso. Broadcasting from Lima, Peru, and Buenos Aires, Argentina, is sometimes received, but not with sufficient regularity to be entirely satisfactory.

The number of receiving sets in use has been estimated at 35,000, about 90 per cent being of American origin and the remainder mostly British and German. Several alternating-current sets have been placed in service and appear to be satisfactory, but they are useful only in the cities. Many important markets still require battery sets. Lighting current is usually supplied at 110 volts, 60 cycles, or 220 volts, 50 cycles, alternating. Short-wave reception is not popular among Chileans, though several foreigners have this equipment.

COLOMBIA

Language, Spanish; area, 482,400 square miles; population, 8,000,000

Radio developments have been greatly discouraged by climatic conditions in Colombia to the point that practically no progress has been made. The principal cities are Bogota, Cartagena, and Barranquilla. The country is generally mountainous. The climate is tropical to the extreme in the lowlands. Static is bad most of the year in all sections. The only reception that is accomplished—and this is said to be unsatisfactory—takes place during January, February, and March.

Colombia has two broadcasting stations at Bogota. These were opened in 1929 and 1930. One operates on a short wave, and there is a possibility that the other will change in the near future, since short-wave reception has been more successful. It has been estimated that 350 receiving sets are in use in Colombia, mostly of American origin. Alternating-current sets are not used. Lighting service characteristics vary considerably between cities. There is no prevailing combination.

ECUADOR

Language, Spanish; area, 118,627 square miles; population, 1,500,000

Ecuador has in the past shown little progress in radio. However, there has recently been a general improvement in radio development, and the number of sets is increasing. Most of the population is of Indian or Negro blood. The principal cities are Guayaquil, Quito, and Cuenca. The entire country is mountainous. The climate is poor for radio, Ecuador being crossed by the Equator. Reception is best from June to September.

Only members of established radio clubs are permitted to own receivers. Reception from Lima, Peru, the nearest station, is not exceptionally good. A recent estimate indicates that some 150 receiving sets are in use, largely American, with some British and German sets. Short-wave reception has met with some success, only short-wave sets at present being sold. There do not appear to be any alternating-current receivers in use. Central-station service is mostly 110-volt, 60-cycle alternating current, but 120 volts is also common, as are frequencies of 40 and 50 cycles.

FALKLAND ISLANDS

Language, English; area, 4,618 square miles; population, 3,510

Because of the great distance from any broadcasting, and that in Spanish, the British Falkland Islands have shown little radio progress. The population is small. Summers are warm and winters cool, reception being poor. About 15 receiving sets are in service, all being of British origin. There is no broadcasting in the islands, and South American stations are received only with difficulty.

FRENCH GUIANA

Language, French; area, 32,000 square miles; population, 44,202

Practically no radio progress has been made in French Guiana. About eight sets are in use, all French. No broadcasting is available for satisfactory reception. All seasons are hot. The only central station provides direct current only, so alternating-current sets can not be used. Short-wave reception has not been developed.

PARAGUAY

Language, Spanish; area, 172,000 square miles; population, 791,469

The principal city of Paraguay is Asuncion. The country is mainly flat. Reception is best from May to September, but from November to March it is seldom possible. Summers are hot and winters warm, with poor receiving conditions.

About 150 receiving sets have been installed. These were purchased through Argentine sources and are of varying origins. One broadcasting station has operated for more than three years in Asuncion, and several Argentine stations are received. No regulations have been adopted, since radio has been little known.

Central-station service is mostly 220-volt, 50-cycle alternating current. Alternating-current receivers have not been introduced, nor are short-wave sets in evidence outside the class interested in " tinkering " with radio.

PERU

Language, Spanish; area, 533,916 square miles; population, 5,500,000

Peru has shown great interest in radio developments, and the country has advanced in this respect beyond some other South American countries where the conditions and the agreements which the Government entered into to secure broadcasting facilities have somewhat retarded progress. Yet the general popularity of radio in Peru has not been seriously checked by these drawbacks. The principal cities are Lima, Arequipa, and Callao. The surface is rugged and mountainous except for a narrow coastal strip. Climatic conditions are not conducive to good reception. The best reception is between July and September. Fair reception may be had from May to October.

A monopoly at one time reserved to the grantee the sole right to broadcast and to deal in radio apparatus. This firm collected license fees from the owners of receiving sets. Being controlled by British interests, it preferred to sell British goods, but since the terms of its concession required that 40 per cent of the material sold be purchased in the United States, the imports were so divided. The buying public, however, demanded American apparatus. After the first American quota had been exhausted and only British materials remained for sale, considerable discontent with the arrangement was shown. Discontent was fomented by dealers who had been unable to make terms with the broadcasting company for the retailing of the apparatus. The Government revoked the concession and in its stead placed the concessionnaire in charge of broadcasting, which became a function of the Government. The receiving license fee is about $4 annually.

Some 18,200 receiving sets are in service, about 70 per cent being American. British, Swedish, and Dutch tubes and sets are also being marketed. There are three broadcasting stations, two being in Lima. No foreign stations can be satisfactorily received. Very few alternating-current receivers have been put into service. Central stations provide 110-volt, 60-cycle alternating current at Lima, but elsewhere both voltage and frequency vary. Short-wave sets are popular, particularly those with changeable coils to work both short and long waves.

SURINAM

Language, Dutch ; area, 54,291 square miles ; population, 142,896

Radio development in Surinam has been almost negligible, and it is to be doubted that the future will show any great improvement. The number of receiving sets has been reported as 18, of various origins. Broadcasting is not available in any satisfactory form. Caracas, Venezuela, and sometimes stations in northern Brazil and the West Indies can be picked up. Hot weather maintains throughout the year. Neither alternating-current nor short-wave receivers have been introduced.

URUGUAY

Language, Spanish ; area, 72,153 square miles ; population, 1,762,451

Uruguay has displayed exceptional interest in radio, and developments there have been much beyond what was to be expected from the existing conditions. The number of receiving sets is increasing rapidly, while broadcasting stations have been opened up in appreciable numbers. Most of the development has been restricted to the Montevideo area, which has the only concentration of population. Further developments appear certain.

The surface of Uruguay is hilly and the climate good for radio, the best season being from April to October.

Radio is under the control of the division of radio communication service. There are no exceptional restrictions on broadcasting. Receiving is freely permitted.

About 17,150 receiving sets are estimated to be in use. American sets are the most popular and in the greatest number, but a number of British and German sets are also in service.

There are now 26 broadcasting stations in Uruguay, all but seven being in Montevideo; Argentine and Brazilian stations are received regularly.

Alternating-current receivers are in use and have generally proved satisfactory. Short-wave reception from the United States is popular. Central-station service is generally at 220-volt, 50-cycle, alternating current, and 220-volt direct current.

VENEZUELA

Language, Spanish ; area, 393,976 square miles ; population, 3,026,818

Radio developments in Venezuela have not been as great as they might have been because of the number of factors retarding the increase of the number of listeners. Climatic conditions are not of the best, and the high receiving-license fee would appear to be prohibitive. The concentration of wealth, however, prevents the license fee from restricting the number of listeners, as those who can afford receiving sets can easily afford this fee.

The principal cities are Caracas and Maracaibo. With the exception of the Orinoco Valley, the country is mountainous. The climate is hot and the humidity is high; radio reception from distances is poor.

Radio is regulated by the Ministry of the Interior, which at one time granted a monopoly giving the concessionnaire the sole right to broadcast and to manufacture, import, and sell radio apparatus, but this was recently revoked. At present it is necessary to secure a permit prior to placing the order, from the Ministry of Interior, for each importation. It is understood that these permits are freely granted. Receiving licenses cost 5 bolivars per month, the proceeds going for the support of broadcasting. About 2,000 receiving sets have been installed. Nearly all are of American origin, though British and Dutch sets are also to be found.

A broadcasting station was established on May, 1926, at Caracas, but operation has since been suspended. Short-wave reception has interested a limited part of the listeners. For the present long-wave reception is impossible. It is thought that alternating-current receivers will be preferred to battery types by future purchasers. Central-station service in Caracas is 190-volt, 25 and 50-cycle alternating current. Elsewhere 110-volt, 60-cycle alternating current is general.

EUROPE

ALBANIA

Language, Albanian; area, 17,374 square miles; population, 831,877

Albania has few conditions which would encourage the development of radio. Summers are hot and winters cool. Reception is good only from October to May. A broadcasting station in Tirana has been reported. Yugoslavian and Italian stations are most easily received. Only 12 receivers have been reported in service, all of German origin. No use of alternating-current or short-wave receivers has been reported.

AUSTRIA

Language, German; area, 32,369 square miles; population, 6,526,661

Austria, despite restrictions, has a high degree of radio development. The climate is good for radio, and, although there is a considerable concentration of wealth, the poorer classes are generally able to afford small receivers. The license fee somewhat restricts this development, however. The populace generally is greatly interested, and broadcasting service from the several Austrian stations and those in neighboring countries using the German language provides a plentiful choice of programs for Austrian reception.

The capital and largest city, Vienna, has a population of about 2,000,000. The country is for the most part mountainous, and the climate is extremely varied, owing to the differences in altitude. The mean annual temperature at Vienna is 40° F. The summers are warm and the winters cold. Radio reception is good in most sections, the season of best reception being from October to March.

A broadcasting monopoly has been granted in the Oesterreich-ischer Radioverkehrs Aktiengesellschaft, a broadcasting company. This company is controlled by the State, which owns 60 per cent of the stock. Its activities are supported by the proceeds from receiving license fees, the amount of which depends upon the use to which the set is to be put and the income of the licensee.

FIGURE 2.—Broadcasting station at Innsbruck, Austria

Control over all activities is maintained through a system of licenses which include broadcasting and receiving, importing, manufacturing, and merchandising. Persons holding a regular license may import radio equipment, but all others must secure a special license for that purpose. Receiving licenses cost 2 schillings ($0.28 in United States currency) per month, but if the licensee's annual income exceeds 8,400 schillings, the fee is 6 schillings per month. Records of all sales must be kept; these are subject to inspection at any time. Merchants are held liable for sales made to persons not licensed to possess radio apparatus. In addition to duty, there is a 5.5 per cent turnover tax which is collected by the customs authorities.

An estimate of the number of receivers, licensed and unlicensed, places the figure at 371,011. Practically all are of Austrian and German manufacture, but a number from various other countries are also in use. American receivers are practically excluded by patent restrictions.

Austria has six stations of which two are in Vienna. One is a short-wave transmitter. Broadcasting from several neighboring countries is received, language making that from Germany particularly valuable.

Alternating-current sets are showing increased popularity. Both 110 and 220-volt central-station services are general, 42 and 50 cycles predominating. Short-wave reception is common only to a few enthusiasts. There is little short-wave broadcasting in Europe, and the hours of American broadcasts are inconvenient.

AZORES

Language, Portuguese; area, 922 square miles; population, 242,613

Although the Azores are situated a great distance from broadcasting of any kind and have comparatively poor reception conditions, radio has proved popular, and a number of sets have been installed. The Azores, lying about 900 miles off the coast of Portugal, are politically part of the Portuguese Republic. Being of volcanic origin, these islands are mountainous and rugged. The climate is warm and equable; frost is unknown, the temperature ranging from 50° to 73.5° F. Radio reception is fair in any season and is best from September to April.

There are no restrictions on the use of receiving sets. According to a recent estimate, radio installations number about 200. A large percentage of receivers are of American origin, but the majority appear to be British. No broadcasting has been done in the Azores, but stations in Spain and Portugal are received without great difficulty. The wave lengths of stations received range from 200 to 3,000 meters.

Only one or two alternating-current receivers are in use, battery sets appearing to give better service at the distances over which receivers must be capable of operating. There is no information as to the use of short-wave sets or adapters, but they should be popular for use under prevailing conditions.

BELGIUM

Language, French; area, 11,752 square miles; population, 7,923,077

Belgium has a high degree of radio development, but it has been retarded by a number of factors. Postwar financial conditions have at times practically abolished the business of radio dealers, but the popularity of broadcasting has served to restore it as soon as prospective purchasers were able to afford the investment. Development in the construction of broadcasting stations has been slow, but this is largely made up by the great number of high-powered stations in neighboring countries.

Brussels, Antwerp, Liege, Ghent, and Mechlin are the principal cities. The northern portion consists of lowlands, which slope to a plateau in the south. The climate is conducive to good radio reception, being similar to that of England. The mean annual temperature is 50.6° F., the mean maximum being 57.2° and the mean minimum 44°. The average annual rainfall is 28.4 inches, but varies considerable in different regions, ranging from 27 to 40 inches a year. Radio reception is good at all times except during the months of June, July, and August, and it is fair even then.

Regulations require that an installation fee and a receiving license fee be paid by owners of receiving sets. Regenerative sets are prohibited. No exceptional restrictions on importing, merchandising, or manufacturing are imposed.

Besides 11 broadcasting stations in Belgium, those in the United Kingdom, France, Germany, the Netherlands, and other countries are received. Statistics indicate that 63,125 licensed installations are in service. French, Belgian, British, and German sets predominate. There is a certain demand for alternating-current receivers. Short-wave sets and adapters are also popular. The prevailing central-station service characteristics are 220 volts, 50 cycles, alternating current.

BULGARIA

Language, Bulgarian; area, 39,824 square miles; population, 5,596,800

Radio has been discouraged in Bulgaria to the point that there is practically no development. There is yet no indication of any appreciable advancement during the next few years. All means of communication such as railways, telephones, telegraphs, and wireless stations are monopolies of the Government. There is no market for apparatus in Bulgaria. Most of the few sets in operation have been brought in by members of the diplomatic corps. The summers are hot and the winters cool. Radio reception is good throughout the year. Radio is administered by the Ministry of Posts and Railways. Receiving licenses costing 200 leva ($1.44 in United States currency) per year for private homes are required. For other places the fee ranges up to 15,000 leva ($110) per year. The penalty for operating a receiving set without a permit is solitary confinement for a period not exceeding one year and a fine of up to 5,000 leva. Licenses for 1,612 sets have been issued, the sets being mostly Austrian and German. Bulgaria has no broadcasting. Reception from neighboring countries is easily accomplished, but language difficulties prevent it from being particularly desirable.

CZECHOSLOVAKIA

Language, Czech, German, and Slovak, and some Hungarian and Ruthenian; area, 54,195 square miles; population, 14,523,186

Czechoslovakia has a high degree of radio development. The Government early adopted an encouraging attitude, and as a result the broadcasting structure is one of the best in the world. The people have found radio interesting and the programs desirable, with the result that a great number of receiving sets have been installed. The climate is good for reception, and the national wealth is so distributed that few people are unable to afford receivers. It is expected that the high rate of advancement that has been carried on for the last few years will continue for some time. The principal cities are Prague and Brunn.

Radio broadcasting is under the Ministry of Posts and Telegraphs, which controls the company having the broadcasting concession. Theoretically individual concessions may be granted to other companies, but none have ever been favorably received. Broadcasting is supported by subscription collected from receiving-set owners. This subscription is 10 crowns ($0.30 in United States currency) per month after the first month, for which no fee is assessed. Licenses are granted to Czechoslovak citizens and to the nationals of other countries which grant the same or greater privileges to Czechoslovak citizens. Importing is prohibited except under license, which is granted for 5 per cent of the value of the shipment. Duty is collected in addition.

Receiving sets in use number about 300,000; 266,333 of which were licensed October 31, 1929. Crystal sets are efficient in most parts of the country and constitute a large proportion of the total in use. Domestic manufacturers supply most of the needs of the market, but some German makes are popular.

Five broadcasting stations are scattered through the country, while Austrian, German, Polish, Hungarian, and other stations are easily received. One of the two in Prague broadcasts on short waves.

Alternating-current receivers are becoming popular, as is equipment for short-wave reception. Both 110 and 220-volt lighting service is provided, mostly at 50 cycles.

DANZIG

Language, German ; area, 754 square miles ; population, 386,000

The Free City of Danzig has displayed a great interest in radio, and developments have been comparatively great. Danzig is situated on the Baltic between the Polish " corridor " and Prussia. Its climate is favorable to radio reception, being best from September to May, although there is considerable difficulty from ship-wireless interference.

Receiving is permitted under license, special permits being required for sets capable of receiving over 700 meters. Some market for sets limited to 700 meters is thus created. A fee of 2½ (Polish) zloty per month (about 28 cents in United States currency) is charged for licenses. A luxury tax of 10 per cent is levied on receiving sets.

Although broadcasting is forbidden by law, a station is operating in Danzig, in conjunction with the German system. Stations in the Baltic States, Poland, Germany, and the Scandinavian countries are received. It is estimated that 155 receiving sets are in use, practically all German.

DENMARK

.Language, Danish ; area, 17,110 square miles ; population, 3,434,555

Interest in radio broadcasting has been high in Denmark, and developments have been encouraged by the Government. The distribution of wealth is such as to enable almost every family desiring radio to purchase a receiver. The climate is excellent for reception, and, although there are no neighboring countries employing the Danish language the similarity of other Scandinavian tongues to Danish and the custom of educating children in German have increased the popularity of foreign stations received in Denmark.

Copenhagen, Aarhus, Odense, and Aalborg are the principal cities. About 57 per cent of the population is rural. The territory is low and undulating. The climate is in general cold and inclement, though somewhat mild in the southern islands. The mean annual temperature at Copenhagen is 46.8° F. and the rainfall 21 inches. Radio reception is good throughout the year but is best from September to May.

Radio is governed by the State Radio Council. Broadcasting is a State monopoly and is supported by the listeners through the medium of a 10-crown annual license fee. No restrictions, excepting the license requirements, have been imposed on the owners of receiving sets. Manufacturing, importing, and merchandising are permitted without restraint.

Four stations are recorded as operating in Denmark. One of these employs short waves. Additional service is obtained from Norwegian, Swedish, German, and British stations.

Receiving sets in use to the number of 343,000 have been licensed; about one-half of these are crystal sets. Domestic manufacturers supply most of the demand. British sets are also popular, and a number of American sets are in use. Socket-power receivers are becoming increasingly popular, about 90 per cent of sales being of this type. Short-wave reception likewise is arousing considerable interest. Central-station service is mostly at 220-volt, 50-cycle alternating current.

ESTONIA

Language, Estonian ; area, 18,355 square miles ; population, 1,110,538

The development of radio in Estonia has been especially high, considering the difficulties. Reception conditions are excellent, but the distribution of wealth is not such as to make it possible for every family to afford radio receivers. The people have become particularly interested in radio, however, and any improvement in general conditions is almost certain to result in increased use of radio. Perhaps.the greatest aid in the promotion of radio activities has been the encouraging attitude of the Government.

Estonia is a flat country bordered by Soviet Russia and Lithuania. It lies east of the Baltic Sea and south of the Gulf of Finland. The capital and principal city is Tallinn, formerly Reval. The language of the country is Estonian, but German and Russian are universally used and understood. The mass of the people are of the peasant class, without high standards of comfort, but the percentage of illiteracy is very low.

The climate is variable, the winters being severe and the summers hot and dry. Radio reception is good throughout the year, especially from September to May. Permits to install receiving sets are required. An annual fee of 9 Eesti krona ($2.40 in United States currency) for crystal sets, 12 Eesti krona ($3.20) for one and two tube sets and 15 Eesti krona ($4) for larger tube sets are assessed. The charge, however, is based on the antenna, and two or more sets on one antenna may be legally used under one license, provided the license covers the set which would pay the highest tax. Two broadcasting stations are operating in Tallinn, and one in Tartu, while Finnish, Latvian, Lithuanian, Russian, Polish, German, and Scandinavian stations are received. Alternating-current receivers are attaining a certain degree of popularity. Short-wave sets have been introduced for some time and seem to be in fair demand. The

FIGURE 3.—A transmitter of Russian manufacture in use at Tallinn, Estonia

preponderance of central-station service is provided at 220-volt, 50-cycle alternating current.

Licensing statistics show that 14,426 receiving sets are in use. About 6,000 of these are tube sets, only 200 being of the socket-power type. Crystal sets account for approximately 8,500. There is no estimate covering illegally operated receivers. Domestic sets are in the majority, and German, British, and American to a fair extent. Very few short-wave sets are in use.

FINLAND

Language, Finnish; area, 149,641 square miles; population, 3,582,406

The development of radio broadcasting and receiving is well advanced in Finland. The population appears to be greatly interested, and the Government has done much to promote broadcasting. The climate is exceptionally good for receiving, and the distribution of wealth appears to be sufficiently extensive to permit all interested people to purchase suitable receivers. The distribution of broadcasting stations is likewise such as to be conducive to good service. The principal cities are Helsingfors (Helsinki), Abo (Turku), Tammerfors (Tampere), Viborg (Vipuri), Wasa (Waasa), Uleaborg (Oulu), Kuopio, and Bjorneborg (Pori). The name given in parentheses in each case is the Finnish name, the Swedish being given first. The country consists of low plains, broken by occasional low hills and ridges. Nearly 80 per cent of the total area is forest and 12 per cent lakes. The winters are severe, the summers hot and dry. Finland has a more temperate climate than any other country in the same latitude, the mean annual temperature being 34° F. and the average annual rainfall 14 inches, although at Helsingfors it is about 20 inches. Radio reception is good during all seasons, with noticeable improvement during fall and winter.

Broadcasting is provided by seven stations scattered through the populous areas. Swedish, Russian, and Baltic stations are also received satisfactorily.

A receiving license fee of 100 Finnish marks ($2 in United States currency) per calendar year is required. Some 90,232 receiving sets are licensed. About 30 per cent are of local manufacture, crystal sets amounting to about one-third of the total. Germany supplies most of the remainder, with Swedish and Dutch sets used in fairly large numbers. Alternating-current receivers are now demanded by urban purchasers. All European programs are available on long waves, and the time that American short-wave programs are receivable begins at midnight or after. Short-wave reception has not made much progress. Lighting service at 220 volts, 50 cycles is provided in most places, but some variation is noted. Helsingfors has 120-volt direct current.

FRANCE

Language, French; area, 212,659 square miles; population, 40,745,874

France is one of the most advanced countries in the world in respect to use of radio. The climate is good for receiving. The people are especially interested in radio, and while there have been financial difficulties preventing a large percentage of the people from investing in receivers, the large population and the fairly even distribution of wealth have promoted the use of radio beyond the proportions maintaining in other countries under similar circumstances. The Government has interested itself in promoting broadcast service, for the Government chain of stations has provided a foundation for the broadcasting system which serves the entire country.

The principal cities of France are Paris, Marseille, Lyon, Bordeaux, Lille, and Strasbourg. The surface generally is flat, but there are border mountain ranges on all of the frontiers except the Belgian and German.

The climate of the different sections varies widely. In the south radio reception is good only during a limited season, while in the north, reception is always good except during the hottest part of the summer. The best reception at Paris is from September to May. Paris has 150 rainy days a year, the total precipitation amounting to about 24 inches. The mean annual temperature is about 50° F.

Broadcasting is permitted by French citizens only. Permits are granted sparingly, apparently to prevent congestion and to guarantee the placing of permits in the hands of organizations qualified to present the best programs.

Broadcasting is supported by the organizations operating the stations. While there is no monopoly, the majority of the stations are owned by the Government and rigid control is exercised over other stations. A reduction of the number to 15 stations of high power has been proposed and will probably be adopted. The project provides for receiving license fees to be continued, and advertising time sales to provide the necessary funds. There are 31 stations well distributed over France, broadcasting on short waves, including 5 which use two or more waves. It is stated that foreign programs are preferred to the French. Various areas receive broadcasts from all parts of Europe.

Receiving set owners are assessed 10 francs annually, the receipt serving as a license. A luxury tax of 12 per cent on sets costing more than 500 francs and on parts costing more than 50 francs was instituted in January, 1926.

Receiving-set license statistics are not made public, but various estimates indicate some 1,500,000, receivers to be in use. Domestic manufacturers supply nearly all of the demand, with British, German, Swiss, and American sets used in small numbers. French equipment is also exported in considerable quantities to Belgium, Spain, Great Britatin, and Italy. South American markets are also receiving considerable attention. A patent pool was found late in 1929, controlling the principal radio patents. It is understood that licenses to import sets or to sell imported sets under these patents will not be granted.

Alteranting-current receivers have been introduced with moderate success. Short-wave receivers are not exceptionally popular. Central stations in France show little uniformity in current characteristics, no particular combinations prevailing.

GERMANY

Language, German ; area, 180,976 square miles ; population, 62,348,782

Germany has a well-advanced development of radio. The broadcasting system sponsored by the Government includes stations in all parts of the Republic, and additional ones are being opened regularly. The purchasing power of the people is generally good, and most families are able to afford a set capable of receiving some one or more of the national stations. The climate is good for receiving, being generally the same as in the southern part of Canada. The people have taken considerable interest in radio and have installed receivers in great numbers.

There are 45 cities in the Republic with populations in excess of 100,000, Berlin and Hamburg both running into millions. The central and southern portions of the country are mountainous.

The climate is temperate and uniform. In the lowlands the mean annual temperature varies from 49° to 52° F. Rainfall is greatest in the Harz Mountains, where the precipitation often exceeds 45 inches per year. The average for the plains regions is 20 inches.

Radio reception is generally good, the season of best reception being from September to May.

Radio broadcasting is under the control of the Government, which owns the equipment of all stations. Broadcasting is done by corporations which have monopolies in each section of the country. These corporations are supported from the proceeds of license fees.

FIGURE 4.—Berlin's funkturm (broadcasting tower), 130 meters (426 feet) high. Transoceanic programs are sometimes sent from this aerial

Under a program of reorganization of the broadcasting system, relay stations are to be discontinued and main stations replaced with others of higher power. Two stations of 60,000 watts (Heilsburg and Muehlacker) are under construction, and are expected to be in service before January 1, 1931.

There are 28 broadcasting stations in Germany. Four short-wave stations are in operation, one using simultaneous long wave. Reception is satisfactorily accomplished from all parts of Europe, Germany being the geographical center of broadcasting on the Continent.

Cheap labor permits German manufacturers to supply the domestic market with sets at very low prices, which reacts unfavorably upon the demand for imported apparatus. The good distribution of broadcasting stations makes cheap sets quite satisfactory. Rigid control of patents by a dominating manufacturer is exercised.

Receiving licenses are granted freely to all applicants except Russians, Poles, and Slovaks. A fee of 24 marks ($5.71 in United States currency) per year is enacted, for which a person is entitled to own and operate as many receiving sets as desired, provided not more than one is in use at any one time.

Receiving-set license statistics show some 3,066,682 authorized, while an additional number, variously estimated, are operated without authority. Nearly all of the sets in use are of German origin, but American and British sets are also in use. Alternating-current receivers are popular, as are short-wave receivers and adapters. Central-station service is about evenly divided between 110 and 220 volts, mostly 60-cycle alternating current.

GIBRALTAR

Language, English; area, 2 square miles; population, 18,061

Radio has been restricted in Gibraltar by a number of conditions, including the great amount of interference from ship stations and the land stations on the Rock. The climate is highly conducive to static. The people generally are interested in broadcast reception, and any improvement in receivers which will permit the reception of Continental stations through the interference should prove popular.

There is no broadcasting in Gibraltar, stations in Spain being most easily received. Reception from the United Kingdom is not unusual. Receiving is permitted without any restrictions except for a 10-shilling license fee collected each year. It is estimated that about 150 receivers are in use in Gibraltar. All of these are believed to be of British origin. Alternating-current receivers are practically useless. Short-wave receivers and adapters are becoming increasingly popular.

GREECE

Language, Greek; area, 49,022 square miles; population, 6,200,000

The restrictive attitude of the Government, maintained until 1926, has limited the development of radio in Greece. The climate is not especially good for reception, and the people are not greatly interested in radio.

Greece is a country that is much broken up, owing to the fact that it consists of a range of partially submerged mountains. Athens, Saloniki, Patras, and Corfu are the principal cities. Greece has hot summers and cold winters; the rainfall is great in some sections. Radio reception is good only from November to February.

Broadcasting is prohibited, but the Government has indicated its intention of creating a broadcasting monopoly as soon as the necessary arrangements can be made. Reception is permitted, under certain restrictions, to Greek citizens, but is prohibited to foreigners. Licenses are required, for which 500 drachmas ($6.50 in United States currency) must be contributed for the benefit of the navy.

Recent estimates indicate about 1,000 receivers to be in use. These are of various origin, particularly American, British, and German.

Greece has no broadcasting, nor is there any in neighboring countries, except the Osmanie station in Turkey, which is at some distance.

Alternating-current receivers have been introduced, but have not yet made much headway. Short-wave reception is not exceptionally popular, since no short-wave broadcasts in Greek are available.

HUNGARY

Language, Magyar; area, 35,901 square miles; population, 8,368,273

While the ownership of receiving sets in Hungary is limited to a proportionately small part of the population, broadcast reception has proved popular and a large number of receivers have been installed. The Government has passively encouraged the use of radio. The climate is good for reception. Owing to the country's position, it is believed that stations in a greater number of countries can be picked up on a given set in Hungary than in any other country. The people are generally interested, and improvement in individual purchasing power of the poorer classes would be almost certain to result in an increased sale of less expensive sets.

The principal cities are Budapest, Szeged, and Debrecen. The surface is mostly flat, though mountains occur in some of the areas adjacent to frontiers. The climate is mild, the summers being warm and the winters cold. There is great variation, however, between different sections.

Radio is under the control of the postal administration, which holds a monopoly on broadcasting through a broadcasting corporation. Stations are supported by proceeds from license fees. Licenses for receiving are issued to all applicants and cost 2½ pengos (45 cents) per month when the set is to be used only for amateur receiving. Higher fees are charged for sets to be used for business purposes. Government inspection and supervision of all sets is required. Manufacturing, importing, and merchandising of radio apparatus are subject to permits issued by the Ministry of Commerce and are under the supervision of the postal authorities.

The only broadcasting station is at Budapest. Considerable dependence is placed on stations in neighboring countries.

Hungary has about 240,000 receivers in use, principally of German and Dutch origin. American sets are preferred, but are too costly when adapted to the high European wave band. Short-wave reception is also arousing interest. Central-station service is provided in 110 and 220 volts, with variations of frequency, mostly 50 and 60 cycles. Socket-power sets have almost completely supplanted battery sets in sales.

ICELAND

Language, Icelandic; area, 39,709 square miles; population, 103,317

Though somewhat isolated by distance, radio has been popular in Iceland ever since the installation of the first sets demonstrated the feasibility of receiving programs broadcast in Denmark, the United Kingdom, and other countries. Since then developments have been fairly rapid.

All but a very few of the inhabitants live in Reykjavik, the chief city. The surface is mainly ice-covered plateaus, with numerous lakes and crater basins. Glaciers cover about 5,000 square miles. There are a number of active volcanoes.

Iceland has two broadcasting stations, at Reykjavik and Akureyri. Scandinavian and North American stations are also received.

The number of receivers in use is estimated at about 50. These are largely of German manufacture. Alternating-current receivers have not yet been introduced. Short-wave reception is popular.

IRISH FREE STATE

Language, Gaelic and English; area, 26,592 square miles; population, 2,972,802

Radio is very popular in the Irish Free State. The attitude of the Government has been one of great encouragement. The climate is exceptionally favorable to broadcast reception, and although there is some interference from ship stations operating in code in the areas near the coast, such interference is at a minimum. There is little difficulty from static.

The principal cities of the Free State are Dublin, Cork, Limerick, and Waterford. The Free State is an undulating plain broken toward the north and west by groups of low hills. A large portion of the total area is occupied by lakes.

The mean annual temperature of Dublin is 50° F., and the rainfall is 40 inches. The season of best reception continues from September to May, but reception is good during the remaining three months.

Broadcasting is a Government monopoly and is supported by licenses. The receiving regulations are very moderate. Licenses are required, however, these costing 10 shillings ($2.43) a year, as in the United Kingdom. There are no exceptional restrictions on manufacturing, importing, or merchandising. The two stations in the Free State and those in the United Kingdom provide satisfactory broadcasting services.

Licensed sets number about 26,000. British sets predominate, but American and German receivers are used in large numbers.

Alternating-current receivers have aroused a great degree of interest. The prevailing current characteristics are 220 volts, 50 cycles, alternating.

ITALY

Language, Italian; area, 119,744 square miles; population, 40,796,000

Italy has shown increased rate of broadcast development during the past few years. Formerly the restrictions and prohibitions imposed by the Government, although intended only for the protection of broadcasters and the service in general, served to arrest development, while the several charges made against the owners of receiving sets were such as to eliminate a large number of people who otherwise would have been prospective purchasers of receivers. This condition no longer exists to the same degree, so that Italy is rapidly becoming one of the leading countries of Europe in broadcast development.

The principal cities are Milan (Milano), Naples (Napoli), Rome (Roma), Turin (Torino), Palermo, and Genoa (Genova). The country has a central mountain range, which slopes to plains along each coast, the southern portion being almost entirely plains.

The climate is generally warm. Temperatures and rainfall vary for different regions, since both latitudes and altitudes vary greatly. At Rome the radio-receiving season extends from November to June.

Radio broadcasting is under the control of the Ministry of Communication. A monopoly for broadcasting has been granted to the Ente Italiane per le audizione Radioqoniche (E. I. A. R.), a corporation organized for that purpose. Licenses costing 3 lire (15 cents) per year are required for the operation of receiving sets, the proceeds accruing to the national treasury. Subscriptions to broadcasting service are compulsory, the funds received being used for the

FIGURE 5.—An American transmitter at a broadcasting station in Italy

purpose of supporting broadcasting stations and providing programs. Listeners are required to pay 72 lire (about $3.80) per annum for this service, but receivers employed for commercial purposes are assessed at varying rates, sometimes as high as 1,500 lire ($80) per annum. The search of homes and other places for illegally operated sets is authorized.

Italy has six broadcasting stations, including one short-wave transmitter, and a certain amount of broadcasting service from neighboring countries.

No set may be installed unless approved by the Ministry of Communications. Samples of sets may be deposited by manufacturers and importers as a check against adherence to types in lieu of individual inspection of sets, which is otherwise required. A sales tax is assessed at the following rates: Tubes, 6 lire ($0.32) ; crystal sets,

12 lire ($0.65) ; loud speakers, 24 lire ($1.25) ; tube sets, 53 lire ($2.80).

Some 250,000 sets are reported to be in service. A majority are of Italian manufacture, but many American, French, and German sets are in use. Alternating-current sets are being sold almost to the complete exclusion of battery sets. The voltage and frequency of central stations vary considerably. Short-wave reception is popular to a certain degree, but because of the lack of short-wave broadcasts in the Italian language, has a limited field.

LATVIA

Language, Lettish ; area, 40,856 square miles ; population, 1,870,520

The development of radio in Latvia has been at a rather high rate. The people are interested in radio, and though the purchasing power of a majority of the population is too low to enable them to afford receivers, the remainder are in sufficient number to make a comparatively good market. The Government has adopted an attitude of general encouragement.

The principal cities are Riga, Libau, Dvinsk, Mitau, and Windau. The climate is similar to that of New York State, and radio reception is good, being best from September to May. However, there is considerable interference along the coast from ship stations. The country is mainly a low plain.

The Post and Telegraph Administration controls radio broadcasting through a monopoly. Receiving licenses are required, costing from 1 ($0.19) to 20 ($3.80) lats per month, the fee for receivers in homes being 2 lats ($0.38). The fee is reduced by 50 per cent for the months of June, July, and August. Permanent permits costing 1 lat are issued to blind persons, disabled veterans, and educational institutions and asylums. A higher rate is assessed on sets to be used commercially. Regenerative sets are prohibited, and government inspection of each installation is required. Fundamentally, manufacturing, importing, and merchandising are government monopolies, although concessions are made. Only such apparatus as does not compete with Latvian manufacturers may be imported. All sets of less than four tubes are under this ban.

There is one broadcasting station at Riga. Additional service is provided by stations in Lithuania, Estonia, Russia, Finland, Sweden, Poland, Germany, and Danzig.

The number of sets licensed totals 30,000. About 70 per cent are crystal receivers. Domestic sets predominate. Alternating-current receivers have supplanted battery-type so far as the demand for new sets is concerned. Lighting-current supply is mostly 220 volts, 50 cycles.

LITHUANIA

Language, Lithuanian ; area, 20,550 square miles ; population, 2,011,173

The development of radio broadcast and reception in Lithuania is well advanced. The people generally are deeply interested in radio, even though only a small part of the population is able to afford receiving sets. The Government encourages the use of radio. Since the population is largely of foreign nationality, broadcasting in all neighboring countries has considerable value in Lithuania. The principal cities are Kovno, Memel, Vilna, Grodno, and Suwalki. The country is an undulating plain. The climate is temperate and very favorable to radio reception through the year, especially from September to May. Radio is administered by the Post and Telegraph Administration. Receiving licenses are issued through the postal system; the cost for sets in homes is 100 lits ($10) per year and for commercial establishments 1,000 and 2,000 lits ($100 and $200) per year. Other fees for various other purposes are charged.

The charges for the registration and stamping of radio apparatus are:

	Lits		Lits
Tube receivers, per tube_____	5	Block condenser _____	0. 50
Crystal sets_____	5	Variable condenser_____	3
Tubes_____	1	" B " batteries of less than 100	
Headsets_____	3	volts _____	2
Loud-speakers_____	10		

Receiving subscriptions of 1 lit per month (in villages) and 2 lits per month (in cities) for crystal sets and of 3 and 5 lits for tube sets is also charged with much higher rates for sets used in commercial institutions. Reception is permitted under a system of licenses. All citizens are permitted to obtain licenses without preliminary arrangements, but foreigners are required to first obtain special authorization from the Foreign Office. Importation and sale are also subject to license. All American equipment must bear Post and Telegraph Administration stamps.

The only broadcasting station is at Kovno. Stations in Russia, Finland, Estonia, Latvia, Germany, and the Scandinavian countries are received.

It is estimated that some 12,000 receiving sets are in use, mostly German. There are a few American sets. One or two alternating-current receivers have been put into service. Lighting service is principally 220 volts, 50 cycles. Short-wave reception is still the property of amateurs.

LUXEMBURG

Language, German; area, 999 square miles; population, 285,524

The development of radio is fairly well advanced. There are some 2,000 receiving sets in operation. One broadcasting station in the city of Luxemburg is in service, and programs from all neighboring countries are received. No alternating-current receivers or short-wave sets have been reported.

MADEIRA

Language, Portuguese; area, 314 square miles; population, 179,002

The climate in Madeira is very poor for reception, static difficulties being the principal retarding agency. The people are interested in radio, however, and a number of receivers have been installed. Future developments should show increased advancement. Estimates place the number of sets in use at 180. It is understood that these are nearly all British and American. There is no broadcasting in Madeira, nor none particularly satisfactory within reasonable receiving distance.

MALTA

Language, English; area, 122 square miles; population, 212,528

Radio has attained a fair degree of popularity in Malta. The chief city is Valetta. The surface is generally low and undulating. The summers hot and the winters mild. Radio reception is fair from November to March.

Broadcasting is prohibited. Reception is subject to permit from the lieutenant governor and to the payment of a license fee of 21 shillings for the first year and 10 shillings each subsequent year. There are no special restrictions on manufacturing, importing, or merchandising.

FIGURE 6.—Transmitting equipment of the short-wave station at Huizen, Netherlands

Receiving sets number about 250. None of these is of the alternating-current type so far as can be learned. Short-wave sets are popular, and this popularity is increasing.

NETHERLANDS

Language, Dutch; area, 13,205 square miles; population, 7,625,938

The development of radio broadcasting and reception has been rapid since it was first introduced into the Netherlands. The Government has been active in encouraging its use. The people are interested in radio, and the general distribution of wealth has enabled almost everyone to purchase a receiver. Although there is considerable interference from ship stations operating in code, satisfactory reception is easy to accomplish. The climate tends toward great extremes and is moist, the mean annual rainfall being about 28 inches. Reception is good from September to May and fair during the summer. The principal cities are Amsterdam, The Hague, Rotterdam, and Utrecht. The surface is low and flat.

Postal authorities must be notified of the installation of a set, but no fees are collected. Broadcasting is supported mainly by voluntary subscriptions from listeners.

Four broadcasting stations are operating in the Netherlands, one broadcasting on short waves. Programs from German, Belgian, French, and British stations are received regularly. Alternating-current receivers are rapidly supplanting battery sets.

A large Dutch firm which controls the principal radio patents has recently become very active in protecting its rights. Several suits were instituted against parties claimed to be infringing without license, and it is understood that the practice of licensing is to be discontinued. In this event, the Dutch market will be strictly under monopoly, and further importation of sets and equipment made impossible. Lighting service is usually at 220-volt, 50-cycle alternating current. Short-wave reception is unusually popular.

Some 152,000 receiving sets are in use. British, Netherland, French, and German sets are used in about equal numbers.

NORWAY

Language, Norwegian; area, 124,964 square miles; population, 2,649,775

The development of broadcast reception in Norway has been good, although until the last two years very little progress has been made. The climate is of the best for radio reception, and there is little in the way of mineral deposits to interfere with good reception. The Government has actively promoted the use of radio, and the people generally appear to be interested. The individual purchasing power and distribution of wealth are such that almost every family desiring to do so is able to purchase a receiving set.

The principal cities are Oslo, Bergen, Stavanger, Drammen, and Trondhjem. The surface is mountainous and broken by numerous valleys and fjords. The climate is tempered by the Gulf Stream, but the central and eastern portions have extremely cold winters. Radio reception, good throughout the year, is best from September to May. Rainfall ranges from 40 to 70 inches in the coastal regions and is about 16 inches in the interior.

The control of radio broadcasting is vested in the telegraph authorities. The use of radio by amateurs is prohibited. Broadcasting concessions for each part of Norway are granted to private broadcasting companies, which receive 16 crowns for each receiving license issued within their respective areas. After five years the stations will revert to the Government. The receiving-license fee of 20 crowns ($5.36) per year is collected from receiving-set owners, the proceeds being used to defray broadcasting expenses. A special Government authorization is required to import radio apparatus.

Eleven broadcasting stations are operating in Norway, one using short waves. Good reception from Swedish, Danish, and other European stations is usual.

Over 70,000 receiving sets have been licensed, and it is estimated that an additional 5,000 are illegally operated. American sets are in little use. Norwegian manufacturers supply a large part of the demand, while Dutch and German sets are also used in considerable numbers. Alternating-curent receivers are in common use, and the number is constantly increasing. Lighting service is usually 220 volts, 50 cycles. Short-wave reception is popular.

POLAND

Language, Polish; area, 149,140 square miles; population, 30,212,962

The climate of Poland is good for radio reception throughout the year, and considerable progress has been made in bringing about increased interest in radio. The Government encourages its use, and the people have displayed more than ordinary interest in it. It is expected that developments of the next few years will show a

FIGURE 7.—A studio of the Polish Broadcasting Co. at Warsaw

considerable increase in the demand for receiving sets. The principal cities are Warsaw, Lwow, Lodz, and Cracow. The surface is entirely of plains. The climate is very good for radio reception, there being no season during which reception is seriously affected.

Radio broadcasting is administered by the Post Office Department. A broadcasting monopoly has been granted to the Polish Radio Co., two-fifths of the stock being held by the State treasury. A license fee of 30 zloty ($3.36) per year is required for amateur receiving sets.

Poland has five broadcasting stations and receives Russian, German, Austrian, and other European broadcasts.

Licensing statistics place the number of receivers at 202,586, of which about 80 per cent are crystal. Polish sets are in the greatest number, with some German, British, and American in use. Over 20 manufacturers are now producing radio equipment in Poland.

Some alternating-current sets have been sold. Various types of lighting service are provided. Short-wave reception is popular among a limited part of the listeners.

PORTUGAL

Language, Portuguese; area, 35,490 square miles; population, 5,628,610

Portugal has a poor climate for radio reception, together with further difficulties provided through mineral deposits over which transmission is difficult. Little interest has been aroused except in the vicinity of Lisbon, and it is expected that at least a few years will pass before developments will reach a stage comparable to other European countries. The principal cities are Lisbon, Oporto, Setubal, and Braga. The country is mountainous, with widely varying climatic characteristics within comparatively small areas, but it is generally hot in the south and cool in the north and very damp throughout. Reception is never very good in any section and is possible only between November and April. Ore deposits are thought to hinder reception seriously in the vicinity of Oporto.

There are no particular restrictions, but a 2 per cent tax is collected by the customs authorities in addition to tariff charges. Some 2,500 receivers are in service. These are of British, German, and American origin. The only broadcasting station is in Lisbon. Reception of Spanish programs is usual, but no reception outside of Lisbon and its vicinity is satisfactory.

So far as is known, no alternating-current receivers are in use. Lighting-service voltages and frequencies vary considerably. Short-wave reception has a limited popularity.

RUMANIA

Language, Rumanian; area, 122,282 square miles; population, 17,393,149

Broadcast reception in Rumania has been of little interest to the public, owing to the attitude of the Government and generally poor receiving conditions. The conditions under which the Government limited the use of radio have been largely overcome, and there now appears to be a hope for greater future developments. In general the situation is such as maintained in most countries during the early days of broadcasting. The country is largely a sloping plain, with temperature ranges from zero to over 100° F., the mean annual temperature at Bucharest being 50° F. The annual rainfall is 25 inches.

Broadcasting is a monopoly, granted to the Societa de Difuzione Radio Pelefonica din Romania, supported by subscriptions costing 600 lei ($3.60). A special permit by the Home Office is required of foreigners. Regenerative sets are prohibited.

A broadcasting station was opened in Bucharest on September 15, 1929. Satisfactory reception from Austrian, Czechoslovak, and Hungarian stations is possible.

Estimates give the number of receiving-set installations at 25,000. German sets predominate, with a limited number of French, British, and American. The American product is preferred in the higher-priced field. Alternating-current sets are proving most popular in the cities. Sales of battery and crystal sets are also increasing. Characteristics of lighting service vary widely.   Short-wave reception is little known except among amateurs.

SOVIET RUSSIA

Language, Russian ; area, 8,144,228 square miles ; population, 147,013,600

The extent of Soviet Russia's radio development is little known. The climate is excellent for reception, but the purchasing power of the people generally is so low that there is little response to the many gestures of the government designed to encourage the use of receiving sets.   It is apparent that a large proportion of those in use are the

FIGURE 8.—A British control board of a broadcasting station at Bucharest, Rumania

property of local organizations and municipalities, operating loud speakers in public places.

Practically all of Russia has warm summers and cold winters. The northern coast has cool summers, while a large part of the southern territory has hot summers.

A news release emanating from the National Bureau of Information states that 500,000 receiving sets are in use.   Claim is made that these are nearly all of Russian manufacture.   There are 45 broadcasting stations listed in the files of the electrical equipment division of the United States Bureau of Foreign and Domestic Commerce. These are scattered throughout Russia and Asiatic Russia.   In various sections European, Chinese, and Japanese stations are received.

SPAIN

Language, Spanish; area, 190,050 square miles; population, 21,763,147

Spanish radio developments have been moderately fast, with the government interested in furthering the use of radio. The climate is good, though not exceptionally so; distant stations are rarely heard, but local service suffers little. There is a great interest on the part of the people, but the purchasing power is largely concentrated in the cities. The well-scattered stations of the broadcasting set-up provide service throughout the country. The principal cities are Madrid, Barcelona, Valencia, Seville, Malaga, Mercia, Saragossa, Cartagena, and Bilbao. The country is mainly a plateau, broken in some parts by mountains, with narrow coastal plains. The climate is hot and dry in the south and temperate in the north. Radio reception is fair from October until April.

Regulations in regard to broadcasting are liberal. Programs are subject to control, and advertising must not exceed five minutes of each hour. Regulations are not rigidly enforced in any respect. Receiving licenses are required and foreigners must obtain special permits. Licenses for sets in homes cost 5 pesetas and in public places 50 pesetas. There are no restrictions on importing, merchandising, and manufacturing, except a requirement that salesmen be licensed.

Spain has 10 scattered broadcasting stations, giving satisfactory service. A plan for a broadcasting system of 19 stations, with a 40,000 watt short-wave key station has been determined upon and is expected to be put into execution during 1930. Programs from French, Italian, Portuguese, and other European stations are received, but the Spanish broadcasts appear to be the most popular.

An estimate recently made gives the number of receivers as 500,000 though only about 90,000 are registered, about 85 per cent of which are cheap tube sets or crystals. About 45 per cent of the high-grade sets sold are American, with an equivalent proportion from Germany. The latter country also supplies some 80 per cent of the low-priced sets. Alternating-current receivers are now demanded by purchasers. Lighting currents are at considerable variation but are mainly 110 or 220 volts, 50 or 60 cycles. There is considerable direct current, and good sets for this power should be introduced successfully. Reports indicate that the majority of the direct-current sets now used are not satisfactory. Short-wave reception is popular.

SWEDEN

Language, Swedish; area, 173,157 square miles; population, 6,087,923

It has been said that the greatest interest in radio has been taken in Sweden. The statistics bear out this statement, no other country except the United States showing a greater per capita development, while a consideration of the average purchasing power in each country serves to place Sweden in advance of the United States under this consideration. The Government has been especially active in the promotion of broadcasting and reception, as a result of which an excellent broadcasting system has been built up throughout the country. Sweden has perhaps the best climate for radio reception in the world. The principal cities are Stockholm, Goteborg, Malmo,

Norrkoping, and Halsingborg. The country has forested highlands in the north, lowlands and lakes in the central parts, and agricultural plains in the south. The climate is mild, owing to the Gulf Stream. The mean February temperature is 25° F., and the August mean is 62° F., at Stockholm. The air in that vicinity is damp, and fogs are frequent; the mean annual rainfall ranges from 18 to 20 inches. Radio reception is good throughout the year, especially from September to May.

Radio is under the control of the Telegraph Administration. A broadcasting monopoly has been granted to a corporation known as " Radiojans," but transmitting licenses are freely issued to amateurs.

FIGURE 9.—Swedish transmitter in a station at Stockholm

and the monopoly has provided facilities for the rebroadcasting of the programs of its stations by amateurs and radio clubs. Sweden now has 32 broadcasting stations scattered through the country, one operating on short waves. Broadcasts from neighboring countries are received readily but are not so popular as the Swedish programs.

Permits to install receiving sets are issued at the rate of 40 crowns ($10.72), while receiving licenses cost 10 crowns ($2.68) per year. Manufacturing, importing, and merchandising are not subject to any exceptional restrictions.

Licenses have been issued for 427,564 receiving sets, with an additional number, not estimated, operated unlawfully. Swedish manufacturers supply a large part of the market, with large numbers of

German and Dutch sets in use. The use of alternating-current receivers in Sweden is advancing rapidly, there being but little demand for battery sets. Lighting service in most sections is at 127 or 220 volts. Short-wave sets and adapters are used to a limited extent.

SWITZERLAND

Language, French, German, and Italian; area, 15,976 square miles; population, 3,987,000

The topography of Switzerland is such as to render radio broadcasting and reception difficult on ordinary types of inexpensive apparatus. The climate, however, is very good, somewhat reducing the deleterious effect of the topography. The people generally appear to be interested, and the Government has aided considerably by per-

FIGURE 10.—Broadcasting church chimes at Zurich, Switzerland. (Photo taken from belfry)

mitting freely the establishment of broadcasting stations and installation of receiving sets, so long as the service itself did not suffer thereby.

The principal cities are Zurich, Geneva, Basel, Lausanne, Berne, and St. Gall. Owing to its mountainous character, Switzerland has a wide variety of climate. Radio reception is good in all altitudes from September to May and in the lower portions throughout the year.

Radio is under the control of the Federal Department of Posts and Railways. Broadcasting concessions are granted for each station, but a nationalized system is under consideration. Permits to operate receiving sets are granted to Swiss citizens only. A preliminary Government inspection of the installation, costing 3 francs

($0.60) is required, the annual assessment being 15 francs ($3), of which the Government retains 20 per cent and the remainder is paid to the broadcasters. No special restrictions are imposed on manufacturers, importers, and merchants.

Licenses have been issued for 77,959 sets, mostly of Swiss and German origin. The trading is so highly competitive that dealers are reluctant to handle American sets unless stocks and repair parts are obtainable in some European free port. The frequent appearance of new models prevents the dealers from profitably carrying more than minimum stocks.

A large portion of the sets in use are crystal type, but their sale has fallen off greatly during the past year. Broadcasting societies are organized under Federal registrations, to operate the stations. Advertising is specifically forbidden. Six broadcasting stations are operating in Switzerland; stations in France, Germany, Austria, and other neighboring countries are also received. Two of the Swiss stations broadcast on short waves. Alternating-current receivers have attained great popularity. Either 110 or 220 volts, alternating current, is available in every city. Short-wave receivers are generally known but little in demand or use.

TURKEY

Language, Turkish, English, and French; area, 282,627 square miles; population, 13,640,810

Turkey's radio development is now in only the primary state and can not yet be said to indicate the country's capacity.

The principal cities of Turkey are Istanbul, with a population of 1,000,000 (the only city having over 60,000), Smyrna, Angora, and Adrianople. The surface of the country is undulating and largely mountainous, with a moderate climate. The mean January temperature at Istanbul is 43° F., and July, 73° F. Rainfall is abundant on the coasts, but the interior is dry. The summers are short and hot and the winters long and cold. Radio reception is best from October to April.

Radio is under the control of the Administration of Posts, Telegraphs, and Telephones. Broadcasting and the sales distribution and installation of receiving sets is a monopoly granted to the Societe Anonyme Turque de Telephonie Sans Fil. Before purchasing receivers, prospective listeners must obtain permits from the company, which also serves as a license for one year, costing 10 Turkish pounds ($44). Renewals are at the same rate. Sets must be available for Government inspection at all times and are subject to confiscation without warning, explanation, or indemnity.

About 5,200 receivers are in service, some 50 per cent being German and 25 per cent French. Turkey has two broadcasting stations, at Osmanie, near Istanbul, and at Angora. The former was shut down in January, 1930, because of financial difficulties, but resumption of service is expected. Some of the higher-powered European stations are received, but there are no other near-by broadcasting stations.

Socket-power sets have attained considerable popularity. Short-wave reception has a limited clientele, but is particularly interesting to that class. Electric service in Istanbul is 50-cycle alternating, some 110 and some 220 volts.

UNITED KINGDOM

Language, English; area, 94,284 square miles; population, 44,173,704

The United Kingdom is one of the countries showing the greatest degree of radio development in the world. Its home development has amply justified the early recognition of the value of Marconi's invention, which it granted after other countries had passed it by. In the field of broadcasting and in all wireless activities the people are highly interested much more in the service than in the means of providing that service—a condition which indicates a solid basis for further advancement. The climate is excellent for radio reception, and the broadcasting system, designed for proper service in all parts of the Kingdom, has proved the most satisfactory of any monopoly system yet adopted.

Radio is controlled by a monopoly vested in the British Broadcasting Corporation, a division of the Post Office Department. Its activities are supported by the proceeds from license fees.

There are 20 broadcasting stations in the United Kingdom, one of which, at Hull, operates only on special occasions, another being a short-wave station. The two stations in the Irish Free State and several on the Continent are also received. A revision of the broadcasting system is in progress. When completed, five regional stations will serve the whole island of Great Britain, each broadcasting two programs on separate wave lengths. One program will be a " chain " broadcast from all five stations, while the other will be local. The first of these regional stations has been completed at Brookman's Park, about 17 miles from London, but the majority of London listeners complain that because of the high power, twin programs interfere not only with each other, but " blanket " all outside reception. This result is claimed to be the fault of receivers and not of the twin-wave system, and work on the other four stations is therefore proceeding with no modification of the plans. Listeners are advised to purchase wave traps to remedy the situation so far as mutual interference is concerned, or " twin-wave traps " if outside stations are desired. Portable sets, formerly very popular in England, may be entirely eliminated from use by the prevailing conditions.

Receiving licenses are issued to all applicants and cost 10 shillings ($2.43) a year. There are no other restrictions on the ownership and operation of sets, nor on importing, manufacturing, or merchandising. The British manufacturing industry, however, has attempted to limit the sale of imported products by granting additional discounts to those dealers who do not handle any imported radio apparatus. This method was tried for over a year and proved so unpopular with most dealers that they refuse to renew agreements. They found the additional discounts insufficient to repay them for the business lost through their failure to handle imported apparatus.

The number of licensed sets in service total 2,515,608. Nearly all of the needs of the British market are supplied by some 2,000 domestic manufacturers, but German and American sets are used in large numbers, with some of French, Italian, Swedish, or other manufacture.

Alternating-current receivers, known as mains sets (equivalent to "socket-power"), are attaining popularity. Lighting service is almost universally 220-volt, 50-cycle alternating current, and under plans now approaching completion, so far as the more important districts are concerned, will be uniformly so. Short-wave reception is very popular.

YUGOSLAVIA

Language, Slavic tongues and German; area, 96,134 square miles; population, 12,017,323.

Radio developments in Yugoslavia have been slow, with few conditions especially encouraging. The people have a low purchasing power and are not generally interested in such advantages as are provided by radio.

The country for the most part is mountainous and the climate temperate, rather similar to our Middle Atlantic States. Reception is good from September to May.

Permits are required for broadcasting stations. Nothing except music may be broadcast. Private persons may not install broadcasting stations or other sending sets. The permission of the Ministry of Posts and Telegraphs is required before a receiving set may be installed. A license fee of 25 dinars (33 cents) per month is charged, 60 per cent of the proceeds being paid over to the broadcasters. Theoretically, foreigners may not obtain this permission, although exceptions are made. In applying for a permit to install a receiving set, the individual must describe his set in detail and indicate the room in which it may be found. Permits may be revoked at any time.

Yugoslavia has some 40,000 receivers in use, nearly all of German or Dutch origin. American sets are known, and those in use give great satisfaction, though the prices are too high for the general market. These sets are all constructed for the long waves used in Europe. There are three broadcasting stations in the country, but good reception from neighboring countries is reported. Some alternating-current sets are in use and are proving satisfactory. Short-wave reception is not common.

ASIA

ADEN

Language, Arabic; area, 9,080 square miles; population, 54,923

The British Protectorate of Aden has had practically no radio development. It is hot at all seasons, and radio reception is difficult, particularly over the distance now necessary. Aden has no broadcasting, but is dependent upon occasional reception from distant stations, none of which can be picked up for satisfactory reception. Only five receivers have been installed. These are in the possession of Americans and Europeans who took them among household effects when going to Aden. Two British short-wave sets have been put into service and have proved highly satisfactory. European and American short-wave stations are received at certain hours, as is the station at Nairobi, Kenya, when operating. The time difference between Nairobi and Aden is 29½ minutes.

FIGURE 11.—A transmitter at Zagreb, Yugoslavia

ARABIA

Language, Arabic; area, 1,200,000 square miles; population, 7,000,000

Arabia has no great radio development, owing principally to the poor climate and the absence of broadcasting. Twelve sets are reported in use, all the property of Europeans and Americans stationed temporarily in Arabia. Summers are hot and winters warm, graduating to cool in the northwestern part. Reception is difficult at all seasons, but the distance from broadcasting is mainly responsible. The nearest broadcasting stations are those at Bombay, Osmanie, and Cairo, none coming in with satisfactory clearness or volume. Short-wave reception from Nairobi, Kenya, should be satisfactory, though so far as is known no short-wave sets have been tried in Arabia except those in Aden.

CEYLON

Language, English; area, 25,332 square miles; population, 5,009,502

Considering the adverse climate and the limited number of people able to afford the investment necessary to obtain radio service, Ceylon has advanced radio development. The Government encourages its use and operates the only broadcasting station on the island. The people able to afford sets are generally interested, finding that it serves the particular needs very satisfactorily. The principal city is Colombo. The climate is hot and damp, and generally poor for radio. The regulations governing radio are similar to those of India, although Ceylon is a separate colony of the British Empire. Some 1,500 receiving installations have been made. American sets are not used to any extent. The station at Colombo and those in India are received regularly. Short-wave reception has a certain limited field. Alternating-current sets are required for Colombo, but battery sets are needed in all other places.

CHINA

Language, Chinese; area, 4,227,170 square miles; population, 400,800,000

Radio developments in China have been seriously retarded by the Government's attitude, which has recently been abandoned in favor of a policy of encouragement and assistance. The Chinese themselves show little interest, but popularity among certain classes is growing perceptibly. The foreigners of nearly all classes are finding radio popular and are installing receiving sets.

Shanghai, Hankow, and Peking have populations in excess of 1,000,000 each. The country's surface consists mainly of plains along the coast, with mountainous regions in several sections. The climate is generally hot and the humidity high. Reception is generally poor.

China now has 14 broadcasting stations, while service is also obtained from Japan, Chosen, Kwantung, and Siberia.

Radio regulations do not impose any exceptional restrictions on broadcasters or owners of receiving sets. Importers, however, are required to submit complete and highly detailed information regarding each shipment of radio equipment to local authorities. The Ministry of Military Administration determines whether an import

permit will be issued. On subsequent applications, the final dispo-
sition of the preceding shipment must also be stated. A fee of $10
and a $2 stamp must be paid with the application.

The more recent estimates indicate that about 10,000 receivers
have been installed. These originated in various countries, principally the United States, Japan, England, France, and Germany.
The construction committee of the nationalist Government opened
a radio factory at Shanghai with 40 workers in February, 1930.
Alternating-current sets are in use only in exceptional cases. Short-
wave receivers are not popular.

CHOSEN

Language, Japanese; area, 84,738 square miles; population, 19,519,927

The development of radio in Chosen has been much greater than
would be expected from a review of the conditions obtaining in the
country. Although wealth is highly concentrated, there are numerous families able to afford the purchase of receivers, and a large
proportion of these have installed them.

The principal city is Keijofu (Seoul), which has a population of
250,000. The climate is generally moderate, but the summers are
hot and rainy. The mean annual rainfall is 36 inches, most of which
falls in July. Reception is good from September to May.

Radio in Chosen is administered through the Japanese Government Bureau of Communications, since this is a Japanese possession.
Japanese regulations are in force, limiting receiving sets to non-
regenerative types not capable of receiving on wave lengths of over
400 meters.

There is one broadcasting station at Seoul; in addition, stations
in Japan, Kwantung, China, and Siberia are received.

An estimate giving the number of receivers as 12,000 has been
reported. American and Japanese receivers are the most popular.
Neither alternating current nor short-wave sets are in use.

FRENCH INDIA

Language, French; area, 196 square miles; population, 273,081

Most of the radio development in French India may be traced
to the developments in British India. The markets in these areas
are generally among the French population. About 50 sets are in
use, all French. French India has no broadcasting, reception being
from stations in British India and Ceylon only. All seasons are
hot and radio reception poor.

FRENCH INDO-CHINA

Language, French; area, 265,004 square miles; population, 19,844,181

Radio developments in French Indo-China have been very slow,
and there is little promise of early development. The climate is
poor for radio reception. The use of receiving sets is prohibited,
but a few sets are in use by Government officials entitled to exception from the prohibition. Practically all of the population is
Asiatic and not especially interested in modern innovations. The
latest estimate is that about 25 sets are in service, but it is believed

that the actual number is much greater. Nearly all are of French manufacture. A short-wave broadcasting station is understood to be operating in Haiphong. Reception from Singapore, Manila, and other cities is unsatisfactory.

HONG KONG

Language, English; area, 391 square miles; population, 662,950

Hong Kong has had little development of radio, and broadcasting stations previously operating there were abandoned for lack of reason for continued operation. There has recently been constructed a new station, however, and it is believed that a greater development will take place.

Americans and Europeans number about 10,000. The principal city is Victoria. The island is a rugged ridge of granite, broken by narrow valleys. Hong Kong is in the typhoon belt and has a rainy season from March to May. From November to March it is comparatively cool, at which time radio reception is fair.

Hong Kong has had a broadcasting station at Victoria since April, 1927. This station formerly sent out only storm warnings and other meteorological data, but in the fall of 1928 was reconstructed and its activities reorganized on a general broadcasting basis.

Receiving license is required, costing 5 Hong Kong dollars per year ($2.20 in United States currency). Receivers licensed number 700, with a number of unlicensed sets also in use. Sets are principally British, though some are American. Socket-power receivers have not proven to be completely satisfactory. Short-wave sets are in the great majority.

INDIA

Language, English; area, 1,805,332 square miles; population, 318,885,980

British India has had considerable difficulty in building up a great radio public. The present unsettled political situation can not be held to be solely responsible for the general lack of interest in radio, as the Indian Broadcasting Co. has never been able to operate at a profit. The company became insolvent in late 1929, since when the Bombay and Calcutta stations have been continued by the Government. In April, 1930, the Government of Mysore State determined upon constructing a station at Bangalore, adding to the Indian service. The Madras city government is said to be considering the establishment of a municipal station. The principal cities are Calcutta, Bombay, Madras, Hyderabad, Rangoon, and Delhi. The great central part of India is a plateau, surrounded by low strips along the coasts and by plains in the north, which are bordered by the Himalaya Mountains. Humidity and temperature are high except during the period from November to January. Radio reception is good from November to May in most sections.

Radio is under the control of the Director General of Posts and Telegraphs. Receiving licenses are issued to all applicants. These cost 10 rupees ($3.65 per year), of which the broadcasting company receives 8. Import permits are required.

The total number of receivers is about 3,600. These are largely American. It is the general belief that American sets are not properly insulated for the Indian climate. A few alternating-current sets are in use and appear to have given satisfactory results, but battery sets are still in demand, as much of India is as yet without electric service. Short-wave sets are popular in the interior and among a certain class of listeners in the population centers.

IRAQ

Language, Arabic; area, 143,240 square miles; population, 3,000,000

There has been practically no development of radio in Iraq, owing to the adverse climate and the distance from broadcasting. The weather is hot at all seasons and radio reception correspondingly poor.

Iraq has no broadcasting, but infrequent reception from European stations is possible. Receiving licenses issued number 31, but of this number 7 sets have been dismantled. The slump is due to the migration to America of the only dealer in Iraq who had any technical radio knowledge.

JAPAN

Language, Japanese; area, 148,756 square miles; population, 59,138,000

Japan is the leading country of Asia in radio development. Before any developments were permitted, the Government made a thorough study of broadcasting and its uses, so that the earliest developments were based on a carefully thought-out plan. This has never been changed in its essentials, and under it progress has been rapid. The climate is good, and the people are interested to a great extent. While wealth is somewhat concentrated, this condition is not as serious as in some other countries, and a large proportion of the population is able to purchase receivers. The principal cities are Tokyo, Kobe, Osaka, Kyoto, and Nagoya. The surface of the country is generally mountainous, being of volcanic origin. The climate is good for radio, although warm and damp. Reception is fair throughout the year and good from September to May.

Radio broadcasting is controlled by the Bureau of Communications, broadcasting permits being issued only to Japanese citizens. Each station licensed has a partial monopoly within certain bounds. Stations are divided into two groups according to their power. Low-powered stations have monopolies in certain small areas, while high-powered stations have monopolies in a large area, which may include several of the areas assigned to local stations. In theory, this would restrict the number of stations which might be received at any point to one high and one low powered station, if all of the stations provided for were operating.

Broadcasting is supported from license fees. Receiving sets may be operated upon payment of the license fee of 1 yen per annum to the Government and a subscription fee of 1 yen per month to the broadcasters. Permits to install are required, and only sets approved by the Bureau of Communications may be used. Manufacturers and importers may deposit a sample set, the approval of which will serve for all additional sets of the same type so long as none of the specifications is changed. Wave lengths of from 150 to 400 meters only may be used.

Japan has 10 broadcasters, including two short-wave Siberian and Chinese stations. Dairen and Seoul stations are also received.

The number of receiving sets is estimated at about 641,774. Japanese manufacturers have supplied a large number of these. Formerly they imported parts, but these, too, are of local manufacture at present. The import market now is for material for the manufacture of parts. Alternating-current receivers have superseded

FIGURE 12.—A Japanese trio of instruments—koto, shakuhachi (flute), and samisen—broadcasting in a studio at Osaka, Japan

battery types, about 50 per cent of the tube sets in use now being of the first kind. Short-wave reception has aroused considerable interest.

KWANTUNG

Language, Japanese; area, 1,305 square miles; population, 1,056,076

There has been a fair degree of radio progress in Kwantung, even though there is but a small portion of the population with sufficient wealth to purchase receivers. Kwantung has hot summers and cold winters, with fair summer and good winter reception.

Sets in use number 3,910, being Japanese, American, and British in origin. One broadcasting station at Dairen is operating. Chinese. Japanese, Siberian, and Korean stations are also received. So far as is known no alternating-current or short-wave sets are in use.

MACAO

Language, Portuguese; area, 4 square miles; population, 74,668

Little radio development has been noted in Macao, although the number of listeners appears to be growing. Summers are hot and winters warm, with comparatively poor reception throughout the year.

About 40 sets are now installed, purchased in all parts of the world. There is no broadcasting, but reception from Hong Kong and, to a lesser extent, from Chinese and Japanese stations, is satisfactory. No alternating-current sets are in use. One or two short-wave receivers are giving little service.

NETHERLAND EAST INDIES

Language, Dutch ; area, 733,642 square miles ; population, 49,534,618

Radio in the Netherland East Indies is not greatly advanced, owing to the late introduction of satisfactory apparatus. The climate is hot and damp, but there is some radio reception of a satisfactory character. There are no exceptional restrictions on the use of radio. Ten broadcasting stations, all operating on short waves, are scattered through the islands. Their services are supplanted by reception from southern continental Asia and the Philippine Islands. A broadcasting monopoly is favored, though it has not yet been put into effect. Developments have been entirely in short waves for local as well as long-distance reception. The short-wave broadcasts from the Netherlands are the programs most appreciated.

Only 106 receivers have been installed. These were largely purchased in the Netherlands and represent various European makes. American sets have not generally proved to be properly constructed for the climatic conditions of the East Indies. Socket-power sets are not popular, since current characteristics, where electricity is available, vary greatly.

PALESTINE

Language, Arabic and French ; area, 900 square miles ; population, 852,268

Several attempts to popularize radio in Palestine have been made, and each has proved successful to a certain extent. On the whole, developments have not warranted the efforts made. The conditions existing are not such as to bring about any great development until broadcasting stations have been established nearer than at present. Summers are hot and winters warm. Reception is poor most of the year and never particularly good.

Palestine has no broadcasting, but Cairo, Osmanie, and the larger European stations are received. Estimates place the number of receiving sets installed at 150. These are largely French with some American, British, and German. No alternating-current or short-wave receivers are known.

PERSIA

Language, Arabic ; area, 628,000 square miles ; population, 10,000,000

The climate and the purchasing power of the people have prevented any development of radio in Persia. The summers are hot and winters cool; reception is never exceptionally good, being almost impossible during the summer. About 300 sets of various origins are in use, owned by foreigners. Persia has no broadcasting, but is dependent upon stations at Bombay, Osmanie, and in Russia, all more than 1,000 miles distant. No alternating-current or short-wave sets have been reported.

SIAM

Language, Siamese; area, 200,148 square miles; population, 9,831,000

Radio has had no development in Siam. Two-thirds of the population are Siamese. The principal city is Bangkok, which has a population of about 750,000. The northern portion of the country is mountainous, the central part is a plateau, and the southern part is covered by plains. There are also numerous islands off the coast. The general climate is fair for radio, except in the mountains and some other sections.

Broadcasting is prohibited for the avowed purpose of preventing the marketing of unsuitable receiving equipment until experiments determine the most effective types of sets for local use. Receiving is nominally allowed under special permits; these permits, however, are not issued. The sets owned represent the property of the governing class and number 25. The origins of these are various. Reception from China, India, and Singapore is not entirely satisfactory. No alternating-current or short-wave sets are in use.

STRAITS SETTLEMENTS

Language, English and native dialects; area, 1,600 square miles; population, 937,099

Radio is popular to a certain extent in the Straits Settlements, but since the popularity is restricted to the whites, only a limited stage of advancement has been noted. The climate is poor for radio, being hot and damp. Half the population is concentrated in Singapore. There are but 20,000 Europeans. A broadcasting station was installed in Singapore in November, 1926, but was closed in 1927. At the present time it is understood that short-wave stations in Singapore and Johore are giving broadcast service. Stations in India, the Philippines, and the Netherland East Indies are received. Receiving licenses are required. About 500 sets are in use, mostly British. So far as is known alternating-current sets are in use. Only short-wave sets can be sold, since satisfactory long wave reception is impossible.

SYRIA

Language, Arabic; area, 60,000 square miles; population, 2,981,863

Radio has not yet been introduced successfully in Syria. The weather is hot in summer and cool in winter, and reception is generally poor.

Some 150 sets have been installed by owners who purchased them prior to going to Syria. Receiving permits are granted freely, costing 5 Syrian gold piasters ($0.96). There is no annual charge. There is no broadcasting, reception from Russia and from Osmanie, Turkey, being depended upon.

OCEANIA

AUSTRALIA

Language, English; area, 2,974,581 square miles; population, 5,495,734

Australia is one of the leading countries of the world in the matter of radio development. Progress there has been exceptionally steady and has attained a high point. The people are deeply interested, and the Government has gone to great lengths in encouraging the use of broadcasts to communicate entertainment and news throughout the Commonwealth. Of the total population 43 per cent are resident of the six capital cities. The principal cities are Sydney, Melbourne, Adelaide, and Brisbane.

Radio developments have been confined to the south coast and the southern part of the eastern and western coasts, these being the more thickly populated areas. The climate of this section is good for radio reception, the best season being from April to September.

Broadcasting is under the control of the Postmaster General. Stations are divided into two categories, those of high and those of low power. There is no restriction as to the number or location of low-powered stations, but high power is permitted to only one station in each of the States, except Victoria, and New South Wales, each of which may have two. These stations are more strictly administered than those of low power and participate in the proceeds from receiving license fees. Arrangements have been made for these stations to be taken over by the Federal Government.

Australia has 19 broadcasting stations. Three of these use double waves, one short and one middle. The Australians take great interest in short-wave broadcasts from American stations. New Zealand is commonly received in eastern Australia.

An annual receiving license, costing 17s. 6d. or 24s., depending on the distance of the receiver from the principal stations, is required. The licensed receivers numbered 309,820 in December, 1928, while varying estimates agree that the number of illegally operated receivers is large. American sets were formerly most popular and in the majority. In 1927 the domestic radio-manufacturing industry became established and by November, 1929, had grown to such proportions that a high tariff was applied to radio products. Early in 1930 a general increase and restriction on imports was applied. Until more data as to the effects of this latter legislation can be obtained, it appears that the Australian market is practically closed to American radio products. British sets are numerous, and a few German receivers are in use.

BRITISH OCEANIA

Language, English; area, 28,365 square miles; population, 480,357

British Oceania, consisting of scattered islands and groups throughout the South Pacific, shows a combined radio development of no mean proportions. Radio has proved particularly popular among the whites stationed in more or less isolated islands for government or trading purposes. Hot weather is usual in all parts of British Oceania at all seasons.

It is estimated that some 250 receivers are in use. Nearly all are of British origin. A new short-wave telephone transmitting station at Suva in the Fiji Islands has been broadcasting music, speeches, and church services on occasion for several months. Regular broadcasting from Australia, New Zealand, Hawaii, and elsewhere is received. Short-wave sets are the most popular.

FRENCH OCEANIA

Language, French; area, 1,520 square miles; population, 31,655

French Oceania has had little radio development. Nearly all of the present demand is for short-wave receivers by European residents. All seasons are hot, with poor reception. About 30 sets are in use. French makes only are represented. No French broadcasting is available, but Hawaiian, Australian, and New Zealand stations, all broadcasting in the English language, are received.

NEW ZEALAND

Language, English; area, 103,862 square miles; population, 1,407,165

New Zealand has a rapidly increasing development of radio broadcasting and reception, but the conditions have been such that the rate of progress is not an accurate indication of the basic development of the country. Soon after broadcasting was introduced in the world, New Zealand had a number of broadcasting and receiving sets. But difficulties arose through patent rights, and for more than a year there was no broadcasting in the islands. Subsequent resumption of broadcasting stimulated developments in the receiving field, and there has since been a steady increase in the number of receivers in use.

The principal cities are Auckland, Wellington, Christchurch, and Dunedin. The eastern slopes of the two main islands are plains, the western portions being volcanic mountains. The climate is mild, but rainfall is abundant. Radio reception is good, especially during the winter months from April to September. Broadcasting is closely supervised by the Government. Receiving licenses are required, costing 30s. per year. Regenerative sets are prohibited.

Twenty broadcasting stations are operating in the principal cities, one in Christchurch using a double wave to give short-wave service. Australian broadcasts are also received.

Some 45,928 receivers are under license in New Zealand. Approximately 60 per cent are of American manufacture, the remainder principally British. About 90 per cent of the tubes sold are American. Socket-power sets suitable for use with 230-volt, 50-cycle current are in demand. Short-wave sets are also popular, though their use is more restricted, amounting to some 10 per cent of the total.

AFRICA

ALGERIA

Language, French and Arabic; area, 222,180 square miles; population, 5,992,770

The development of radio in Algeria has been restricted mainly to the French residents, among whom there has been an appreciable increase in its use. Radio provides contact with France which otherwise is impossible. The native population is not interested. Hot summers and cool winters are the rule. Static is bad, especially during the summer. The total number of sets is estimated at 9,500. French products predominate. Alternating-current receivers have met with little success. Short waves have a certain popularity as a means of better reception from France. A broadcasting station is operating in Algiers.

ANGOLA

Language, Portuguese; area, 484,800 square miles; population, 2,481,956

Angola has not seen any great development in radio. The class to be interested are the Portuguese, and there is no Portuguese broadcasting nearer than Portugal or Brazil. Summers are hot and winters warm. Reception is poor. The only stations which may be received regularly are those in the Union of South Africa. About 50 receiving installations have been made, mostly representing British and American makes. There are no alternating-current or short-wave sets, so far as can be ascertained.

BASUTOLAND

Language, native dialects; area, 11,716 square miles; population, 515,781

Radio developments have been limited in the native State of Basutoland. Summers are warm and winters cool, with corresponding receiving conditions. The only broadcasting received is that from stations in the Union of South Africa. Not over 10 sets are in use. These are understood to be of British manufacture. Alternating-current receivers have not yet been introduced. One or two of the receivers in use have been equipped for short-wave reception.

BECHUANALAND

Languages, English and native dialects; area, 275,000 square miles; population, 154,983

There are only a few whites in Bechuanaland, and the number of receiving sets is accordingly restricted. Estimates indicate only 15 installed, mostly British. The stations of the Union of South Africa are received regularly.

BELGIAN CONGO

Language, French; area, 909,654 square miles; population, 8,500,000

Developments in radio in Belgian Congo are limited to the high-powered sets maintained on the coast for reception of European broadcasts. All seasons are hot, and reception is correspondingly poor. There is no near-by broadcasting. But six sets are in service, all probably of Belgian origin. Short-wave receivers should be satisfactory for use in the Congo, but no information as to their use is available.

BRITISH SOMALILAND

Language, Arabic; area, 68,000 square miles; population, 347,000

There is practically no development of radio in British Somaliland. The entire year is hot, and static is bad. Only five installations have been made, all of British sets. The only near-by broadcasting station is that at Nariobi, Kenya.

BRITISH WEST AFRICA

Language, Arabic; area, 493,628 square miles; population, 22,681,696

The scattered colonies of British West Africa show little progress in the development of radio. All of British West Africa lies within the zone where all seasons are hot, and static conditions are correspondingly bad. No broadcasting stations are operating in West Africa, the more powerful European stations being depended upon for what reception is possible. Altogether, some 50 sets are reported in use, and it is believed that only British makes are represented. No alternating-current sets are in use anywhere in British West Africa. Short-wave receivers are popular and are used at many points to keep in touch with the United Kingdom.

CANARY ISLANDS

Language, Spanish; area, 2,807 square miles; population, 481,555

The people of the Canary Islands have shown a great interest in radio, but developments have been limited by the low purchasing power of the people and the lack of sufficiently powerful broadcasting stations to serve the entire group.

This group of islands is of volcanic origin and includes seven large inhabited islands and many islets. Radio reception is good from November to April.

Radio is controlled through the Director General of Communications. Broadcasting is permitted to Spanish citizens, and licenses are issued on the payment of a fee. Receiving installations require permits costing 5 to 50 pesetas, according to the use to which the set is to be put. A special type of permit is provided for foreigners.

One broadcasting station is operating, while conditions are occasionally favorable for receiving from Spain.

The number of receivers installed is estimated at 200. A large part of these are of American manufacture. Various European makes are also represented. Alternating-current sets have not been put into use. Interest is now centered on short waves, because of atmospheric conditions and more varied reception.

EGYPT

Language, Arabic; area, 347,840 square miles; population, 14,168,756

Radio has been limited in Egypt by the Government's failure to provide regulations for broadcasting, but it has proved very popular. European broadcasting is regularly received and has brought about a high rate of development. It is expected that the establishment of an officially recognized broadcasting station or system would greatly improve the situation.

The populated section of the country is the Nile Valley, especially the delta region. The climate is fair for radio, and reception is good from November to May.

There are two broadcasting stations in Cairo. The identity of the broadcaster is known to the public, but officials are careful to avoid " learning officially " of them since any cognizance would probably necessitate closing the stations. European broadcasts, particularly from Osmanie, are received.

About 4,000 receivers are in service. British sets are the most popular, French and American also being used extensively. A small number of alternating-current receivers has been put into use. Short-wave reception has been popular.

ETHIOPIA

Language, Amharic; area, 350,000 square miles; population, 10,000,000

Ethiopia has the smallest degree of radio development of any country in the world. Only two receiving sets have been reported in this country, but that this number was increased by the importation of several gift sets at the time of the Emperor's coronation in November, 1930, is well known. Members of the royal family, the priesthood, and foreign legations may be considered as the principal buyers of receivers. Summers are hot, winters are warm, and reception is poor throughout the year. The nearest broadcasting is at Nairobi, Kenya. No regulations have been adopted.

FRENCH EQUATORIAL AFRICA

Language, Arabic; area, 982,049 square miles; population, 2,845,936

French Equatorial Africa, aside from the coasts, is principally desert, and little of the area is involved in radio developments. In the vicinity of St. Louis, Senegal, there has been an appreciable amount of progress made.

Summers are hot; winters are warm in the north and hot in the south. Climatic conditions are poor throughout the year. There is little reception, the more powerful stations of Europe providing what service is available.

Some 500 receiving installations have been made. Most of these sets are French. Some short-wave sets have been put into service to receive from stations in northern Africa and France. Sets for this purpose might find a good demand.

FRENCH MOROCCO

Language, French; area, 213,000 square miles; population, 4,229,146

There is a considerable degree of radio development in French Morocco among the French and other Europeans there, but little interest has been aroused among the native Moroccans. It appears that the ability to keep in direct touch with Europe is the principal motive. Summers are hot and winters cool. Reception is good during winter but poor in the summer.

Three broadcasting stations are operating, while Algerian, French, and Spanish stations are also received. Two of the stations use short waves, one operating on a double wave. There are about 2,500 receivers in use, largely French. There are a few alternating-current sets in use, but the service is not satisfactory. The current at Casablanca is 110 volts, 50 cycles, but there is much variation in other localities. Short waves have proved valuable in the French-controlled areas of Africa, and short-wave sets are constantly becoming more numerous.

ITALIAN AFRICA

Language, Arabic; area, 879,435 square miles; population, 2,200,000

The scattered colonies of Italy in Africa have shown only limited interest in radio, there being little in their characteristics to encourage any great developments. The climate is generally poor for radio and the people interested few in number. The distance from broadcasting further limits the field. There is no broadcasting in Italian Africa. Tripoli receives Italian stations and other European broadcasts. Estimates indicate that a total of about 250 sets are in use. Most of them are Italian and a number of British manufacture. Short-wave reception has a certain degree of popularity, since by this means programs from Rome can be picked up.

KENYA

Language, Arabic; area, 245,000 square miles; population, 2,575,789

Kenya has not exhibited especially great interest in radio, but with the establishment of a new broadcasting station at Nairobi greater developments are expected. The summers are hot and winters warm, with resultingly poor reception from distant stations. The number of sets in use is estimated at 250, nearly all British. As yet alternating-current sets have not been introduced. Short-wave reception is becoming popular more rapidly than reception in the broadcast wave band because stations in Johannesburg and England as well as the new local station may be received through the former medium.

LIBERIA

Language, English; area, 36,834 square miles; population, 1,500,000

There has been as yet no development of radio in Liberia; summers and winters are both hot, with poor reception resulting. Only five receivers have been installed, three of them being American. The broadcasting from European stations is depended upon for programs. Alternating-current receivers are not used.

MADAGASCAR

Language, French; area, 225,707 square miles; population, 3,598,728

Radio has not had any great development in Madagascar but is gaining in popularity. Several short-wave stations which may be used for broadcasting are now contemplated.

The principal cities are Antananarivo and Tamatave. In general the island is a plateau; there are several extinct volcanoes. The climate is tropical. From June to November it is cool and dry; during the remainder of the year rain is frequent and the temperature high.

The only broadcasting available for average sets is that from South African stations, although some of the more powerful receivers pick up European programs. French regulations are in force.

About 150 receiving sets are reported to be in use. These are French, brought from France chiefly by officials assigned to posts in Madagascar. No alternating-current sets are in use. Some experimentation with the use of short waves for picking up Eiffel Tower programs has been carried out with success.

MOZAMBIQUE

Language, Portuguese; area, 428,132 square miles; population, 3,160,500

The development of radiobroadcast reception in Mozambique has not been great. Only a small per cent of the population are

Europeans.   The principal cities are Lourenco Marques and Beira. The country is mainly mountainous.   The rainy season lasts from November to March.   The coasts are hot, but the highlands are temperate.   The Chief of Posts and Telegraphs has authority over all radiobroadcasting activities.

About 75 receivers have been installed, representing various European and American makes.   The only broadcasting available is that from the Union of South Africa and Kenya, all of which is in English.   Alternating-current receivers are as yet unknown. Short-wave reception is not particularly popular, inasmuch as there are no short-wave broadcasts in the Portuguese language.

NORTHERN RHODESIA

Language, English ; area, 291,000 square miles ; population, 1,154,624

The distance from broadcasting has hindered the development of radio in Northern Rhodesia.   All seasons are hot, with poor reception conditions.   There are only 25 sets in the colony, mostly British. Stations in Kenya and in the Union of South Africa are received. No alternating-current sets are used.   Short-wave reception is arousing some interest since the commencement of short-wave broadcasts from Johannesburg and Nairobi.

SOUTHERN RHODESIA

Language, English ; area, 148,575 square miles ; population, 873,647

Southern Rhodesia has shown a great interest in radio, but the developments have been limited by the distance from broadcasting stations and the expense of the types of sets necessary.   Summers are hot and winters warm, reception being poor.

Regulations provide for the payment of a license fee annually, amounting to £2 ($9.75) per year for sets within 50 miles of the nearest broadcasting station, and 15 s. ($3.55) per year for those over 250 miles, with intermediate rates for distances of between 50 and 250 miles.

About 150 receiving sets have been installed.   Many are British and a few American.   Programs are received from stations in the Union of South Africa and Kenya.   Short-wave reception is becoming increasingly popular.

SOUTHWEST AFRICA

Language, German ; area, 322,000 square miles ; population, 227,739

Interest in radio is growing in Southwest Africa, but, because of the distance from broadcasting stations, little has been accomplished as yet.   The Government is generally interested in radio development, but the small proportion of white population will probably limit advancement for some years.   All seasons are warm, with reception fair throughout the year.   Receiving installations number 50, principally British.   Reception is possible only from stations in the Union of South Africa.   Alternating-current sets are practically unknown.   Short-wave reception is becoming popular.

SPANISH AFRICA

Language, Spanish; area, 140,000 square miles; population, 980,000

Aside from the Canary Islands, there has been little progress made by radio in Spanish Africa. Although radio is popular among the few whites, conditions are not favorable to its promotion, the distance from broadcasting stations in all cases being the principal retarding factor. In all of Spanish Africa summers are hot and winters warm, with poor reception.

There is no broadcasting in any part of Spanish Africa, aside from the Canary Islands. Rio de Oro and Spanish Morocco, as well as the Canary Islands and French Africa, receive broadcasts from Spain.

The total number of sets in use is estimated at 150, including several American and various European types. Neither alternating-current nor short-wave receivers have been introduced.

SWAZILAND

Language, native dialects; area, 6,678 square miles; population, 117,877

Radio has had no development in Swaziland. Summers are hot and winters warm, reception being poor at all seasons. Only five receivers have been installed, all believed to be British. Broadcasting from South African stations is received.

TANGANYIKA

Language, Arabic; area, 373,494 square miles; population, 4,123,493

Radio development in Tanganyika has been limited to a considerable extent by the distance from broadcasting, but the establishment of the new station in Kenya is expected to improve this condition. It is hot at all seasons, with poor reception. About 10 receiving installations are in service, mostly British.

TUNISIA

Language, French; area, 50,000 square miles; population, 2,159,758

The French and other Europeans in Tunisia have shown considerable interest in radio, and developments are comparatively well advanced. Though the climate is not the best, reception from France is easily accomplished, while the broadcasters in Tunisia provide programs of local interest. Summers are hot and winters warm. Static is bad throughout the year.

Three broadcasting stations are operating in Tunisia, one on short waves. French broadcasts from Algeria, Morocco, and France are received, as well as other European stations. Receiving licenses are required, costing 20 francs per year. A recent estimate indicates that about 1,000 sets are in service. The majority are French, the remainder of various makes. Short-wave reception is meeting with considerable success and is arousing some interest.

UNION OF SOUTH AFRICA

Language, English and Dutch ; area, 472,347 square miles ; population, 6,928,580

Radio in the Union of South Africa has shown considerable development. The Government has taken a great interest in promoting the use of broadcasting. The whites are particularly enthusiastic, and, while the financial end of broadcasting has proved a difficult problem, it is apparent that progress will continue. Radio dealers have agreed to contribute 10 per cent of their net profits in radio toward the cost of broadcasting and to include the cost of the license in the sale price of each set, giving a voucher for which the broadcasting company will exchange a license. Meanwhile, the Government has under consideration the abolition of licenses and using instead a 25 per cent import tax, most of which would be paid over to the broadcasters. Newspapers have taken a position adverse to radio, however, considering it a competitor in the field of advertising, with resulting friction that has somewhat retarded its development.

The principal cities are Johannesburg, Cape Town, Durban, Pretoria, Port Elizabeth, and Benoni. About 1,500,000 of the population are white. The country for the most part consists of plains. Radio reception is always good and is best from June to August.

The postmaster general has supervision over radio matters. Broadcasting is a regional monopoly, each station being licensed to operate exclusively within a certain territory for a period of five years.

Three broadcasting stations are now operating in the Union of South Africa. One of these uses double waves to provide short-wave transmission. While reception from Europe and the Americas is frequently accomplished, it is not very satisfactory. Receiving set owners are subjected to the payment of license fees ranging from £1 for sets situated over 200 miles from the nearest broadcasting station to £1 15s. for sets under 100 miles. The intermediate charge is £1 5s. Higher rates are provided for sets used elsewhere than in homes.

The licensed receivers in service have a total of 20,000, while a large number of unlicensed sets are known to be in use. British sets predominate, but American makes are popular and a large number are in use.

Some interest in alternating-current sets has been aroused. Short-wave reception has been popular for several years, particularly among the exceptionally large class of amateurs.

ZANZIBAR

Language, Arabic ; area, 1,020 square miles ; population, 215,879

There has been practically no promotion of radio in Zanzibar. Five receivers are in use, all British. The only programs satisfactorily received are from Kenya. All seasons are hot, with poor reception.

U. S. DEPARTMENT OF COMMERCE
R. P. LAMONT, Secretary

BUREAU OF FOREIGN AND DOMESTIC COMMERCE
FREDERICK M. FEIKER, Director

BROADCAST ADVERTISING IN ASIA AFRICA, AUSTRALIA AND OCEANIA

Trade Information Bulletin No. 799

UNITED STATES
GOVERNMENT PRINTING OFFICE
WASHINGTON: 1932

FOREWORD

This is the third of a series of bulletins answering some of the questions with respect to the feasibility of employing radio as an advertising medium for American products in foreign lands. In certain countries commercial broadcasting is definitely prohibited; in others the restrictions upon owners of radio sets are such as to discourage their general use. In most countries existing regulations are, with a few exceptions, unfavorable to the development of commercial broadcasting.

The brief country-by-country outline presented herewith gives the status of commercial broadcasting in scattered countries of Asia, Africa, Australia, and Oceania at the middle of 1931. This issue completes the bureau's survey of commercial broadcasting, two bulletins having already been published, one covering the Western Hemisphere, except the United States and Canada (Broadcast Advertising in Latin America, Trade Information Bulletin No. 771) and the other covering European countries, except Soviet Russia (Broadcast Advertising in Europe, Trade Information Bulletin No. 787).

This bulletin, issued jointly by the electrical equipment and specialties divisions of the Bureau of Foreign and Domestic Commerce, was compiled by E. D. Schutrumpf of the latter division from reports submitted by the foreign representatives of the Department of Commerce and Department of State. The electrical equipment division has a wide variety of information available on foreign markets for radio equipment.

FREDERICK M. FEIKER,

Director, Bureau of Foreign and Domestic Commerce.

MAY, 1932.

(II)

BROADCAST ADVERTISING IN ASIA, AFRICA, AUSTRALIA, AND OCEANIA

INTRODUCTION

Radio broadcasting in Asia, Africa, Australia, and Oceania is, with few exceptions, under direct governmental control, and regulations are in effect for most countries. The tax or license fee for receiver-set ownership is in general practice.

While several countries have made considerable progress in radio development, commercial broadcasting is not generally favored. Of the countries permitting such advertising, only Australia and the Union of South Africa are making noticeable progress, and these have profited by the interest of their Governments in promoting broadcasting. China has been retarded by the Government's attitude, but efforts are being made toward a better relation between radio interests and the Government. Activities at this time are at a minimum, owing to unsettled conditions. Although radio has been limited in Egypt by the Government's failure to provide regulations for broadcasting, it has proved very popular.

Each of the countries permitting commercial broadcasting must be considered separately because of varying facilities and possibilities for the promotion of American products. As a whole, there are definite limitations in these countries because ownership of receivers is, with one or two exceptions, confined to a very small portion of the population, and because of the restrictions regarding types of programs and time limits for broadcast advertising. Such broadcasting in the countries involved, however, encounters problems practically identical with those affecting other types of advertising, such as language, prejudices, differences in buying habits, etc., discussion of which appears in the following pages.

While the information in this bulletin was gleaned largely by first-hand contact and observation by the foreign representatives of the Department of Commerce and Department of State in the summer of 1931, it can not be considered complete and final. It should prove of value of American firms that would consider radio as a medium with a more personal touch to add to their advertising campaigns. In most cases the rates have been furnished by the station managers, but no responsibility can be assumed by the Department of Commerce for their accuracy.

ASIA

CHINA

The conditions under which commercial broadcasting is carried on within the territory that the world calls China are so varied that the following text is arranged to treat separately Manchuria, North China, and South China. There have been no reports indicating that any of the stations discussed have been shut down in recent weeks owing to the political and military troubles in the Far East.

MANCHURIA

By Assistant Trade Commissioner C. E. Christopherson, Mukden

There are only two broadcasting stations in Manchuria which accept commercial advertising. These are the Northeast Radio, Liaoning broadcasting station at Mukden, call letters COMK, wave length 410 meters, power 2,000 watts, and the Northeast Radio Harbin broadcasting station at Harbin, call letters COHB, 445 meters, 1,000 watts. The officials of the Mukden station also control the Harbin station.

There is also a broadcasting station at Dairen, call letters JQAK, but it does not accept commercial advertising. It is owned and operated by the bureau of communications of the Kwantung Government and hence under Japanese supervision.

Practically no commercial advertising has actually been accepted by the Mukden station as yet, but a schedule of rates has been adopted. Rates are charged by the word, 40 words being the standard unit and 70 words the maximum. The following rates are for broadcasting once each evening: 40 words, one day, Mex. $1; one week, Mex. $6; half a month, Mex. $11; one month, Mex. $20; 70 words, one day, Mex. $1.50; one week, Mex. $9; half a month, Mex. $17; and one month, Mex. $32. (Mexican $1 equals $0.23 in United States currency.) For an extra broadcast during the day there is an additional charge of one-half the above rate.

Station COHB at Harbin quotes the following rates, in Mexican dollars:

| Item | Advertising [1] | | Records [2]—1 record | |
	For 10 words	For 1 minute	Talking	Music
One time	5.00	25.00	15.00	1.50
One week	25.00	150.00	80.00	10.50
15 days	40.00	275.00	125.00	22.50
One month	75.00	500.00	200.00	45.00

[1] Rate is increased 50 per cent for the second 10 words and 25 per cent for each additional 10 words above 20. Advertisements may be in Chinese, Russian, English, or French.
[2] Records are announced by the COHB announcer.

Some local talent is probably available for station COMK, but as none has yet been used rates are not available. Local talent is available for station COHB. The charge for orchestras is 10 gold yen per hour. (1 gold yen equals $0.50 in United States currency.)

Records can be used and should be recorded for 75 revolutions per minute for station COMK. Station COHB uses an American reproducer. These stations have not contracted with any local, American, or other agency for the sale of broadcasting time to advertisers.

No commercial advertising is being broadcast from Mukden. Among the commodities advertised by the Harbin station are machinery, household equipment, phonograph records, bicycles, and automobiles. Broadcasting from Mukden should be in the Chinese language, but Harbin uses Chinese or Russian.

NORTH CHINA

By Assistant Trade Commissioner Louis C. Venator, Tientsin

Although there are three broadcasting stations in North China, the presentation of purely entertainment programs has, in the past, been limited to occasional and spasmodic private and governmental enterprise and no commercial advertising by air has as yet been undertaken.

Two of the existing stations are operated by the Government; they broadcast entertainment programs along with certain political propaganda between scheduled hours, during which they handle commercial messages. These stations are COTN, Tientsin, wave length 480 meters, power 500 watts, and XOPP (formerly COPK), Peiping, wave length 320 meters, power 1,000 watts. Both are operated by the Northeast Radio Broadcasting Co. (Ltd.), a Government agency. The one private station, call letters CRC, wave length 280 meters, power 500 watts, has been out of operation for almost a year, but during the time of its activity handled entertainment features at the expense of the owner, one of the principal radio dealers of Tientsin. He contemplates reopening his station on a commercial basis.

Government regulations and restrictions and fairly heavy license fees and taxes seem to be the deterrent factors to private establishment of broadcasting stations.

There is no basis for even estimating the potentialities of radio advertising in North China. A Chinese household sufficiently well-to-do to own a radio usually has servants who do the household shopping, and they purchase most of the commodities which are used. If directly commanded they will probably purchase a particular brand of article; otherwise they customarily buy that brand which they themselves prefer. It would thus appear that the classes of commodities likely to benefit to any extent from radio broadcasting in North China would be luxuries and semiluxuries.

Broadcast advertising would of necessity be directed to the Chinese, and the native style of entertainment would be desirable. Local orchestras, singers, and other entertainment features are available in considerable numbers, but no schedule of charges for radio work has been established. The effectiveness of programs in English would be negligible.

SOUTH CHINA

By Assistant Trade Commissioner Edgar W. O'Harow, Shanghai

Radio broadcasting, and in consequence advertising by radio, has never gained much headway in China, owing to governmental supervision. Broadcasting is viewed by the Government as a dangerous instrumentality for the dissemination of propaganda inimical to the welfare of the country. The result is that stations previously established are now under Government control or have entirely ceased operations.

Another attempt is being made to sponsor advertising by radio by the China Broadcast (Ltd.) operating its new station XCBL on the premises of Millington (Ltd.), 113 Avenue Edward VII, Shanghai, which broadcast its first test program on May 14, 1931. This promises to be a successful venture, since the necessary license to operate was obtained from the National Government, because a limited amount of Chinese capital is invested in the new company, and because it is so organized as to encourage confidence in the success of the new venture.

China Broadcast (Ltd.) is sponsored by Reuters (Ltd.), world-wide news service, and Millington (Ltd.), an established British firm of advertising agents, who have charge of the business organization and management of the new enterprise. The new station has a power of 400 watts which the management hopes to increase to 1,000 watts in the near future. The wave length is 235 meters. The studios consist of two broadcasting rooms, reception room, and offices. An entirely new and modern transmitter was installed. The generating set was constructed locally, but American parts, Philips tubes, and Telefunken amplifier and microphone are used. A brochure published by China Broadcast late in 1931 listed 40 firms as program sponsors, indicating a substantial support of this new enterprise.

The actual operation and management of the station is under the direction of an American. Correspondence should be addressed to the China Broadcast (Ltd.), care of Millington (Ltd.), 113 Avenue Edward VII, Shanghai. The method of handling programs will be patterned after that of American chains. Reuters (Ltd.) will supply foreign news and a commercial service which will be broadcast twice daily. This will comprise lectures in English prepared by professional teachers for the benefit of Chinese students. The broadcasting will be continuous from 11.30 a. m. to 2 p. m. and 4.30 p. m. to midnight. A band of 12 instrumentalists has been engaged to provide musical selections, and plans are in hand for broadcasting Sunday religious services. Other developments are expected to take place, such as broadcasting by remote control from various places of amusement in Shanghai and perhaps the transmission of programs by wire to Nanking for rebroadcast by the new large station being completed there.

It has been unofficially estimated that there are approximately 5,000 radio sets in use in Shanghai and in the immediate neighborhood. It may be assumed that radio advertising will often reach a community of at least 25,000 people. Once there is a continuous broadcast in Shanghai there is no doubt that the listeners will increase materially. The majority, of course, will be Chinese, and the greater part of the programs will be in the Chinese language.

There are two other broadcasting stations operating in Shanghai which have facilities for advertising by radio. These are the Telling Radio Broadcasting Studio, 462 Avenue Joffre, and Amateurs Radio Home, 323 Kiangse Road, call letters, XGAH; wave length, 240 meters; power, 50 watts. However, these are small stations, which operate intermittently and are not organized on a scale to handle broadcasting in a manner similar to the larger organizations.

Rates charged for studio time per month for one period (15 minutes each) a week by station XCBL are as follows: From 11 to 11.45, 50 Shanghai taels [1]; 12 to 1.45, 60 taels; 2 to 4.45, 40 taels; 5 and 5.15, 50 taels; 5.30 to 6, 55 taels; 6.15 to 6.45, 60 taels; 7 to 7.15, 65 taels; 7.30 to 7.45, 70 taels; 8 to 8.15, 75 taels; 8.30 to 9, 80 taels; 9.15 to 10, 75 taels; and 10.15 to 11,70 taels.

Prices for special talent are in addition to regular rates charged per hour for studio time as above. For one program per week for a month, the orchestras listed charge as follows (currency in taels): Gypsy (7 musicians), 110; Spanish (8 musicians), 120; Italian (7 musicians), 100; Russian (9 musicians), 120; Hungarian (7 musicians),

---

[1] The Shanghai tael varies with the price of silver, but has recently been quoted at about 32 cents in United States currency.

110; Chinese (6 to 8 musicians), 140; Symphony (12 musicians), 150; Symphonette (8 musicians), 120; quartet (4 musicians), 75; quartet (4 to 5 musicians), 90; quartet (8 musicians), 120; trio (3 musicians), 60; trio (violin, cello, and harp), 70.

If more than one program per week is desired, the prices are as follows: Two per week, plus 50 per cent; three, 65 per cent; four, 80 per cent; five, 90 per cent; six, 100 per cent; daily program (exclusive services), 125 per cent additional.

Newspaper space has been used to advertise commercial broadcasts.

Records can be used. The rates charged do not differ from the price charged for station time. Prices for special programs are in addition to regulation station time. Records should be made for a speed of 78 revolutions per minute.

Commercial concerns in Shanghai have contracted for broadcasting time to advertise the following: Radios, radio products and equipment, phonographs, office appliances, electrical products, cameras and photographic supplies, radio and telegraphic instruments, automobiles, jewelry, theater programs, men's furnishings, interior decorations, credit investigations, stock quotations, real estate, and a popular American restaurant.

Programs are broadcast in both English and Chinese, and announcements are made in both languages. Records prepared in the English language may be used effectively in Shanghai. A translation of the record into Chinese will be made and a synopsis given in Chinese prior to broadcasting in English.

Canton, in southern China near Hong Kong, has a radio station, CAB, operating on 435 meters with 1,000 watts power. Commercial advertising is not permitted by the Government.

HONG KONG

By Assistant Trade Commissioner David M. Maynard

As far as ascertainable, there are no broadcasting stations in this territory that accept commercial advertising. One station located at Hong Kong and controlled by the Government is station ZBW, 355 meters, 1,500 watts. As yet the Government has not permitted advertising to be broadcast.

The manager of the Hong Kong branch of a well-known advertising firm has been endeavoring to secure the permission of the Hong Kong Government to broadcast on the local station. He reports little progress in this direction.

It is customary to broadcast phonograph records. The names of these records and their distributors are published in the daily papers and the distributors of the records are also announced over the air. This provides advertising for the local music stores, which at present costs them only the loan of the records.

FRENCH INDO-CHINA

By American Consul Henry S. Waterman, Saigon

There is only one broadcasting station in French Indo-China, Radio Saigon, owned by Compagnie Franco-Indochinoise Radiophonie. This station broadcasts on two wave lengths, 49.05 and 358 meters. Its programs have been received in the United States.

The unit for announcements is 40 words in one language only. The text must be furnished by the advertiser, as well as the translation, if there is any. The company declines all responsibility for the correctness of a translation which it makes itself, in the event the subscriber does not furnish one. The announcements can be made in French, English, Cantonese, Annamite, and Cambodian, but announcements may not be in different languages.

The following statement shows the prices according to the number of announcements per 3-month period:

	Piasters [2]
1 announcement per month (total of 3 broadcasts)	30
2 announcements per month (total of 6 broadcasts)	54
3 announcements per month (total of 9 broadcasts)	72
5 announcements per month (total of 15 broadcasts)	105
10 announcements per month (total of 30 broadcasts)	180
15 announcements per month (total of 45 broadcasts)	225
30 announcements per month (total of 90 broadcasts)	360

Advertising contracts are established and signed for a first period of three months, renewable automatically for another three months if the client does not give one month's notice in advance, to stop his subscription. Renewals are thus made continuously without other notice for a period of three months each.

The European orchestra used by the Compagnie Franco-Indochinoise de Radiophonie costs 200 piasters per concert of 1 hour; between musical numbers different advertisements are broadcast. The price of a native orchestra is 25 piasters per concert, which lasts three-quarters of an hour, under the same conditions as above.

Concerts broadcast by records cost 15 piasters each, for 30 minutes, whether the music is native or European, under the same conditions as above. The speed desired for records is 78 revolutions per minute.

Local singers can be obtained, the price varying according to the quality of the talent. The company believes that it can furnish acceptable singers for 50 piasters per concert.

Broadcast advertising has just been introduced in French Indo-China and a few local companies are using this medium. The products advertised are photographic appliances, pharmaceutical products, and agricultural and metallurgical products, as well as various publications. No American companies have as yet contracted for broadcasting advertisements.

Although broadcasting may be done in French, English, Cantonese, Annamite, and Cambodian, it is suggested that English be entirely eliminated from consideration, as it would not be understood. French should be the principal language used, although alternating announcements may be made in Annamite, Cambodian, or Cantonese, particularly if the advertised products such as agricultural equipment and supplies, certain foodstuffs, and possibly automotive supplies are used by the natives of these races.

Assuming that there are approximately 1,000 receiving nets in French Indo-China, it may be considered that radio advertising is not of wide applicability as yet. On the other hand, should an American company decide to use this service, it could probably arrange with the Compangnie Franco-Indochinoise de Radiophonie to broadcast a special program having a particular appeal to whichever section of the population it is desired to reach and in that manner be able to obtain contact with a considerable buying public.

---

[2] 1 piaster equals 10 francs, or approximately 40 cents in United States currency.

JAPAN

By Assistant Trade Commissioner H. B. Titus, Tokyo

All broadcasting stations in Japan are members of one association, which is under direct Government control. No program may be broadcast until it has been submitted to and approved by the Imperial Japanese Department of Communications. The regulations under which the broadcasting company operates do not allow it to broadcast advertising programs or political speeches. During a recent political campaign special permission was granted to two of the ministers of the cabinet to make political speeches over the broadcasting system, but this was an unusual event.

NETHERLAND EAST INDIES

By Assistant Trade Commissioner Carl H. Boehringer, Batavia

According to local authorities, the Government broadcasting station does not accept advertising, and it is illegal for privately operated broadcasting stations to accept advertising.

Practically all programs now being broadcast consist of gramophone records. The local stations are using the Dutch language, but the programs of the Government broadcast transmitter at Bandoeng, Java, are announced in Dutch, French, German, and English.

SIAM

By Assistant Trade Commissioner Joe D. Walstrom, Bangkok

There are no broadcasting stations in Siam which accept commercial advertising at the present time, although the radio authorities are considering the matter and it is possible that broadcasting time will be sold in the future.

All broadcasting comes under the supervision of the Siamese Government (Ministry of Commerce and Communications). There are no privately operated stations. Each owner of a radio set is required to obtain a license and pay a small annual fee; dealers in radio accessories must pay an annual shop tax. A small amount of revenue is obtained from these sources, and the remainder of the expense is borne by the Government.

STRAITS SETTLEMENTS

There are no commercial broadcasting stations in British Malaya.

SYRIA

By American Consul J. Thayer Gilman, Beirut

Except for a very small amateur station, no broadcasting stations exist in Syria, the nearest one being situated at Angora, Turkey. Stations in Moscow, Union of Socialist Soviet Republics, which is on the same meridian as Beirut, are popular, since programs begin early. Programs from Rome, Berlin, Prague, London, Paris, etc., are all obtainable with powerful sets, but owing to the difference in time, the more distant stations, starting their programs at 9 o'clock, are not heard in Syria until about midnight. Radios rank distinctly in the luxury class and are available to a limited wealthy group, as only the barest necessities of life are obtained by the general population.

CEYLON

By American Consul Stillman W. Wells, Colombo

The only broadcasting station in Ceylon is owned and operated by the Ceylon Government, and no commercial broadcasting is permitted.

AFRICA

EGYPT

By Commercial Attaché Charles E. Dickerson, jr., Cairo

There are at present only two broadcasting stations in operation in Egypt, both of which accept commercial advertising. These stations are owned by J. P. Sheridan & Co., 23 Sharia Madabegh, Cairo, and the Heliopolis Broadcasting Station, 12 Rue Nubar Pasha, Cairo, owner and operator, Gabriel M. Tabet. J. P. Sheridan & Co. reports that it is increasing the power of its station in the near future to 1,000 watts, and obtaining a high-tension generator from the United States for this purpose. The new power will make the station heard in Syria and at Khartoum, Sudan. At present it is heard all over Egypt. The Heliopolis broadcasting station has a 500-watt transmitter.

The Sheridan station states that its advertising rates are 5 cents per word for short contracts and 2½ cents per word for long contracts. For sponsored programs it charges a flat rate of $25 per hour for the use of its studio. Musical programs, either Arabic or European, if of superior quality, usually cost another $25 maximum.

The other firm gives its rates as follows: One announcement per day of 5 words, 5 piasters per word; 10 words, 4 piasters; 20 words, 3 piasters; monthly rate for one announcement per day, 10 words, 300 piasters for one month; 20 words, 400 piasters for one month; 350 piasters for three months; 300 piasters for one year; 50 words, 450 piasters for one month, 400 piasters for three months, 250 piasters for one year. For sponsored programs a flat rate of $15 per hour is charged for the use of the studio. Musical programs, either Arabic, or European, if of superior quality, cost about $25 in addition. Good local talent is available.

Phonograph records can be used. If a flat program is given on records, the Sheridan station charges the same as for a sponsored program, i. e., at the rate of $25 an hour, with minimum of $5 per program. The Heliopolis station charges corresponding rates, $15 per hour for the use of the studio.

The first of the two firms advises that its phonograph turntables operate at 78 revolutions per minute and it has a complete system of fading from one table to the other. The second firm states that its turntables are adjustable as regards speed.

J. P. Sheridan & Co. report that it has broadcast advertising for the past 13 months on behalf of several prominent concerns principally local, including department stores, hotels, piano dealers, etc. Last year from May to August it carried a sponsored program for an American dentifrice, and in 1931 it also broadcast a 3-month sponsored program for an American razor manufacturer.

The Heliopolis station advises that it has 1-year advertising contracts with the following advertisers, through their local representatives: Two American automobile manufacturers, two American producers of radios, an American tire company, and a German piano company. This firm also states that it has numerous other short-term contracts with local firms.

Arabic and French are principally used in Egyptian broadcasting. Very little English is used. Phonograph concert and dance records in English are, however, popular and in daily use.

UNION OF SOUTH AFRICA

By Commercial Attaché Samuel H. Day, Johannesburg

Radio broadcasting in South Africa is a monopoly controlled by the African Broadcasting Co. (Ltd.), Orpheum Building, Joubert Street, Johannesburg. The three principal broadcasting stations now accept commercial advertising. They are as follows: Johannesburg, station ZTJ, two wave lengths simultaneously, one 450 meters and the other 49.4 meters, with a power of 15,000 watts; Cape Town, station ZTC, 370 meters, 1,000 watts; Durban, station ZTD, 410 meters, 1,000 watts.

Substations are being installed at Bloemfontein and Pretoria. These relay stations will use 510 and 300 meters respectively.

The broadcast advertising rights are entirely in the hands of the African Amalgamated Advertising Contractors (Ltd.), 88 Fox Street, Johannesburg, to whom all inquiries should be addressed.

The charges for commercial broadcast advertising per "mention" are as follows: Johannesburg, £3; Cape Town, £3; and Durban, £2 5s. These rates are on the understanding that not less that 13 mentions will be put over during each year. A mention consists of a message of not less than 15 words broadcast during the evening hours. Each mention is interspersed between items of the evening's program.

In addition to mentions, arrangements can be made for sponsored concerts, either complete with concert party or made up from a selection of phonograph records. In either case, the services of the studio announcer are available in introducing the concert or phonograph program. These sponsored concerts may be arranged for either half-hour or hour periods. The charge per station for half-hour concerts is £15. Should 12 concerts or more be booked during the year then the charge per concert per station is reduced to £12 10s. For concerts up to one hour, the charge per concert per station is £20.

Local talent of all kinds is available, in the form of orchestras, singers, and entertainers. The charges vary greatly, but on the whole may be comparable with medium grades of similar talent obtainable in the United States.

Phonograph records may be used. The speed may be either 75 or 33⅓ revolutions per minute, according to American practice.

Among the leading firms now employing radio broadcasting for advertising are the White Horse Distillers; H. & H. Sulston (hosiery dealers); D. W. Gibbs (manufacturers of dental preparations and soaps); Phillips, S. A. (radio apparatus); A. Wander (beverage manufacturer); Cadbury Frye (chocolates and cocoas), as well as various American manufacturers of watches, petroleum products, and other commodities.

Although both English and Afrikaans may be employed, the principal language used is English. In fact, the widespread knowledge of English even by the Afrikaans section of the population is such that English can be used effectively.

At present there are about 30,000 licensed radio receiving sets in South Africa, so it is estimated that approximately 150,000 persons would be the present maximum number to be reached by radio programs.

AUSTRALIA

H. P. Van Blarcom, Assistant Trade Commissioner, Sydney, Australia

TYPES OF STATIONS

The use of radio as a means of advertising has come into considerable prominence in Australia in recent years. During the latter part of 1924 the postmaster general's department issued regulations providing for "A" and "B" class stations, the A class broadcasters to receive their revenue from the listeners' license fees, while the B class stations were to obtain revenue through advertising or other means. The A stations were to refrain from broadcasting paid advertising programs.

During the latter part of 1929 the Federal Government announced the establishment of a national broadcasting service whereby all A stations would be taken over by the Government and all programs would be arranged by a single organization to be known as the Australian Broadcasting Co. (Ltd.). The establishment of the national service left the radio advertising field to the B class stations, but the popularity of radio was apparently not sufficient to warrant much expense in advertising. There were only nine B stations in operation in 1925, but the number increased to over 30 by July, 1931.

Every B class broadcasting station now in operation is prepared to accept advertising. In some cases, efforts have been made to link up a station in each capital city in a Commonwealth broadcast. At the present time stations 2UW, Sydney; 3DB, Melbourne; 4DC, Brisbane; 5AD, Adelaide; and 6ML, Perth, are in a Federal broadcasting network, which will provide for chain advertising. However, past experience with nation-wide hookups has indicated considerable difficulty in picking up the program for rebroadcasting purposes, owing to interference, land-line difficulties, and other causes. On several occasions B stations have linked together for national broadcasts of political speeches, cricket matches, etc., and the results in some cases have been quite satisfactory.

There has also been a federation of B class stations formed for the purpose of protecting the mutual interests of station operators, and it is understood that arrangements might be made through the secretary of this federation (G. L. Chilvera, Collins House, Collins Street, Melbourne, Victoria) by which the same advertisement may be broadcast from every B station in Australia.

Fifty per cent of Australia's total population of 6,500,000 is in the metropolitan areas of the capital cities. For this reason it would be expected that, if stations in these cities were selected for purposes of radio advertising, the larger proportion of the radio listeners would be reached. A further example of the advantages of this course may be indicated by the report that practically 70 per cent of the licensed radio receivers in New South Wales are within a 25-mile radius of Sydney. The same condition appears to be true with regard to the

capital cities of the other States. In any event, for purposes of good-
will advertising, one station in each of these cities (Sydney,
Melbourne, Brisbane, Adelaide, Perth, and Hobart) would probably
provide service for the great majority of the 330,000 licensed radio
sets in the Commonwealth.

The following is a list of B stations accepting commercial advertising:

AUSTRALIAN RADIO BROADCASTING STATIONS ACCEPTING ADVERTISING

Name and address	Call	Power, in watts	Wave length, in meters	Remarks
NEW SOUTH WALES				
Moss Vale Broadcasting Service (Ltd.), North St., Moss Vale.	2MV	50	245.8	Advertising agents, Amalgamated Wireless (A/sia), York St., Sydney.
2AY Publicity Service, 610 Dean St., Albury.	2AY	50	202.7	Do.
Electric Utilities Supply Co., 617 George St., Sydney.	2UE	1,000	293	Advertising agents (exclusive), Reuters (Ltd.), 15 Castlereagh St., Sydney
Broadcasting Station 2GB, Adyar House, 29 Bligh St., Sydney.	2GB	3,000	316	Handles own advertising.
Radio Broadcasting (Ltd.), Palings Bldgs., 16 Ash St., Sydney.	2UW	800	267	Do.
Trades Hall Broadcasting Station, Trades Hall, Goulburn St., Sydney.	2KY	1,500	280	Do.
Lismore Broadcasting Station, 173 Molesworth St., Lismore.	2XN	50	224	Advertising agents (not exclusive), Amalgamated Wireless (A/sia) (Ltd.).
Airsales Broadcasting Co., Civic Centre, Newcastle.	2HD	200	270	Do.
Mockler Bros., Howick St., Bathurst	2MK	250	260	Station reported to be experimental, probably handles own advertising.
M. J. Oliver, 432 Peel St., Tamworth (station at Gunneday).	2MO	50	225.5	Handles own advertising.
Goulburn Broadcasting Co. (Ltd.), P. O. Box 88, Goulburn.[1]	2GN	50		Will handle own advertising, but will possibly have nonexclusive arrangement with Amalgamated Wireless (A/sia) (Ltd.).
Station 2CA, Canberra, F. C. T.[1]	2CA	50	285.5	Probably will handle own advertising.
Newcastle Broadcasting Co. (Ltd.), Newcastle.[1]	2KO	200	212	Do.
Broken Hill Broadcasting Co. (Ltd.), Broken Hill.[1]	2XL	250	219	Do.
VICTORIA				
3DB Broadcasting Co. Pty. (Ltd.), 36 Flinders St., Melbourne.	3DB	500	255	Handles own advertising; represented in the United States by J. B. Powers, 250 Park Ave., New York.
Nilsens Broadcasting Service, 45 Bourke St., Melbourne.	3UZ	500	319	Handles own advertising.
Wangaratta Broadcasting Pty. (Ltd.), Reid St., Wangaratta.	3WR	200	238	Do.
Ballarat Broadcasters Pty. (Ltd.), Sturt St. Ballarat.	3BA	50	231	Do.
Geelong Broadcasters Pty. (Ltd.), Malop St., Geelong.	3GL	50	214	Do.
Industrial Printing & Publishing Co., Strand Buildings, Elizabeth St., Melbourne.	3KZ	500	222	Do.
Amalgamated Wireless (A/sia) (Ltd.), Broadcasting Station 3BO, Kangaroo Flat, Bendigo[1]	3BO	200	307.7	All advertising handled through Amalgamated Wireless (A/sia), Sydney.
Western Broadcasting Co. (Ltd.), Hamilton.[1]	3HA	200	297	Will probably handle own advertising.
Swan Hill Broadcasting Co., Swan Hill[1]	3SH	50	278	Do.
Gippsland Broadcasting Service Trafalgar (Ltd.), Contingent St., Trafalgar. (P. O. Box 89.)[1]	3TR			Do.

[1] Not yet in operation.

AUSTRALIAN RADIO BROADCASTING STATIONS ACCEPTING ADVERTISING—Con.

Name and address	Call	Power, in watts	Wave length, in meters	Remarks
QUEENSLAND				
J. B. Chandler & Co., 43 Adelaide St., Brisbane.	4BC	200	262	Handles own advertising.
Brisbane Broadcasting Co. (Ltd.), King House, Queen St., Brisbane.	4BK	200	233	Reuters (Ltd.), Queen St., Brisbane, exclusive advertising agents.
Gold Radio Service, Ruthven St., Toowoomba.	4GR	50	294	Handles own advertising but states advertising open to any agent at 15 per cent commission.
Amalgamated Wireless (A/sia), Broadcasting Station 4TO, Townsville.	4TO	------	------	All advertising handled through Amalgamated Wireless (A/sia), Sydney.
Broadcasters (Aust.), Brisbane.	4BH	600	217	Probably handles own advertising.
SOUTH AUSTRALIA				
The Advertiser Broadcasting Station, Waymouth St., Adelaide.	5AD	1,000	229	Handles own advertising; will accept contract from accredited agent; United States representative, J. B. Powers, 250 Park Ave., New York.
Sports Radio Broadcasting Co. (Ltd.), 81 Flinders St., Adelaide.	5KA	1,000	250	Handles own advertising.
5DN Pty. (Ltd.), 2 Montpelier St. Parkside, Adelaide.	5DN	500	313	Reported to be experimental; probably handles own advertising.
WESTERN AUSTRALIA				
Musgrove's (Ltd.), Lyric House, Murray St., Perth.	6ML	300	297	Handles own advertising.
TASMANIA				
Commercial Broadcasters Pty. (Ltd.), 80 Elizabeth St., Hobart.	7HO	50	337	Do.
Findlay & Wills Broadcasters Pty. (Ltd.), Brisbane St., Launceston.	7LA	100	273	Handles own advertising; also on nonexclusive basis through Amalgamated Wireless (A/sia).

RATES

The number of licensed listeners in Australia has continued to increase despite a somewhat serious setback during 1930. It is remarkable, under present business conditions, that the radio industry has continued to expand. Yet the decreasing returns of general business have made it necessary for the operators of B class stations to make a special effort to obtain some form of advertising revenue.

The type of advertising program has undergone a rather striking change during the past two years resulting in a dual-rate system, one based on time, the other on the number of words in an advertising message. The sponsored program had been used in the majority of cases until the early part of 1930, but it is alleged by some users that the returns did not justify the cost.

The reduction in sponsored programs has resulted in the direct-advertising program. Every broadcasting station is equipped with a turntable for broadcasting recorded music; in fact, the evening programs of most of the stations are devoted almost entirely to this type of broadcasting. The station supplies recorded musical programs, while the advertiser pays only for the words necessary to broadcast a short announcement regarding his product or service. By adopting this form of radio advertising the broadcasting stations have increased their range of advertisers to include department stores, shops, grocery stores, drug stores, and a host of small concerns or individuals who might otherwise be unable to pay for sponsored programs.

Programs from the B stations in Sydney are not received by many listeners in Victoria, and the same is true of the B stations in the other cities. The popular radio receivers are apparently not powerful enough for interstate reception; this factor quite naturally limits the field for any sponsored program. The fact that the recorded program is more extensively used may prove advantageous to American companies considering the use of radio in Australia. The public is already accustomed to the recorded program and will possibly accept programs with advertising announcements included in the records.

American companies contemplating the use of recorded radio advertising programs in Australia should carefully consider the voice, tone, enunciation, and diction of the announcer, as well as the construction of the announcement itself. Australians find proper English decidedly more to their liking than characteristic American expressions.

The question of the cost of recorded programs with records supplied by oversea organizations is rather uncertain, but it would appear that the broadcasting stations would in the majority of cases refrain from charging for musical numbers, charging only for the announcement whether it was given by the radio announcer or broadcast from a record. The length of the announcement has been limited by most stations to 100 words, with proportionate charges for a greater number.

Rates quoted by the various stations for sponsored programs are as follows:

	Evening			Daytime		
	1 hour	Half hour	Quarter hour	1 hour	Half hour	Quarter hour
3DB, MELBOURNE	£ s. d.	£ s. d.	£ s. d.	£ s. d.	£ s. d.	£ s. d.
Number of programs:						
Casual	15 0 0	9 0 0	4 16 0	5 0 0	2 10 0	1 5 0
13	14 7 6	8 12 6	4 12 0	4 15 0	2 7 6	1 3 9
26	13 15 0	8 5 0	4 8 0	4 10 0	2 5 0	1 2 6
39	13 2 0	7 17 0	4 4 0	4 5 0	2 2 6	1 1 3
52	12 10 0	7 10 0	4 0 0	4 0 0	2 0 0	1 0 0
3KZ, MELBOURNE						
Number of programs:						
Casual	12 10 0	7 10 0	----------	2 10 0	1 10 0	----------
5	12 5 0	7 7 6	----------	2 5 0	1 6 0	----------
13	11 17 6	7 2 6	----------	2 0 0	1 3 0	----------
39	10 12 6	6 7 6	----------	1 15 0	1 0 0	----------
52	10 0 0	6 0 0	----------	1 10 0	0 17 6	----------
2BG, SYDNEY						
Number of programs:						
Casual	27 0 0	14 0 0	7 5 0	(1)	----------	----------
13	25 0 0	13 0 0	6 15 0	(1)	----------	----------
26	23 10 0	12 5 0	6 7 6	(1)	----------	----------
39	22 0 0	11 10 0	6 0 0	(1)	----------	----------
52	20 0 0	10 10 0	5 10 0	(1)	----------	----------
2UW, SYDNEY						
Base rate	18 0 0	9 10 0	5 0 0	----------		----------
5KA, ADELAIDE						
Number of programs:						
Casual	8 10 0	4 0 0	----------	2 10 0	1 10 0	----------
5	8 5 0	3 17 6	----------	2 5 0	1 5 0	----------
13	7 17 6	3 12 6	----------	2 0 0	1 2 6	----------
39	6 12 6	3 0 0	----------	1 15 0	1 0 0	----------
52	6 0 0	2 17 6	----------	1 10 0	0 17 6	----------

[1] 50 per cent of evening rates.

	Evening			Daytime		
	1 hour	Half hour	Quarter hour	1 hour	Half hour	Quarter hour
5AD, Adelaide	£ s. d.	£ s. d.	£ s. d.	£ s. d.	£ s. d.	£ s. d.
Base rate	10 0 0	9 0 0	3 10 0	5 0 0	3 0 0	1 15 0
4BK, Brisbane						
Number of programs:						
Casual	14 0 0	9 0 0	----------	2 10 0	----------	----------
6	12 18 0	8 2 0	----------	2 7 0	----------	----------
12	12 14 0	8 0 0	----------	2 4 0	----------	----------
24	12 10 0	7 18 0	----------	2 1 0	----------	----------
36	12 8 0	7 16 0	----------	1 19 0	----------	----------
52	12 5 0	7 10 0	----------	1 17 0	----------	----------
104	12 0 0	7 5 0	----------	1 15 0	----------	----------
156	11 0 0	7 0 0	----------	1 12 0	----------	----------
312	10 0 0	6 0 0	----------	1 8 6	----------	----------
4BC, Brisbane [2]						
Base rate	12 10 0	7 10 0	4 0 0	5 0 0	2 10 0	1 5 0
7HO, Hobart						
Number of programs:						
Casual	7 10 0	4 10 0	2 10 0	2 10 0	1 10 0	0 15 0
13	5 18 6	3 11 3	1 18 0	2 7 6	1 3 9	0 12 6
26	5 12 6	3 7 6	1 16 0	2 5 0	1 2 6	0 11 3
39	5 6 3	3 3 9	1 14 0	2 2 6	1 1 3	1 10 6
52	5 0 0	3 0 0	1 12 0	2 0 0	1 0 0	0 10 0
6ML, Perth						
Number of programs:						
Casual	10 0 0	6 0 0	3 10 0	5 0 0	2 10 0	1 5 0
13	9 10 0	5 14 0	3 6 5	4 15 0	2 7 6	1 3 9
26	9 0 0	5 8 0	3 3 0	4 10 0	2 5 0	1 2 6
39	8 10 0	4 17 6	3 0 0	4 5 0	2 2 6	1 1 3
52	8 0 0	4 17 0	2 17 6	4 0 0	2 0 0	1 0 0

[2] Discounts of 5 to 20 per cent allowed for long-term contracts.

The schedules for direct advertising by short announcements among Australian stations are as follows:

Item	Evening	Daytime	No time specified
3DB, Melbourne			
	£ s. d.	£ s. d.	£ s. d.
100 words or less (extra 3d. per word)	----------	----------	1 0 0
Talks and lectures (minimum, 5 minutes), per minute	0 15 0	0 7 6	----------
3KZ, Melbourne			
Announcement, 130 words or less:			
Casual	0 12 6	0 8 6	----------
24 advertisements	0 11 6	0 7 6	----------
78 advertisements	0 11 0	0 7 0	----------
156 advertisements	0 10 6	0 6 6	----------
312 advertisements	0 10 0	0 6 0	----------
2GB, Sydney			
Announcement, 100 words: [1]			
1 to 6	1 12 6	1 1 0	----------
7 to 24	1 8 0	0 19 0	----------
25 to 78	1 6 0	0 18 0	----------
79 to 156	1 4 0	0 17 0	----------
157 to 312	1 2 0	0 16 0	----------
Over 312	1 0 0		

[1] A reduction of 1 shilling is allowed on less desirable hours in the daytime and from 1 to 3 shillings for less desirable evening hours.

Item	Evening	Daytime	No time specified
2UW, Sydney	£ s. d.	£ s. d.	£ s. d.
Announcement, 100 words (minimum 3 announcements)	1 10 0	0 15 0	
2 early each morning, per week		6 0 0	
Mid-day (Monday to Friday):			
5 half hours, per week		10 0 0	
5 quarter hours, per week		6 0 0	
Women's session, 2-minute talk			0 15 0
Talks and lectures (minimum 5 minutes), per minute			0 10 0
5KA, Adelaide			
Announcement, 130 words:			
Casual	0 10 0	0 8 6	
24 advertisements	0 9 0	0 7 6	
78 advertisements	0 8 0	0 6 6	
156 advertisements	0 7 0	0 5 0	
5AD, Adelaide			
Announcement, 100 words or less	1 10 0	1 0 0	
Working description of industry (maximum 30 minutes)			10 0 0
Talks and lectures (minimum 5 minutes), per minute	0 15 6	0 7 6	
4BK, Brisbane			
Announcement, 60 words:			
Casual	0 12 6	0 8 6	
24	0 11 6	0 7 6	
78	0 11 0	0 7 0	
156	0 10 6	0 6 6	
312	0 10 0	0 6 0	
4BC, Brisbane [2]			
Announcement, 100 words or less	1 0 0	0 7 6	
Women's radio service, 100 words			0 10 0
7HO, Hobart			
Announcement, 100 words or less			0 10 6
24			0 9 6
78			0 9 0
156			0 8 6
312			0 8 0
Talks and lectures (minimum 5 minutes), per minute	0 5 0	0 2 6	
6ML, Perth			
Announcement, 10 words or less	0 12 6	0 8 6	
24	0 12 0	0 8 0	
78	0 11 3	0 7 6	
156	0 10 6	0 7 0	
312	0 9 9	0 6 6	
Talks and lectures (minimum 5 minutes), per minute	0 10 0	0 5 0	

[2] Discounts of 5 to 20 per cent allowed for long-term contracts.

LOCAL TALENT

While orchestras, instrumentalists, singers, comedians, etc., are available in all the capital cities, there is apparently some dearth of available talent in the smaller broadcasting centers. Orchestras, however, do not have the national reputations that American organizations enjoy, although they probably have good followings within their own metropolitan areas. Singers and comedians who have been on vaudeville circuits are probably known to a greater extent than any other performers, but their charges in many cases may be somewhat higher than the averages given herein.

The firms that have in the past used the radio for sponsored programs have found it necessary to hold one or two rehearsals for each session; since it is necessary to pay all performers for rehearsals, the cost of the sponsored programs is considerably increased.

In view of the direct method of advertising which is in vogue at the present time, it is estimated that 80 to 90 per cent of the broadcasting time is composed of recorded numbers, particularly in the evening.

The Federal wage award rates govern the cost of orchestras, musicians, etc., but it is understood that these rates do not apply to amateur performers or to nonunion members, although it is advisable for all stations or all promoters of sponsored programs to conform as closely as possible to the standard rates.

The rates for a 12-piece orchestra range from a minimum of about $27 to as high as $90 an hour, depending on contiguous engagements and the extent of the conductor's fee. Allowance for the cost of rehearsals would have to be added. The cost of singers, comedians, or other individual performers ranges normally from 10s. 6d. per hour to £1 1s. for two items. Regular talent at the larger metropolitan studios cost up to £3 3s. for two songs or performances. Discounts up to 20 per cent apply when a number of engagements (6 or more) are contracted for.

USE OF RECORDS

All broadcasting stations in Australia, even the A class Government-controlled stations, have facilities for broadcasting recorded programs. The new stations under construction and those contemplated are making provision for turntables, in view of the requirements of direct advertising and the present difficulties and costs in the way of sponsored programs.

The record facilities provided for each B station now in operation are as follows:

USE OF RECORDS IN AUSTRALIAN RADIO BROADCASTING

Station	Type of turntable	Revolutions per minute	Extra charge for records
NEW SOUTH WALES			
2MV, Moss Vale	Single and double	78	None.
2AY, Albury	Double	33⅓	Do.
2UE, Sydney	do	75	Do.
2GB, Sydney	Single and double	[1] 75	Do.
2UW, Sydney	Double	78	Do.
2KY, Sydney	Single (could install double)	80	Do.
2XN, Lismore	do	78	Do.
2HD, Newcastle	Single (will have double in near future).	33⅓ and 75	15s. charge for each 18-inch record.
2MO, Gunnedah	Single	78	None.
2GN, Goulburn	Single and double	33⅓ and 75	Do.
2CA, Canberra, F. C. T.	Double	[1] 78	Do.
VICTORIA			
3DB, Melbourne	Double	33⅓ and 78	None.
3UZ, Melbourne	do	75 to 80	Do.
3WR, Wangaratta	Single and double	78	Rates slightly lower for recorded programs.
3BA, Ballarat	Double	33⅓ and 78	None.
3GL, Geelong	do	78	Extra charge for special program.
QUEENSLAND			
4BC, Brisbane	Single and double	33⅓ and 75	None.
4BK, Brisbane	{ Double	78	Do.
	{ Single	33	Do.
4GR, Toowoomba	Double	33⅓ and 78	Do.
SOUTH AUSTRALIA			
5AD, Adelaide	Double	33⅓ and 78	None.
5KA, Adelaide	{ Double	75	Do.
	{ Single	33⅓	Do.
WEST AUSTRALIA			
6ML, Perth	Double	33⅓ and 78	Additional fee for program arrangement.
TASMANIA			
7HO, Hobart	Single and double	75 to 78	None.
7LA, Launceston	Double	78	Do.

[1] Can provide 33⅓ if necessary.

Many of the advertising firms in Australia handle radio advertising. A canvass of the various B class stations, however, reveals that only one advertising firm has obtained any exclusive agency contracts. Reuters (Ltd.), 15 Castlereagh Street, Sydney, New South Wales, and Queen Street, Brisbane, Queensland, with offices in other capital cities has obtained exclusive contracts with stations 2UE, Sydney, and 4BK, Brisbane.

Amalgamated Wireless (A/sia), 47 York Street, Sydney, owns and will operate stations 3BO, Bendigo, Victoria, and 4TO, Townsville, Queensland, and will handle the advertising for these two stations. This company also handles advertising on a nonexclusive basis for the following stations: 2AY, Albury, New South Wales; 2XN, Lismore, New South Wales, 2HD, Newcastle, New South Wales; 2MV, Moss Vale, New South Wales; and 7LA, Launceston, Tasmania. It is also reported to be in a position to accept advertising for all B stations in Australia, either direct, or through Reuters for the two stations mentioned above. Amalgamated Wireless has constructed a number of the stations in Australia, and in view of this fact has considerable technical ability at its command.

Few Australian agencies have gone into radio advertising seriously, so it is suggested that careful inquiry be made with regard to any specific agency's ability to handle this class of work satisfactorily. With recorded programs, this suggestion usually would not apply, as most, if not all, of the advertising material would probably be supplied by the advertiser. With sponsored programs, however, this question would undoubtedly require serious consideration.

COMMODITIES ADVERTISED

The number of firms throughout the Commonwealth using radio as an advertising medium is estimated to be between 1,500 and 2,000, indicating the patronage of many small houses. Almost every type of commodity produced or sold in Australia appears to be advertised over the radio, even down to the small shops, such as beauty parlors, men's furnishing stores, retail grocers, etc.

The types of firms using radio advertising comprise the following: Radio manufacturers and retailers, music houses, clothing dealers, department stores, liquor manufacturers, show manufacturers and retailers, tire retreading shops, furniture houses, groceries (wholesale and retail), biscuit manufacturers, sports organization, taxicab companies, tobacco manufacturers, motion-picture theaters, hardware merchants, heating fuel manufacturers, drug, perfume, and soap manufacturers, motor-car dealers, hotels, stock and station (cattle ranch) agents, confectionery manufacturers, steamship and travel agencies, gasoline and oil distributors, household electrical appliance manufacturers and dealers, canneries, paint manufacturers, newspapers, and hosiery manufacturers.

Some firms have advertised their products in more than one city, and it would appear that in some cases local agents or distributors have undertaken the advertising at their own expense.

OCEANIA

NEW ZEALAND

By Assistant Trade Commissioner Charles F. Kunkel

Radio advertising in New Zealand is not permitted. The Government policy relating to this phase of radio transmitting is outlined in regulation No. 28, reading as follows:

Subject to the provisions of regulation 29 hereof, neither direct nor indirect advertising shall be undertaken by the licensee from any broadcasting station, unless specially authorized by the minister.

Regulation No. 29 reads:

A broadcasting station shall not be used for the dissemination of propaganda of a controversial nature, but shall be restricted to matter of an educative, informational, or entertaining character, such as news, lectures, useful information, religious services, musical or elocutionary entertainment, and other items of general public interest as may be approved by the minister from time to time.

PHILIPPINE ISLANDS

By Trade Commissioner E. D. Hester, Manila

There are two broadcasting stations in Manila which accept commercial advertising. They are Radio Manila (station KZRM), operated by the Radio Corporation of the Philippine Islands, Insular Life Building, Plaza Moraga, Manila, which has three wave lengths, 413, 48.94, and 31.35 meters, power 1,000 watts; and Beck's Radio (station KZIB), operated by I. Beck (Inc.), 89–91 Escolta, Manila, which has a wave length of 333.3 meters, power 1,000 watts. Arrangements can be made for station KZIB through I. Beck & Co., 331 Fourth Avenue, New York City.

Rates charged for sponsored time are: Radio Manila, 20 pesos for first quarter hour, 1 peso for each additional minute; Beck's Radio, by contract, 50 to 60 pesos per hour, depending on time of day and amount of time used.

Three types of local talent are available at approximately the same rate at both studios: Singers and instrumental soloists, 5 to 20 pesos per hour in addition to time rate; orchestras, 20 to 30 pesos per hour in addition to time rate; declaimers and monologuists, 5 to 20 pesos per hour in addition to time rate.

Records can be used at both stations; in fact, over 50 per cent of the sponsored time programs is in recorded music. No charge is made for sponsored record music. In either studio, should the advertiser wish to supply his own records containing advertising matter, he will be charged the usual flat rates for sponsored time consumed. Both studios are equipped to use records at 75 and 33⅓ revolutions per minute.

Companies now using radio advertise the following commodities: Automobiles, motor spirits and lubricating oil, and cigars and cigarettes. A real estate firm also uses this form of advertising.

The preferred language is English, but both companies are equipped to handle advertising in Spanish, Tagalog, or Visayan. Singers and declaimers use principally English, but Spanish songs and folk songs in the native dialects are frequently used. Not only can English language records be used effectively, but they are the preferred medium since English is the common language in the Philippine Islands, spoken by 50 per cent of the inhabitants and by almost every radio owner or prospective purchaser. Spanish is spoken by about 8 per cent of the population, but practically all those who speak Spanish also speak English.

HAWAII

Data furnished by Federal Radio Commission, Washington, D. C.

There are two radio stations in the Territory of Hawaii which do commercial broadcasting. Station KGMB, licensed in the name of the Honolulu Broadcasting Co. (Ltd.), 119 Merchant Street, Honolulu, has a wave length of 227 meters and a power of 250 watts. This station is licensed to operate unlimited time. According to the latest application for renewal of license, the types of programs broadcast weekly by this station are as follows: Entertainment, 33 hours; religious, 2 hours; commercial, 30 hours; educational, 3 hours; agricultural, 3 hours; fraternal, 2 hours; markets, 2 hours; and weather news, 4 hours.

Radio station KGU is licensed in the name of Marional A. Mulrony & Advertiser Publishing Co. (Ltd.), Advertiser Square, Kapolani and South Streets, Honolulu. It is associated with an American broadcasting chain and has a wave length of 400 meters, power 1,000 watts. This station is licensed to operate with limited time. According to the latest application for renewal of license, the programs of this station are as follows: Entertainment, 49 per cent; religious, 2 per cent; commercial, 25 per cent; educational, 10 per cent; agricultural, 3 per cent; welfare, 5 per cent; fraternal, 1 per cent; markets, news, and weather report, 5 per cent.

O

BROADCAST ADVERTISING IN EUROPE

INTRODUCTION

Radio broadcasting in European countries has developed on a basis almost entirely different from that in the United States. Commercial programs are the exception, not the rule. Hence the possibilities of effective coverage of the Continent by broadcast advertising are limited, and changes from existing systems will probably be infrequent.

There is uniformity in the " European system " of radio only in reception, since most Governments require a tax or license fee for receiver-set ownership. As for broadcasting, there is no general practice among European countries, each State having regulations peculiar to its own government.

Broadcasting is a governmental monopoly in some countries, with operation of the stations either in the hands of an official branch of the Government or a clublike association responsible to the Government. In other countries private and Government stations are operated side by side, with the private broadcaster accepting advertising and the State radio refusing it. In a few other countries all broadcasting as well as reception is prohibited by law.

The accompanying table indicates briefly the status of broadcasting and reception and commercial advertising in each of the European countries.

RECEIVERS, BROADCASTING STATIONS, AND ACCEPTANCE OF ADVERTISING IN EUROPEAN COUNTRIES (EXCEPT SOVIET RUSSIA)

Country	Number of licensed receivers[1]	Number of broadcasting stations[2]	Foreign advertising accepted	Country	Number of licensed receivers[1]	Number of broadcasting stations[2]	Foreign advertising accepted
Albania	12	-------		Lithuania	12,000	1	No.
Austria	439,322	6	No.	Luxemburg	2,000	1	Yes.
Azores	250	-------		Madeira	180	-------	
Belgium	133,016	12	No.	Malta	386	-------	
Bulgaria	1,612			Netherlands	278,891	7	No.
Czechoslovakia	336,222	5	No.	Norway	95,292	12	Yes.
Danzig	16,000	1	(3).	Poland	296,921	6	Yes.
Denmark	437,244	4	No.	Portugal	5,000	8	No.
Estonia	15,869	2	Yes.	Rumania	40,000	1	Yes.
Finland	106,559	7	No.	Spain	550,000	15	Yes.[5]
France	500,000	30	Yes.[4]	Sweden	461,721	33	No.
Germany	3,731,948	30	No.	Switzerland	103,808	6	No.
Gibraltar	150	-------		United Kingdom	3,930,577	21	No.
Greece	1,500	-------		Turkey	7,500	2	Yes.
Hungary	308,009	2	No.	Vatican City	(3)	1	No.
Iceland	3,500	2	(2).	Yugoslavia	42,000	3	Yes.
Irish Free State	26,000	2	No.				
Italy	126,000	12	Yes.	Europe, total	12,048,923	233	
Latvia	39,434	1	No.				

[1] Estimated; it is known also that in some countries "bootleg" sets operate without licenses.
[2] Including short-wave stations.
[3] Not known.
[4] By private stations.
[5] 2 stations only.

To estimate the feasibility of broadcast advertising in Europe, each country must be studied individually. In Germany, for example, considerable advertising is accepted from domestic concerns, but time can not be sold to foreigners. In France the Government owns and operates numerous stations, but they do not broadcast direct advertising. On the other hand, privately owned French stations allow limited commercial mention of advertised goods, and the number of products and services advertised is surprising. No radio advertising of any character is permitted in the United Kingdom, but stations in the Irish Free State accept domestic accounts.

Another important factor the American advertiser should consider in continental broadcasting is the common reception of foreign programs. With political boundaries in some cases only a few hundred miles apart, the ether waves easily carry one national program into half a dozen different countries. The language factor is also evident in continental broadcasting. In Yugoslavia alone, for example, three different languages are used by the three broadcasting stations.

Reception is by no means as popular as in the United States, since the cost of sets and the taxes levied thereon make listening prohibitive to a great part of the population. Yet there are opportunities for exploitation of American products and services over the air, despite a variety of governmental restrictions and natural economic limitations. These are pointed out in the following pages.

While the information in this bulletin can not be considered complete and final, it should prove of value to American concerns contemplating the use of radio for advertising purposes in Europe. Where rates are mentioned, they are to be considered as indicative only. In most cases they have been obtained directly from station managers, but no responsibility can be assumed by the Department of Commerce for their accuracy.

AUSTRIA

By American Commercial Attaché D. F. Spencer, Vienna

There are no radio stations in Austria which accept commercial advertising.

Broadcasting is in charge of a private company, jointly formed by the Government, certain large banks, and leading industrial companies, which is known as the Ravag. This company, which in reality is a club, had on March 31, 1931, a total of 387,290 members. Each member pays a monthly fee of 2 schillings (about 28 cents) and an additional fee of 1½ schillings (approximately 21 cents). Payments are made through the post offices. From the money raised in this manner a variety of excellent programs are given. Music, literature, science, current topics, and the weather reports are the chief fields from which these programs are drawn. The radio public seems to prefer to pay for selected programs with an absence of advertising, for an attempt was made unsuccessfully some time ago to introduce commercial broadcasting.

When a retailer sells a receiving set he is obliged to give the name and address of the buyer. The latter must then make his monthly payments to the broadcasting company. Failure to carry out the payments as stipulated may cause a fine of 30 schillings (about $4.28). Makers of homemade sets must also account for all sets produced, even if used by the maker himself.

BELGIUM

All of the major broadcasting stations in Belgium are operated by the Institut National Belge de Radiophonie, a Government organization, and do not accept commercial advertising.

Radio Schaerbeek, the most important privately owned station, 76 Avenue Clays, Brussels, call letters ON4FO, operating on 251 meters with a power of 500 watts, had been broadcasting daily from 12.30 p. m. to 12 midnight and accepting advertising programs from some 200 subscribers, but it was closed December 31, 1931.

CZECHOSLOVAKIA

All broadcasting stations in Czechoslovakia are owned or controlled by the Government, and no commercial broadcasting is permitted. According to information furnished by the Ministry of Posts and Telegraphs, it is not likely that permission will be granted for such advertising in the near future.

DENMARK

Broadcast advertising is not definitely prohibited. Broadcasting is governed by the State Radio Council but the stations are owned by the Ministry of War, whose policy precludes all possibility of utilizing the radio for commercial advertising. The monopoly system was adopted to prevent the projection of advertising into radio programs.

ESTONIA

By J. Reintam, of the American Consulate, Tallinn

The sole rights of radio broadcasting in Estonia have been granted by the Government on concession basis to a private concern, O/ü Raadio Ringhääling, of Tallinn. This company operates two broadcasting stations, one in Tallinn and the other in Tartu. The power of the transmitter at Tallinn is 10 kilowatts and the wave length 296.15 meters. The Tartu station is linked with the studio at Tallinn and is used principally for relaying the Tallinn programs for reception in the southern part of Estonia. The power of the Tartu relay station is 2 kilowatts and its wave length 475 meters.

Under the provisions of the Government concession contract (the O/ü Raadio Ringhääling is not permitted to broadcast) commercial advertising is not permitted between the various numbers on the regular programs. This means that the broadcasting company is obliged to designate a special time for transmission of commercial advertising.

The advertising period now immediately precedes the afternoon program, 10 minutes having been designated for this purpose by the company. Up to the present time this short period has been adequate to cover the present demand for commercial advertising.

Since the O/ü Raadio Ringhääling has full authority to extend the time for broadcasting of advertisements, it is entirely possible for it to sell to any advertiser any period of time not occupied by its scheduled programs. Such advertiser will be permitted to use the time according to his own discretion. This means that the advertiser can arrange a special program of his own and broadcast announcements between numbers.

The time schedule which the radio company uses for broadcasting its own programs is as follows:

On week days:
Monday, 6.30 to 9.30 p. m.
Tuesday, 6.30 to 9.30 p. m.
Wednesday, 6 to 9.30 p. m.
Thursday, 6.30 to 9.30 p. m.
Friday, 6.30 to 9.30 p. m.
Saturday, 6 to 11 p. m.
On Sundays and holidays: From 10 a. m. to 5 p. m. and from 6.30 p. m. to 10 p. m.

There are about 14,000 receiving sets now in use in Estonia.

Orders for commercial advertising are accepted direct by O/ü Raadio Ringhääling, Estonia teatrimaja, Tallin, Estonia.

RATES

The rates charged local advertisers are 0.5 Estonian crowns ($0.0133) per word or 2 crowns ($0.53) per minute. The rate per word is charged when the text of advertisement is read before the microphone by the announcer of the broadcasting company, and the time rate when the advertiser furnishes his own announcer or when a phonograph record is played. However, records have hitherto not been used for this purpose.

Thus far the broadcasting company has received no advertising from foreign countries, and therefore no definite rates have been fixed for this purpose. It is understood, however, that the rates for foreign advertisers would be approximately 100 per cent higher than the rates charged to domestic concerns. A precedent to this policy has already been created by an American religious society which rents one hour's time, paying therefor the rate of 125 Estonia krooni ($33). This rate includes the use of the broadcasting company's studio.

LOCAL TALENT

The musical programs consist, as a rule, of performances by local orchestras, singers, various instrumental soloists, and phonograph music. The broadcasting company maintains its own orchestra of 12 members. Te soloists, however, are hired for each individual performance.

The rates paid to local talent for solo performances range from 15 to 25 Estonian crowns ($4 to $6.67) for about 20 minutes of actual performance time. The rate for outside orchestras and bands is about 11 crowns ($2.93) per player for a broadcast of one hour or more. However, owing to the general depression and the predominance of sound film in motion-picture theaters there is some unemployment among musicians and bands can be hired at somewhat lower rates.

USE OF RECORDS

The broadcasting company has in its studio two devices for the playing of phonograph records. One is a regular American phonograph. The other is a double-disk device of local construction, with electrical pick up, which permits continuous playing of numbers requiring more than one record.

The speed of both instruments is normally 78 revolutions per minute, but they can be regulated. The phonograph was used before the installation of the electrical reproducer and now is kept in the studio only for emergency cases.

Advertising records are played at the usual time rates.

PRESENT USERS OF BROADCAST ADVERTISING

Radio advertising has been used in Estonia only by local concerns. The principal advertisers are motion-picture theaters, which announce their new programs regularly by radio. Other advertisers are various newly established stores, and also products for general consumption such as tea, cocoa, etc. These other advertisers are not very regular and contract only for one to five programs at a time.

LANGUAGE

The language spoken is Estonian. In the cities a certain percentage of German Balts, Russians, and Jews reside, and although most of these understand Estonian, business places in the cities use three languages—namely, Estonian, German and Russian. However, radio advertising has been done in the Estonian language alone. English is little known in Estonia and its use is out of the question.

PROSPECTS FOR RADIO ADVERTISING

The Estonian Government is said to be contemplating the direct operation of radio broadcasting facilities, and it will probably prepare an entirely new scheme for broadcast advertising. It is understood that there is a possibility of the adoption of the system now being used in the United States. The new arrangement would possibly not go into effect before the middle of 1932.

FINLAND

Broadcast advertising is forbidden by terms of the contract between the company that holds that monopoly, namely Finlands Rundradio A. B. of Helsingfors, and the State. The only advertising that is done at present is the announcing of the name of the company furnishing free phonograph records for programs.

FRANCE

By American Trade Commissioner Louis Hall, Paris

France is one of the most advanced countries in the world in respect to the use of radio. The climate is good for receiving. The people are especially interested in radio, and while there have been financial difficulties preventing a large percentage of the people from investing in receivers, radio programs have a popularity more common than in most other countries of Europe. The Government has interested itself in promoting broadcast service, for the Government chain of stations has provided a foundation for the broadcasting system which serves the entire country. Stations are owned both by the Government and by private concerns.

According to latest information available, the broadcasting stations belonging to the French State (stations of Eiffel Tower, Ecole Superieure des P. T. T., Lille, Strasbourg, Lyon-la-Doua, Grenoble, Marseille, Montpellier, Toulouse, Borteaux, Limoges, and Rennes) do not carry any direct advertising. Until the Parliament votes "organic texts" concerning broadcasting, these stations are authorized to place their broadcasting under the patronage of commercial firms. The latter take care of the expenses incurred in connection with the artistic concerts or theatrical representations thus placed under their patronage. The name, address, and specialty of the firm offering the program are indicated only three times during a presentation.

It is rumored that this arrangement will be terminated in the near future. All above-mentioned stations are equipped to broadcast from phonograph records, if necessary. No advertising is broadcast by record.

The quality of the programs broadcast, with but few exceptions, is such that listeners, including the French, tune in frequently on foreign programs, especially those from the German and English stations. The private stations are remarkably well equipped and appear to enjoy considerable financial means. The Government stations are older and do not compete in their entertainment programs with the commercial stations.

Out of about 30 stations in France, only 11 have furnished detail data concerning their facilities. These are:

City	Name of station	Wave length in meters	Power, in watts	Record speed, in revolutions per minute
Paris	Radio Paris	1,725 2,650	13,500	All.
Do	Radio LL	368 61	1,500	50–100
Do	Petit Parisien	331	500	78–80
Do	Radio Vitus	310 61	2,000	33⅓, 78, 80
Agen [1]				
Beziers	Radio Beziers	220	1,500	78
Bordeaux	Radio Sud-Ouest	250	5,000	78
Fecamp	Radio Normandie	(2)	(2)	80
Juan-les-Pins	Radio Cote d'Azur	248	250	(2)
Lyon	Radio Lyon	291 40.2	500	78
Toulouse	(2)	381	8,000	78–80

[1] Wrecked by the inundations in southwestern France in the late spring of 1931.
[2] Not known.

LOCAL TALENT

Paris, of course, offers almost unlimited possibilities in the way of radio talent. The cost varies to a great extent depending on the reputation of the artist, musicians being paid from 50 to 150 francs per program, while theatrical and other artists can be enagaged at from 100 to 1,500 francs. No scale is available for talent in the provincial centers, but the same principle applies as to their being well known. Artists engaged must be paid by the advertiser.

RECORDS

Radio Paris is equipped for using records, but the programs comprising records are available only to record manufacturers or retailers. No reduced rates are granted to them, on the theory that there is excellent advertising value in such broadcasting. Records of any speed can be used.

Other stations are equipped to broadcast records on a commercial basis.

AGENCIES SELLING BROADCASTING TIME

A number of stations have intrusted the sale of broadcasting time to the agencies indicated: Radio Paris—Informations et Publicite, 50 Rue de Chateaudun, Paris; Petit Parisien—Poste Radiophonique du Petit Parisien, 118 Champs Elysees, Paris; Radio Toulouse—Radio Lyon, Radio Sud-Ouest. Radio Beziers has two commissionaires—Radio Informations, 51 Rue d'Alsace-Lorraine, Toulouse, and Service de Publicite Radiophonique, 118 Champs Elysees, Paris. Radio Normandie handles the sale of its time for France, but the agency for England is International Broadcasting Co., 11 Hallam Street, London; Radio Cote d'Azur sells through Publicis, 62 Boulevard de Strasbourg, Paris.

ENTERPRISES AND COMMODITIES ADVERTISED

A variety of products is now being advertised over the radio, of which the following list of concerns and products is representative: Automobiles, cigarettes, coal dealers, department stores, dry cells, electrical equipment and electric bulbs, fire extinguishers, foodstuffs (such as preserves, breakfast foods, beverages, cheese, biscuits, groceries, chocolate, cakes, and jam), central heating plants, radiators, hotels, insectiides, watches, knitting wool, liquor, magazines and newspapers of interest to radio amateurs, motion-picture theaters, office appliances, oil, opticians, paints, pharmaceutical products, phonographs and records, pianos, shoe polish, individual towns and cities, radio sets and equipment, wireless apparatus, razors, restaurants, safes, schools, sprays, telephone and radio accessories, toilet preparations such as tooth paste and soap, wearing apparel, and wall paper.

RATES

Although there is at present a large volume of broadcast advertising in France, rates are not thoroughly stabilized and are by no means uniform. Radio Paris, for example, issues no rate card, each contract being negotiated after a study of its peculiar requirements.

Radio LL quotes regular rates as follows: Advertisements of about 5 lines, 250 francs; 10 lines, 400 francs; 25 lines, 800 francs; talk of about 50 lines, 1,000 francs; address of about 10 minutes, 2,000 francs; concert of chamber music by station LL orchestra,

2,000 francs; with vocal or instrumental soloists, according to estimate. It offers a reduction of 10 per cent for a series of 10, and 20 per cent for 25 broadcasts.

Petit Parisien charges 1,500 francs for a half-hour broadcast of recorded music and 3,000 francs for one and a half hours of orchestra concert; special artists cost extra. Brief announcements are charged for at the following word rates: ten, 275 francs; twenty, 300 francs; thirty, 325 francs; forty, 350 francs, with 5 francs per supplementary word.

Radio Vitus quotes in more detail. For short announcements, 300 francs for 20 words, 15 francs for extra words up to 30 maximum; 500 francs for 40 words, with 20 francs for each extra word up to 50 maximum. A half-hour broadcast of selected records with two 20-word announcements is quoted at 1,500 francs; an "artistic" concert of one hour (12 to 15 musicians and artists) of popular music with three 20-word announcements, 3,500 francs; an hour's broadcast of a "gala" concert (20 to 25 musicians and artists of note) with three 20-word announcements, 8,000 francs. All of these rates are subject to discounts of 5, 10, and 15 per cent on contracts covering 30, 100, or 300 broadcasts, respectively.

Radio Toulouse publishes an elaborate rate card which takes into account the relative value of the various times of day. One 40-word announcement between 5 and 7 p. m. costs 100 francs; for thirty times a month, 2,300 francs; for thirty times a month on a yearly contract, 1,900 francs. The prices for a similar announcement between 8.30 and 10 p. m. are 500, 12,000, and 11,000 francs respectively. Concert broadcasts of an hour cost 4,000 francs between 5 and 8.30 p. m. or 10 and 12 p. m., and 6,000 francs between 8.30 and 10 p. m.

Radio Lyon charges 80 francs for a single 40-word announcement; on a six months' contract, a monthly rate of 320 francs for 4 announcements per month, 700 francs for 10 per month, 1,000 francs for 15 per month, and 1,800 francs for 30 announcements per month. Concerts of recorded music are broadcast at 1,000 francs per hour. Advertisers wishing to give an orchestral or other original broadcast pay the artists in addition to the time rate.

Radio Sud-Ouest quotes announcement rates similar to Radio Lyon, but charges 500 francs per hour's broadcast of records. Artists are paid by advertisers.

Radio Beziers has an hourly rate of 250 francs for concerts and recorded programs. A single announcement of 40 words costs 50 francs. On six months' contract the scale runs from 200 francs per month for 4 announcements to 1,200 francs per month for 30 announcements.

Radio Normandie differentiates between daytime and evening broadcasts. One announcement costs 250 francs, 25 daytime announcements during a year cost 50 francs each, while 100 or more cost 25 francs each. In the evening 25 would cost 100 francs each, and over 100 would cost 50 francs each. The hour rate for record concerts is 750 francs by day, 1,500 francs in the evening.

By Radio Cote d'Azur announcements are offered at 1 p. m. or 8.30 p. m. and may consist of four typewritten lines. Rates: 150 francs for one, 1,200 francs for ten, 7,000 francs for one hundred, or 18,000 francs for three hundred sixty-five per year. The rate card of this station does not provide for the sale of broadcast time in any other way.

GERMANY

By American Trade Commissioner A. Douglas Cook, Berlin

Radio advertising is common in Germany but not available to foreign firms. It is administered and controlled by the Federal Postal Ministry by means of a branch in the juridical form of a limited liability company in which the Postal Ministry is the sole participant. The name of this advertising branch is Deutsche Reichs-Postreklame G. m. b. H. (German Federal Post-Advertising Co.), which has offices in all German cities where there are broadcasting stations, as well as in other important commercial centers. All contracts for radio programs must be made with the Deutsche Reichs-Postreklame G. m. b. H., and it in turn pays the various stations for the use of their time. The stations are as follows:

Operating company	City	Wave length, in meters	Power, in watts
Funkstunde A. G	Berlin	419	1,700
	Berlin (East)	284	600
	Mageburg	284	600
	Stettin	284	600
Mitteldeutscher Rundfunk A. G	Leipzig	253	2,300
	Dresden	319	300
Deutsche Stunde in Bayern G. m. b. H	Munich	533	1,700
	Augsburg	560	300
	Nuernberg	239	2,300
	Kaiserlautern	270	300
Suedwestdeutscher Rundfunk A. G	Frankfort on the Main	390	1,700
	Kassel	246	300
Nordischer Rundfunk A. G	Hamburg	372	1,700
	Bremen	316	300
	Flensburg	219	600
	Hannover	566	300
	Kiel	232	300
Sueddeutscher Rundfunk A. G	Stuttgart (Muehlacker)	360	60,000
	Freiburg	569	300
Ostmarken Rundfunk A. G	Koenigsberg	277	1,700
	Danzig [1]	453	250
Schlesische Funkstunde A. G	Heilsburg		60,000
	Breslau	325	1,700
	Gleiwitz	259	5,600
Westdeutscher Rundfunk A. G	Cologne	227	1,700
	Aachen (Aix la Chapelle)	227	300
	Muenster	227	600
	Langenberg	473	17,000
Deutsche Welle G. m. b. H. (Deutschland-sender).	Koenigswusterhausen (near Berlin)	1,633	35,000

[1] Danzig station (call letter PTB) is operated by the Post Office Department of Danzig and is a relay station of the Koenigsburg station.

Advertising programs may be sent out at certain intervals from all German stations with the exception of that at Koenigswusterhausen, known as " Deutschlandsender." However, no foreign firms may have their products advertised over any of the German broadcasting stations. This ruling is aimed particularly at imported goods. Exceptions, however, have been made in the case of two large foreign manufacturers, one American, having plants in Germany. It was held that these firms could be regarded, in so far as radio broadcasting is concerned, as German firms, since they were incorporated in Germany, paid taxes in the country, manufactured articles, and gave substantial employment to German workers.

ADVERTISING PROGRAMS

At most German stations the advertising program runs from 8.15 to 9 a. m. or around noon. The postal authorities advise that it has been found most important to reach the women hearers before the daily shopping tour is undertaken, and consequently these hours have been selected.

Radio advertising in Germany falls into three general categories— namely, short remarks, lectures, and propaganda remarks.

The " lectures " usually last 10 minutes and, if time permits, may be listed in the official program; they are usually given by one of the announcers on the pay roll of the station, though in special cases the advertiser may employ vaudeville or cabaret artists or other outside talent.

The so-called propaganda remarks are usually given by the announcer of the station at intervals in a program of phonograph records, no mention of the firm being made in the printed program. A regular " propaganda-remarks " program usually takes about one and one-half minutes to repeat and contains 15 typewritten lines. This type of program is also accepted up to 30 typewritten lines, for which a double fee is charged. If the 15 typewritten lines are to be broadcast by means of a record, it should correspond to one and one-half minutes ordinary talking.

" Short remarks " run up to five typewritten lines and last about 30 seconds. The costs for this type of program are half of those for the " propaganda remarks."

RATES

The following rates are charged by the various German broadcasting stations:

Station	Prices, in marks		Station	Prices, in marks	
	Re-marks	Lec-tures		Re-marks	Lec-tures
Berlin (including Stettin and Magdeburg)	200	600	Kiel (including Flensburg)	56	300
Bremen	40	210	Cologne (including Aachen)	40	200
Breslau (including Gleiwitz)	60	200	Koenigsburg, Prussia	60	200
Dresden (including Leipzig)	60	200	Langenberg	50	250
Frankfurt on the Main	60	200	Leipzig (including Dresden)	60	200
Freiburg, Baden	35	130	Munich (including Nuernberg and Augsburg)	80	300
Hamburg	80	420	Muenster, Westphalia		200
Hannover	56	300	Suedfunk Muehlacker	150	500
Kassel	40	150			

Exceptionally good local talent is available in Germany. A nationally known entertainer would charge from 400 to 600 marks for a 15-minute program.

Phonograph records may be used; the rate is the same as for studio programs. Records should be made for a speed of 78 revolutions per minute.

Among the German firms and products being advertised are the following: Department stores, foodstuffs, summer and winter resorts, dairy products, radio articles, phonograph records, and leather goods.

German is the only language used in radio advertising.

GREECE

Broadcasting is prohibited, but the Government has indicated its intention of creating a broadcasting monopoly as soon as the necessary arrangements can be made. Reception is permitted, under certain restrictions, to Greek citizens, but it is prohibited to foreigners.

HUNGARY

Radio broadcasting is a Government monopoly in Hungary, and broadcast advertising is prohibited by ministerial decree.

IRISH FREE STATE

By American Vice Consul Edwin J. King, Dublin

Radio is controlled by the Irish Free State Government. Commercial broadcasting has only recently been introduced, but programs advertising goods in competition with Irish products are not accepted.

The Government has entered into an arrangement with the Irish Radio Publicity Co. (of which Col. F. C. Russell is the manager), of Dublin, to transmit programs, which are broadcast at Dublin and relayed at the Cork station.

The Bublin station, with call letters of 2RN, has a wave length of 413 meters and a power of 1,500 watts. The station has three well-equipped broadcasting rooms.

The cost of advertising programs per hour varies, according to the type of program, between £25 for a phonograph concert and £40 for a full orchestral and vocal program. No special records are employed, the programs being made up from the ordinary records available. The speed used is 78 revolutions per minute.

Local talent is available for orchestral and vocal programs, and all advertising programs are broadcast in the English language.

Among the products now advertised are the following: American and English tooth paste, cigarettes, chocolate, corn flour, jam, marmalade, confectionery, and a monthly magazine.

ITALY

By American Commercial Attaché Mowatt M. Mitchell, Rome

Radio broadcasting in Italy is a monopoly controlled by Ente Italiano Audizione Radiofonica, Corso Italia 1, of Milan. All the stations accept commercial advertising and have granted the sole right to negotiate said transmissions to Societa Italiana Pubblicita Radiofonica Anonima (S. I. P. R. A.), Via Bertola, No. 40, of Turin. The stations are as follows:

Call letter	City	Wave length, in meters	Power, in watts	Call letter	City	Wave length, in meters	Power, in watts
IBZ	Bolzano	453	200	Not assigned	Palermo	(1)	3,000
IGE	Genoa	385	1,200	IRO	Rome	441	3,000
IMI	Milan	501	7,000	IIAX	do	45	(1)
INA	Naples	331	1,500	ITO	Turin	272	7,000

1 Not known.

A new schedule of rates for radio broadcasting was issued July 1, 1931. Broadcasting of announcements without guaranty of a minimum number of words by sponsor runs from 2 lire daytime and 4 lire evening per word for the smaller stations, such as Trieste and Palermo, to 6 lire daytime and 12 lire evening for Milan. (One lire equals about 5 cents, United States currency.) The rates for more than one station range from 5.50 lire per word daytime and 14 lire evening to 22 lire daytime and 44 lire evening for all Italian stations. With a guaranty by the sponsor of a minimum of words to be used within periods ranging up to six months, the rates are scaled down proportionately. For instance, a guaranty by the sponsor of a minimum of 3,000 words to be used within six months from date of contract would cost 4 lire per word in the daytime and 8 lire per word in the evening for the Milan station.

LOCAL TALENT

Local talent is available, but the charges vary according to the importance and renown of the artists. The cost ranges down from 15,000 lire each evening for exceptional artists, although some are available at 8,000 lire; a singer of average ability asks from 4,000 to 5,000 lire; a good orchestra director from 3,000 to 5,000 lire. However, the orchestra can be secured directly from the company owning all the Italian broadcasting stations, at terms to be agreed upon (2,000 lire per hour on an average).

RECORDS

Records can be used, the cost of time being the same as for personal broadcasts. The speed of records is from 78 to 80 revolutions per minute.

COMMODITIES ADVERTISED

There are some 400 Italian firms using broadcast advertising. With the exception of the two sponsors of the programs described below, these firms pay a fixed rate per word. The commodities advertised include radio sets, phonographs and records, shoes, carpets, furniture, gas stoves, toilet specialties, wines, liquors, olive oil, household utensils, textiles, gloves, automobiles, automobile schools, garden seeds, soaps, sports goods, watches, biscuits, candy, tooth paste, and a variety of other articles.

A radio manufacturer gives a classic concert once a week. He engages high-class artists and an orchestra conducted by a director of national reputation.

The maker of a special kind of spaghetti also gives weekly concerts and variety shows, for which the best of talent is engaged. These concerts usually last about an hour.

LANGUAGE

Broadcasting in Italy is nearly all in the Italian language. Records prepared in the English language could be utilized if approved by the broadcasting company. However, the general knowledge of English is very limited.

LATVIA

The Riga broadcasting station, the only one in Latvia, is owned and operated by the Government. No advertising has ever been permitted by the station and no change in policy is expected in the near future.

LITHUANIA

Radio control in Lithuania is a function of the postal administration of the Ministry of Communications, whose policy precludes all possibility of broadcast advertising.

LUXEMBURG

By American Trade Commissioner C. C. Frick, Brussels, Belgium

The Government of the Grand Duchy of Luxemburg, on June 19, 1931, granted a charter to the Compagnie Luxembourgeoise de Radiodiffusion to erect and operate a broadcasting station. This company is capitalized at 15,000,000 francs.

The charter stipulates that the station shall be located within 15 kilometers of the city of Luxemburg and have a minimum power of 100 kilowatts. A modulated high-frequency transmission system must be used. The wave length of the station is not yet known.

The company is authorized to accept and broadcast paid advertising and to relay foreign programs containing advertising. No rates have been determined.

NETHERLANDS

By American Commercial Attaché Jesse F. Van Wickel, The Hague

Broadcast advertising is strictly prohibited in The Netherlands by the law of May 15, 1930.

All the broadcasting organizations are financed exclusively by voluntary contributions paid by their members. Several organizations owing to insufficient funds to finance expensive programs, commonly resort to broadcasting phonograph records as an inexpensive means to fill the bulk of their programs, while considerable time is also devoted to lectures pertaining to the political or religious leanings of the subject organizations. The make, number, title, etc., of each record is announced before it is played, and repeated at the end. In a measure, this practice is indirect advertising. A similar instance is that of an orchestra consisting of employees of a well-known factory playing at one of the radio stations and being announced as the orchestra of the factory in question. It is apparent that such announcements have advertising value, but it has not yet been decided by the radio board whether or not radio programs sponsored by business firms are within the provisions of the law.

NORWAY

By American Trade Commissioner Gudrun Carlson, Oslo

Radio as a means for advertising has never assumed any importance in Norway. At present the tendency appears to be in the direction of decreased rather than increased use of radio time for advertising. It is not possible to predict the future, since the Storting (Parliament) is expected to decide later in what manner and by whom broadcasting is to be controlled and directed.

All arrangements for advertising are made in the Kringkasting-selskapet A/S of Oslo. Seven other stations serve as relays, and no separate accounts are accepted by them.

The only time now allowed for advertising is between 7 and 7.15 p. m. each evening. A short period previously set aside in the forenoon has now been eliminated. There are no restrictions against foreign firms purchasing time, but so far Norwegian companies have made chief use of this medium.

The present rate is 2 crowns per word, with a minimum charge of 50 crowns, with the following rebate for broadcasts in series: Three times, 10 per cent; six times, 15 per cent; ten times, 25 per cent; and fifty times, $33\frac{1}{3}$ per cent. The following rebates are also given for one-time announcements: 75 to 124 words, 10 per cent; 124 to 149 words, 15 per cent; and 150 or more words, 25 per cent.

Programs consist usually of short talks, often instructive or humorous, music being employed on a small scale. Local talent is available for such purposes, but the cost varies with the type of music and the reputation of the artists.

Records can be used, and any standard size is acceptable, since the studio is equipped for all types of plates. When music or records form the program the rate is usually 200 crowns for 10 minutes but the broadcasting company will furnish rates for any special or different kinds of performances to be given.

The broadcasting company has so far dealt with firms buying advertising time, but there is no objection to dealing with an advertising agency handling accounts for foreign companies.

Various commodities are advertised by radio. One of the most successful series has been sponsored by a local manufacturer of electric ranges. The Norwegian language is preferred for broadcasting, but all the Scandinavian languages are understood.

POLAND

By American Trade Commissioner Gilbert Redfern, Warsaw

The sale of radio advertising time in the American manner is not yet practised in Poland. Polskie Radjo controls and operates the broadcasting stations in this country and uses advertisements in the form of simple announcements, or by entertainment talks and dialogues. This advertising has been of a strictly local character, although it could be applied to foreign products. Rates are quoted on a word basis and not by time required.

The principal Polish advertisers are government and social institutions. Trade advertising is confined largely to articles of primary necessity, such as food products, clothing, household furnishing, etc.

Polskie Radjo has designated an American broadcasting chain (whose name may be secured on application to the Specialities Division of the U. S. Bureau of Foreign and Domestic Commerce) as its sole representative in the United States. The chain under this agreement is authorized to sell to American concerns commercial advertising time over the main Warsaw broadcasting station, and prospective American advertisers are accordingly advised to address their inquiries to the American agent.

The language principally used in broadcasting is Polish. Records prepared in the English language could not be effectively used.

PORTUGAL

By American Commercial Attaché Richard C. Long, Lisbon

While there is considerable interest in radio in Portugal, the situation has not yet developed to the point where commercial broadcasting.stations have been established, and the only existing stations are operated by amateurs. There are approximately 10 amateur stations which broadcast musical programs at irregular intervals, the music usually being supplied by ordinary phonograph records. These do not sell time for advertising and are prohibited by law from doing so. No Portuguese firms use broadcasting facilities for advertising. Since little attention is devoted to other forms of adverising in Portugal, future possibilities of broadcast advertising are problematical.

RUMANIA

By American Trade Commissioner Kenneth M. Hill, Bucharest

There is only one radio broadcasting station in Rumania which accepts commercial advertising, and this only under strict supervision. It is the Societate Romana de Radiofuziune, Strada General Berthelot 60, Bucharest. The broadcasting is done from Otopeni, located a short distance from Bucharest. The managing director of the company is Ing. Carnu Munteanu and the secretary, Ing. Sorin Betolian.

Broadcast advertising is charged for by the word and not by the hour. The system is entirely different from that in use in the United States, and advertisers have not adopted the practice of hiring the studio facilities for private programs. At present radio advertising consists only of short announcements interspersed throughout the program in such manner as the following: " The XYZ silk stocking wears longer, looks better, and gives greater satisfaction; on sale by Smith's department store, Bucharest." Such advertising is charged at the rate of from 20 to 30 lei (12 to 18 cents) per word. The nearest thing to the American " radio hour " now given in Rumania is the period from noon to 2 o'clock, when the local phonograph stores furnish the latest records. After each record the make, name, and number is announced.

Local talent is available. The cost of an orchestra of five men for a concert of about one hour and a half is reported to be 4,000 lei, or about $24. Singers also are readily obtainable, but no standard price for services exists.

Records can be used at a price of 300 lei (about $1.80) per record. Records now in use are adjusted to a speed of 78 revolutions per minute.

Commercial advertising through the Bucharest radio broadcasting company is concessioned to the Advertul Publishing Co., Strada Sarindar, Bucharest. The radio company itself does not negotiate advertising contracts. According to the terms of the concession, the company is prohibited from inserting more than 1,000 words per day into the broadcast. In view of the growing popularity of radio advertising, however, it is possible that some changes may be made within the next year. Practically all of the leading stores of Bucharest are reported to be using radio advertising. Among the principal lines advertised are women's wear, food products, automobiles, radio sets, and specialty lines.

Rumanian is the only language which should be used normally for advertising purposes. Records of music, songs, etc., with only small amounts of English might be acceptable, but the general knowledge of English is limited.

SPAIN

By American Commercial Attaché Charles A. Livengood, Madrid

There are two Spanish companies operating broadcasting stations which accept commercial advertising. They are Union Radio S. A., Piu Margall 10, Madrid, and Radio Asturias S. A., J. Tartiere 2, Oviedo.

The Union Radio owns and operates the principal broadcasting stations in Spain, the central station being located in Madrid, with other stations in Barcelona, Cartagena, San Sebastian, and Seville.

As last reported, the stations in Spain are identified and equipped as follows:

Call letter	City	Wave length, in meters	Power, in watts	Call letter	City	Wave length, in meters	Power, in watts
EAJ18	Almeria	251	200	EAJ7	Madrid	424	1,500
EAJ1	Barcelona	349	7,500	EAM	do	30.7	(1)
EAJ13	do	268	10,000	EAJ19	Oviedo	368	30
EAJ15	Cartagena	246	100	EAJ5	San Sebastian	365	1,000
EAJ2	Madrid	400	750	Not known	Seville	365	(1)

1 Not known.

The regulations and rates charged for various classes of broadcast advertising by the two companies are given in the following schedules:

UNION RADIO S. A.

General conditions.—Texts to be broadcast must be in the company's possession 30 hours beforehand and must be delivered during office hours.

A written order, 36 hours before the time set for broadcasting, is required if a text is to be withdrawn or substituted.

The fee for the seal must be paid by the advertiser.

If an advertiser does not fulfill the contract signed by him or fails to submit texts for broadcasting, the Union Radio S. A. will charge him for the total number of words contracted for but not broadcast and at the prices quoted in advance.

The Union Radio S. A. reserves the right to postpone the broadcasting of texts contracted for if it is oversupplied with material for that purpose or for other reasons.

No verbal promise or concession made to advertisers shall be binding unless it is stipulated in the contract.

No text may be broadcast without the approval of the directors.

All advertising contracts must be for a period of one year.

The Union Radio S. A. reserves the right to change the prices quoted in this schedule.

The rates for announcements without a specified time for broadcasting are:

Item	Minimum text	Price per word, in pesetas	Item	Minimum text	Price per word in pesetas
Announcements without a fixed number of words	*Words*	2. 50	By annual contracts to be broadcast in 1 year:	*Words*	
By monthly contracts to be broadcast in 30 days:			Over 1,080 words	3	2. 15
Over 90 words	3	2. 40	Over 2,160 words	6	2. 00
Over 180 words	6	2. 25	Over 3,600 words	10	1. 90
Over 300 words	10	2. 10	Over 5,400 words	15	1. 70
Over 450 words	15	1. 90	Over 7,200 words	20	1. 55
Over 600 words	20	1. 75	Over 12,000 words	25	1. 35
Over 1,000 words	25	1. 50	Over 36,000 words	25	1. 25
Over 3,000 words	25	1. 40	Over 60,000 words	25	1. 10
Over 5,000 words	25	1. 25			

If certain hours are specified, the charges are insreased 50 per cent.

There are three broadcastings daily of 20 minutes from 8 to 9. The price for this service is subject to a 50 per cent discount from the rates shown in the schedule in the table above.

The rate for broadcasting at noon hours 11.45 to 12.15 p. m. is: For each text with a right to 10 words, 3 pesetas; each additional word, 0.25 peseta.

Preference section:[1] Minimum text, four words, 30 pesetas; each additional word, 6 pesetas. Discounts: If contract calls for one text daily for one year, 20 per cent; if for three texts daily for one year, 30 per cent. The charge is 50 per cent extra if broadcasting time is specified.

Preference section:[2] Minimum text, four words, 20 pesetas; each additional word, 4 pesetas. Discounts: By contracting for one text daily for one year, 20 per cent; for three texts daily for one year, 30 per cent. The charge is 50 per cent extra if broadcasting time is specified.

Advertising by means of lectures or talks (without specifying broadcasting time):

Pesetas

Maximum duration, 1 minute, about 100 words _____ 150
Maximum duration, 2 minutes, about 200 words _____ 250
Maximum duration, 3 minutes, about 300 words _____ 350
Maximum duration, 4 minutes, about 400 words _____ 425
Maximum duration, 5 minutes, about 500 words _____ 500

Discounts: By contracting for five talks or lectures per month, or 30 per year, 10 per cent discount; by contracting for 10 talks or lectures per month, or 60 per year, 15 per cent; by contracting for 30 talks or lectures per month, or 180 in one year, 25 per cent. This rate is 50 per cent extra if the time for broadcasting is specified.

Broadcastings of one hour devoted to or organized by an advertising firm subject to the special regulations of the Union Radio: After-dinner or afternoon talks, 1,000 pesetas; night talks, 1,500 pesetas.

Financial meetings, sessions, broadcastings, and drawing of shares and bonds, dividend payments: Each word, 2 pesetas; news, per word, 5 pesetas.

Disks and cylinders, without specifying time for broadcasting: Broadcasting one cylinder or disk, mentioning the name of the firm (five words as a max-

---

[1] These announcements are broadcast at certain hours when they will attract most attention, after the announcer has said: " EAJ7, Union Radio, Madrid."

[2] Will be broadcast as the first of each group of announcements or after the speaker has announced: " EAJ7 " during intervals.

imum), 60 pesetas; arranging for 15 to 19 broadcastings per month, each 40 pesetas; arranging for 30 broadcastings per month, each 30 pesetas. The rate is 50 per cent extra if broadcasting time is specified.

Book announcements: Each word, 0.50 peseta, except name of advertising firm, author, and title of work, which will be billed at 2 pesetas per word. There are experienced persons to prepare news talks. Such announcements will be made during the period of time devoted to book reviews or during the after-dinner hour. Duration one minute, 40 pesetas; duration two minutes, 75 pesetas. Discounts: By contracting for four talks per month, 10 per cent. Criticisms of books will be broadcast during the book review hour.

Dances, teas, festivals, etc. (after-dinner broadcasting) each word, 1 peseta. Society news (trips, balls, baptisms, marriages, etc.), each word, 2 pesetas. Sports (after-dinner broadcasting), notices of contests, horse races, bull fights, etc., each word, 1 peseta.

For other forms of announcements, dates, etc., prices will be quoted on request.

ASTURIAS RADIO OF OVIEDO

General rates: Pesetas per word

From   1 to 10 words per day_____ 1.00
From 11 to 25 words per day_____ .75
From 25 to 50 words per day_____ .57

Contracts:

Announcements of from 1 to 10 words per day—
Up to 10 day per month_____ .95
Up to 20 days per month_____ .90
Up to 30 days per month_____ .85

Announcements of from 11 to 25 words per day—
Up to 10 days per month_____ .71
Up to 20 days per month_____ .675
Up to 30 days per month_____ .637

Announcements of from 26 to 50 words per day—
Up to 10 days per month_____ .554
Up to 20 days per month_____ .507
Up to 30 days per month_____ .478

Minimum collected per day and announcement, 4 pesetas. For special announcements, request prices stating clearly the kind of announcement to be broadcast. Taxes shall be charged to the advertiser. Payments are in advance.

Local talent, in the way of artists, singers, and orchestras, is available at all the broadcasting stations. It is not possible to give approximate cost per hour for such services, this depending upon the caliber of the talent employed, duration of contract, hours of broadcasting, class of advertising, etc.

The Radio Asturias gives an approximate estimate of cost per hour for broadcast advertising, of medium importance, of 125 pesetas. The Union Radio quotes rates per hour in the schedule listed herein.

The Union Radio uses records of all speeds, rates for which have already been quoted. The Radio Asturias states that it uses phonograph records of the speeds current on the market. The rates charged are subject to agreement with the company.

Union Radio has contracted for the sale of advertising time with various national and European agencies, but none American. The sale of time may also be arranged directly with the company.

Radio Asturias has not contracted for the sale of advertising time with any agencies, and such sales are made by the company itself.

The Spanish language is used almost exclusively in radio advertising. As only a very small percentage of the population understands English, records prepared in the English language can not be effectively used.

SWEDEN

Julius Rabe, manager of Aktb. Radiojanst, Kungsgatan 8, Stockholm, the Government-controlled company in charge of all public broadcasting, states that Government regulations prohibit any commercial advertising.

SWITZERLAND

Any advertising broadcast by radio, direct or indirect, is forbidden, no matter whether it is paid for or not.

TURKEY

By American Commercial Attaché Julian E. Gillespie, Istanbul

Radio broadcasting is a State monopoly in Turkey, and exclusive rights until 1937 have been granted by the Government to Telsiz Telefon T. A. S. of Istanbul.

Regular programs are broadcast daily, between 6 and 11.30 p. m., from two stations. The station in Istanbul operates on a wave length of 1,200 meters, while the Ankara station, works on a wave length of 2,000 meters. Both have ample power for clear reception in all parts of the country.

It is estimated that there are between 4,000 and 5,000 receiving sets in Turkey at the present time, the largest number being in Istanbul. Other cities such as Izmir, Ankara, and Bursa also have a considerable number, but there are few in the rural districts.

ADVERTISING AND RATES

The volume of radio advertising is extremely limited, consisting only of short talks describing and recommending commodities being offered for sale. No form of entertainment accompanies these talks, which on the average take less than one minute to broadcast. The rates charged per word for this service are as follows: 1 to 5 words, 50 piasters; [3] 6 to 10 words, 40 piasters; 11 to 50 words, 25 piasters; and 51 to 100 words, 15 piasters. If the same advertisement is repeated five times or five advertisements of various wordings are given at the same time a rebate of 10 per cent is allowed on these rates.

The Telsiz Telefon T. A. S. has no rates on a time basis. However, if it receives a specific proposal it will quote a rate either for a sigle advertisement or a contract price for any number of programs during a specific period. The approximate charge for one-half hour would be 100 Turkish pounds. This charge would include a five or six piece orchestra, supplied by the studio. However, the company does not now have time contracts either with local or foreign advertisers.

RECORDS

The broadcasting company recently established a rate for advertising records, but so far no individual or firm has taken advantage of

---

[3] One piaster equivalent to about one-half of 1 cent in United States currency; 100 piasters in 1 Turkish pound, which is equivalent to $0.47.

this medium. The charge is 2 Turkish pounds per minute or fraction thereof. Records should be made for a speed of 78 revolutions per minute.

LOCAL TALENT AND LANGUAGE

With regard to the availibility of local talent, should the advertiser wish to arrange for the performance independently of the studio and pay the company only for time used, there are small orchestras, mostly of the jazz variety, which play at private parties, dances, etc., with which arrangements can be made. The broadcasting company, however, does not quote a rate on time alone unless it receives a specific proposal.

The language used for broadcasting is Turkish and to a limited extent French. The number of English-speaking people in Turkey is relatively small.

CONCLUSION

It is questionable whether radio broadcasting is an effective means of advertising in Turkey at the present time. There is a comparatively small number of receivers in use, and they are concentrated in the larger cities. Another factor is that the quality of the average program broadcast locally is so far below those broadcast by the European stations that many radio owners prefer to listen to foreign programs.

UNITED KINGDOM

Radio is controlled by a monopoly vested in the British Broadcasting Corporation (formerly a division of the post office department), and no commercial advertising is accepted. The system of listeners' licenses is in effect, and the projection of advertising into radio broadcasting appears to be opposed by listeners as well as by the Government.

YUGOSLAVIA

By Commercial Attaché Emil Kekich, Belgrade

There are three Yugoslav broadcasting stations accepting commercial advertising: Radio A. D., of Belgrade, wave length 432 meters, power 2,500 watts; Radio Zagreb, of Zagreb, 307 meters, 700 watts; Radio Ljubljana, of Ljubljana, 569 meters, 3,000 watts.

Commercial broadcasting is being done on a relatively small scale, but it probably will increase in the future. Comparatively few well-known international concerns use broadcasting facilities, and these are for the most part radio concerns such as Philips, Telefunken, and local radio apparatus distributors. Local products such as soap, confectionery, watches, etc., are also advertised.

Rates for advertising are based on time, with the copy generally limited to four typewritten lines, broadcast once daily at 100 dinars (1 dinar equals $0.0177), or 2,500 dinars per month. This monthly rate may also include, by arrangement, two or three broadcasts daily. Broadcasting in the evening is limited to 10 minutes of advertising text. Exclusive rates are charged for special broadcasts, amounting to an increase of 50 per cent over those mentioned. Stations do not contract with local or any other agencies for the sale of broadcasting time.

Local talent is available at all the stations. In Belgrade an hour's radio concert (16 musicians) costs an aggregate of 2,500 dinars. The Zagreb radio orchestra costs 1.200 dinars an hour, plus 800 dinars for the station's fee in the evening or 400 dinars station fee for daylight broadcast. The symphony orchestra (40 to 45 musicians) at Belgrade broadcasts for an hour at an approximate cost of 10,000 dinars. The comparable program in Zagreb is somewhat less in cost. A solo singer of the best grade may be engaged for 30 minutes at 2,000 dinars.

Records may be used in Zagreb and Ljubljana, although they are not recommended by the stations. The rates for records of 3.5 to 4 minutes duration are about 3,500 dinars monthly for one broadcast daily. In Belgrade reproduction of records for musical performance as advertising is not permitted, excepting advertising for phonograph records. Concerts by records of one hour cost 2,500 dinars in Belgrade, and in the cases of reproduction of whole operas there is a reduction of 50 per cent. Records should be made for 75 to 80 revolutions per minute.

The Belgrade station uses the Serbian, the Zagreb station Croatian, and the Ljubljana station the Slovenian language. Broadcasting in English would not be effective.

○

U. S. DEPARTMENT OF COMMERCE
R. P. LAMONT, Secretary

BUREAU OF FOREIGN AND DOMESTIC COMMERCE
FREDERICK M. FEIKER, Director

BROADCAST ADVERTISING
IN LATIN AMERICA

Trade Information Bulletin No. 771

UNITED STATES
GOVERNMENT PRINTING OFFICE
WASHINGTON : 1931

FOREWORD

Until now many questions have been unanswered as to the feasibility of employing radio as an advertising medium for American products in foreign lands. In certain countries commercial broadcasting is definitely prohibited; in others the restrictions upon owners of radio sets are such as to discourage their general use. In Latin America existing regulations are, in general, favorable to the development of this form of publicity.

The brief country-by-country outline presented herewith is intended to sketch the status of commercial broadcasting in the Western Hemisphere outside the United States and Canada at the middle of 1931. A similar review covering the more important commercial countries in the rest of the world will be made available shortly.

Recent radio publications issued by the Bureau of Foreign and Domestic Commerce have been considered highly valuable by the radio industry. The latest of these bulletins is Radio Markets of the World, 1930 (Trade Promotion Series No. 109; price, 20 cents). This handbook of radio development in foreign countries lists all the known broadcasting stations outside the United States, with their power and wave lengths. In addition it presents a comprehensive survey of broadcasting and reception in each country, indicating restrictions in force, the type of reception, and other factors of similar interest. It would be advisable for the reader to have this bulletin at hand for ready reference in gaging the feasibility of broadcast advertising in the various Latin American countries.

American concerns are reminded that the Bureau of Foreign and Domestic Commerce will be glad to supply, upon specific inquiry, what additional information it may have available on broadcast advertising in any individual country.

FREDERICK M. FEIKER, *Director*,
Bureau of Foreign and Domestic Commerce.

SEPTEMBER, 1931.

BROADCAST ADVERTISING IN LATIN AMERICA

Compiled in Specialties Division by E. D. Schutrumpf from reports submitted by the foreign representatives of the Department of Commerce and the Department of State

INTRODUCTION

In no country of the world is radio advertising used, directly and indirectly, as extensively as in the United States. Its success as a medium here has led to widespread interest as to its possible success in foreign countries. The increasing trend, especially among smaller stations, toward " electrical transcriptions " has stimulated that interest, so that to-day several American firms are already sponsoring broadcasting records, with advertising, on foreign radio stations.

The language factor is a prime consideration in foreign broadcasting. In Latin America, except in Portuguese-speaking Brazil, the Spanish language is almost universally used.

In certain countries there are restrictions, both on broadcasting and reception, through governmental control of radio stations and through the license method of receiver-set ownership. The countries treated in this publication are those which are known to accept commercial advertising.

Another radio characteristic of Latin America is that ownership of receivers is largely confined to a relatively small portion of the total population. Only the well-to-do people have sets, yet these are the ones most likely to purchase goods advertised over the air, since many of the poorer classes lack the necessary buying power. However, there are accentuations and exceptions to this generality, which are discussed under the head of each country in this publication.

In former years climatic conditions were great hindrances to suitable reception in the warm, humid countries, but with the installation of improved transmission equipment in recent years, this difficulty has been partially overcome. However, reception in summer is nowhere as good as it is in winter, and North American concerns using the radio in Central and South America should not forget the difference in seasons on either side of the Equator. This factor is important both in planning campaigns and in the actual presentation of programs.

Latin Americans are naturally lovers of high-class music. And while the quality of their own native music may not have a general appeal in North America, their artists perform to the delight and satisfaction of their countrymen. Hence, some advertisers have found it desirable to sponsor local orchestras and singers of good reputation in preference to records made in the United States.

(1)

The data in this bulletin were gleaned largely by first-hand contact and observation by the foreign representatives of the Department of Commerce and Department of State in the early summer of 1931. Where rates are mentioned either for broadcasting time or for the services of artists or announcers, they are to be considered as indicative only. In most cases they have been obtained from the station managers, but no responsibility can be assumed by the Department of Commerce with respect to their accuracy.

SOUTH AMERICA

ARGENTINA

By Assistant Trade Commissioner Charles H. Ducoté, Buenos Aires

PRINCIPAL BROADCASTING STATIONS

Of 29 principal broadcasting stations in Argentina, 19 are located in Buenos Aires. All, with the exception of that operated by the municipality of Buenos Aires, station LS1, accept commercial advertising. (A list of stations appears at the end of this section.)

It is the usual practice for the owner of a broadcasting station to provide the musical or other talent, and after the presentation of each selection, advertising announcements are made. In a few cases the sponsoring firm engages its own entertainers. The system of radio " hours " used largely in the United States, during which brief advertising announcements are made, is employed here to but a very small extent. The American system has been under consideration for some time, but it appears to be the general belief that it is not suited to this country.

Two important factors impede the greater development of radio broadcasting. These are the general lack of variety of the programs and the too great insistence upon advertising announcements. In addition, there may be mentioned the interference among stations and the unsatisfactory transmission from some of the stations.

It is generally considered that among the stations in the front rank as regards quality of programs, discretion in the use of advertising matter, and quality of transmission are the following: LR4, Radio Splendid; LS9, La Voz del Aire; LS1, Broadcasting Municipal; LR8, Radio Cine Paris; LS5, Radio Rivadavia, and one or two others.

The management of a good proportion of the Argentine broadcasting stations is divided into three principal groups. The first, operated by Jaime Yankelevich, consists of stations LP4, Radio Porteño; LR6, Radio Mitre; LR3, Radio Nacional; LS6, Radio Bijou; LT3, Soc. Rural de Cerealistas de Rosario; LU2, Radio Nacional of Bahia Blanca; LV2, Radio Central of Cordoba; and LT4, Radio del Parque of Mendoza. The second group, managed by Prieto y Schroeder, includes stations LR2, Radio Prieto; LR9, Radio Fenix; and LS2, Radio Prieto. The third group, managed by Antonio Devoto and Benjamin Gache, consists of stations LR4, Radio Splendid; LS5, Radio Rivadavia; and LS3, Radio Mayo. The first group is called the " Primera Cadena Argentina de Broadcastings," and from time to time it broadcasts " chain " programs.

4

The rates charged for advertising by radio vary widely. Several of the stations have published tariffs, but the rates are nevertheless adjusted according to the importance of the firm, the amount of time involved, the quality of the musical or other programs to be trasmitted, and other such factors. The basic rate schedules of several of the stations are shown below.

Station LS9.—Monthly rates for one 15-minute broadcast a week, 200 paper pesos;[1] for one half-hour broadcast a week, 300 pesos; two 15-minute broadcasts a week, 300 pesos; two half-hour broadcasts a week, 450 pesos; one 15-minute broadcast every other day, 450 pesos; one half-hour broadcast every other day, 700 pesos; one daily 15-minute broadcast, 600 pesos; one daily half-hour broadcast, 1,000 pesos.

The same station will put announcements on the air at the following rate per month: 5 a day of 15 words or less, 360 pesos; 5 a day for 35 words or less, 525 pesos; 10 a day of 15 words or less, 600 pesos; 10 a day of 35 words or less, 900 pesos; 15 a day for 15 words or less, 810 pesos; 15 a day for 35 words or less, 1,125 pesos; 20 a day of 15 words or less, 960 pesos; 20 a day for 35 words or less, 1,200 pesos; 25 a day of 15 words or less, 1,050 pesos; 25 a day of 35 words or less, 1,350 pesos; 30 a day of 15 words or less, 1,080 pesos; 30 a day of 35 words or less, 1,440 pesos.

In the case of long-time contracts, discounts are allowed as follows: For 3 months, 3 per cent; for 6 months, 10 per cent; and for 12 months, 20 per cent.

Station LR8.—For one 15-minute broadcast per day, 450 pesos per month; text of announcements during each broadcast not to exceed 50 words; 4 announcements daily, 275 pesos per month; 7 announcements daily, 400 pesos per month; 15 announcements daily, 700 pesos per month, with text of announcements not to exceed 25 words each.

Stations LR3 and LR6.—For one broadcast per day (rates quoted per month), 15 minutes, 800 pesos; 30 minutes, 1,400 pesos; 60 minutes, 2,200 pesos. For 5 announcements daily, 500 pesos per month; 10 announcements daily, 900 pesos per month; 15 announcements daily, 1,300 pesos per month; 20 announcements daily, 1,500 pesos per month.

The Primera Cadena Argentina de Broadcastings quotes the following rates for the use of its time: 15 minutes a day, 3,000 pesos a month; 30 minutes a day, 5,000 pesos a month; 5 announcements nightly, 1,000 pesos a month.

Station LP4 offers the same rates as stations LR3 and LR6, with a 20 per cent discount.

AVAILABILITY OF LOCAL TALENT

Entertainment material in radio broadcasts consists of music by local musicians or from records, speeches, dramatic selections, recitations, etc. As regards classical music, it is the opinion that local performers have not the capabilities of the average performers whose

[1] The paper peso is equivalent to about 42 cents in United States currency.

efforts · are recorded on the best American phonograph records, although the quality of some of the programs rendered by certain artists, such as those from the Teatro Colon, is high. Orchestras especially skilled in playing "national" music, such as "tangos," "rancheras," and the like—which music makes up an important proportion—are naturally available. Either records are used or the actual playing of the orchestras themselves is transmitted. It is interesting to note that many listeners are not able to distinguish records of "national" music from the playing of the same music by the actual orchestra or one of about equal quality when transmission in both cases is handled by the better broadcasting stations. This naturally tends to increase the use of records. While there is ample local talent available, it is believed that phonograph records will continue to be used, owing to their low cost and because of their value in supplementing actual entertainers.

There is a wide variation in the cost of orchestras and singers available for broadcasting purposes. One station, for instance, paid about 1,100 paper pesos a month for an orchestra of five pieces, playing so-called classical music one hour a day. An orchestra of six persons, playing "national" music two hours a day, charged about 1,800 pesos a month. These rates are for orchestras of average ability. A very few orchestras playing "national" music, having national renown through phonograph recording, appearances at theaters, etc., must be paid much more. One station was charged 700 paper pesos per hour by the "Gardel" band. This station indicated that the rates charged by local orchestras for five to six performances varied from 25 to 250 pesos per hour per day.

The rates charged by very good sopranos, tenors, and other singers are said to average about 100 pesos per hour. Singers whose names are less known are paid less, and may be obtained sometimes for 25 pesos per hour. Second-rate singers were obtained by one good broadcasting station for as little as 10 pesos per hour.

In the foregoing rates, given per hour, performers are called upon to act only during intervals between advertising announcements, and although the rates are paid per hour, the actual performance time may be considerably less than one hour. There are very few, if any, performers especially renowned for their work in radio broadcasting.

One well-known station during 1929 spent 70,000 pesos in supplying performers for its programs.

The relative amount of time spent in advertisements as compared with that devoted to entertainment may be as low as 20 per cent in the best stations and as high as 50 per cent in the stations of minor importance.

USE OF RECORDS

Phonograph records are used considerably by the broadcasting stations, and all of them have extensive record libraries. Advertising rates do not differ materially whether records are used or whether performers appear personally. In a few cases advertisers may supply their own entertainment numbers, in which case a difference is made in the charge for using the station's facilities. The usual record speed used in local transmission is about 75 revolutions per minute. Standard records as made by the well-known American and European manufacturers are used.

SALE OF ADVERTISING TIME

Hitherto all time has been sold to the advertisers directly by the station. Arrangements are now under way by which some stations will offer broadcasting time through accredited agents in the United States. It should be noted that there is intensive competition among the stations for the business available, and as a result there has been price cutting among the smaller stations.

LANGUAGES USED IN BROADCASTING

For announcement Spanish is the language almost universally used. From time to time broadcasting is done in English or some other language than Spanish, but the amount of such broadcasting is very small in comparison with that done in Spanish. This is true not only of advertising but also of entertainment numbers and speeches. Songs are very often sung in many languages other than Spanish. Records with advertising material in the English language would, it is stated by station owners, meet with very little success in Argentina.

PROGRAM LISTINGS AND CHIEF STATIONS

A typical schedule of early evening programs, from 4 to 9 p. m., as listed in a Buenos Aires newspaper announcement, is shown below:

LR8.—Ministerio de Agricultura bulletin; typical orchestra; tales by "La Maestrita." Records: (1) Mignon, overture, (2) Danza Eslava, (3) Chant Hindu, (4) Ariette, song by Cora Lacosta, soprano, (5) Capricho Italiano (records), Fiocca la Neve, (7) Stormelatrice, song by C. Lacosts, (8) Romanza de fa.

LR4.—Classical orchestra; duet by Fleruquin-Febré; guitar by Rodriguez and Chazarreta; news; classical orchestra.

LR1.—Records.

LR5.—Classical quartette; recitations; songs by Emilia Amat; records.

LS5.—Classical orchestra; songs by Juanita and Aurora Rivero; dance music by jazz.

LS9.—Tales for children; records; news; recitations; song and guitar.

LP4.—Handel quartette; Rondalla; recitations; songs; typical orchestra; records "Nollina"; comedy by Angelina Pagano Co.

LR3.—Guitar duet, "Una hora en la Pampa," Angelina Pagano Co.; songs; records.

LP6.—Records; special program.

LS2, LR2, and LR9.—Sonia Tarrecosky; Carmen de Larmen de Lerma; duet Paniche; Mimi Pinsonett; E. Orse.

LS3.—Grain market reports; records; dance music.

The principal radio broadcasting stations, their wave lengths, and power are shown below:

PRINCIPAL BROADCASTING STATIONS IN ARGENTINA

City	Call letters	Name of station	Wave length, meters	Power, watts
Buenos Aires	LR1	Radio Cultura	380	500
Do	LR2	Radio Prieto	345	10,000
Do	LR3	Radio Nacional	316	5,000
Do	LR4	Radio Splendid	303	10,000
Do	LR5	Radio Excelsior	361	3,000
Do	LR6	Radio Mitre	330	5,000
Do	LR7	Radio Buenos Aires	400	7,000
Do	LR8	Radio Cine Paris	270.9	10,000
Do	LR9	Radio Fenix	291.2	10,000
Do	LS1	Broadcasting Municipal	423	5,000
Do	LS2	Radio Prieto	252	10,000
Do	LS3	Radio Mayo	236.2	1,000
Do	LS4 [1]	Radio Telefunken	262	4,000
Do	LS5	Radio Rivadavia	280.5	10,000
Do	LS6 [1]	Radio Bijou	222.2	3,000
Do	LS8	Radio Sarmiento	243.9	10,000
Do	LS9	La Voz del Aire	215.8	10,000
Do	LP4	Radio Portena	448	5,000
Do	LP6	Casa America	509	([2])
City of La Plata	LP8	Univ. de La Plata	438	1,000
Concordia	LT1	Radio Rural	370.3	1,000
Rosario	LT3	Soc. Rural de Cer	275.3	3,000
Mendoza	LT4	Radio del Parque	340	4,500
Parana	LT5	Diario El Litoral	240	500
San Juan	LT6	S. A. Bodegas Grattigna	411	5,000
Cordoba	LV2	Radio Central	328.9	1,000
Rosario	LV5	Radio Rosario	218.9	500
Do	LV6	Casa Roca Soler	279.1	100
Bahia Blanca	LU2	Radio Nacional	375	5,000

[1] Not now operating.   [2] Not known.

BOLIVIA

By American Vice Consul Paul C. Daniels, La Paz

There is only one broadcasting station in Bolivia, the Radio Nacional de Bolivia, station CPX, at La Paz. It can be heard throughout Bolivia, northern Argentina and Chile, in all Peru, and in part of Brazil.

Rates quoted by this station are as follows: For one hour, 50 bolivianos ($18 in U. S. currency); for one-half hour, 30 bolivianos ($11). These rates are subject to change every three months, except in the case of contracts for longer periods of time.

It is possible to contract local talent for broadcasting purposes, such as singers, orchestras, and musicians, who can play either native Bolivian or classical music. Programs can be drawn up using this talent for a minimum of 50 bolivianos per hour, in addition to the cost of station time. Prices paid for local artists vary, of course, depending on the number of persons performing and their ability.

Records may be used for commercial broadcasting, but they must be provided by the sponsors at their own expense. In this case the only fee charged by the studio is the regular fee of 50 bolivianos per hour. At present station CPX uses only records of 75 revolutions per minute. It is stated, however, that within a few weeks there will be equipment installed to accommodate records of 33⅓ revolutions per minute.

The local broadcasting station has no contracts or concessions for the sale of time with any agency, either Bolivian or foreign.

The facilities of the studio are at present used for advertising the following: American automobiles, general importers; local brewery, soda water, soft drinks; local jeweler, importing from Germany; local stockbroker and money exchange; steamship agent; imported men's furnishings; local race track; three local theaters; international cable station; national charity lottery; local tax-collecting agency; ladies' apparel, novelties; and one evening paper and two morning papers broadcasting news items.

Programs should be transmitted in Spanish to be fully effective. However, songs in English can occasionally be used, or instrumental records with only incidental English. All announcing should be in Spanish.

BRAZIL

By Assistant Trade Commissioner J. Winsor Ives, Rio de Janeiro

PRINCIPAL BROADCASTING STATIONS

Advertising by broadcasting in Brazil has become increasingly important during the past three years, owing to the growing number of radios in use and the proven effectiveness of this medium for reaching the better-class population. Although this group is decidedly in the minority, it represents an important potential outlet for luxury items and other goods falling into a price class beyond the reach of the mass buying power. As last reported, the stations making commercial broadcasts are identified and equipped as follows:

Call letter	Name of station	Wave length	Power	City
		Meters	*Watts*	
PRAA	Radio Sociedade do Rio de Janeiro	400	1,000	Rio de Janeiro.
PRAC	Radio Sociedade Mayrink Veiga	350	500	Do.
PRAD	Radio Educadora do Brazil	326	50	Do.
PRAP	Radio Club de Pernambuco	425	3,000	Pernambuco.
PRAG	Radio Sociedade Gaucha	425	3,000	Porto Alegre.
PRAS	Radio Club de Santos	335	1,000	Santos.
PRAE	Sociedade Radio Educadora Paulista	368	1,000	Sao Paulo.
PRAR	Radio Sociedade Record	298	500	Do.

RATES

No set schedules of time rates are issued by any of the stations handling advertising. Local firms buying time seem to prefer to shop around, hoping the stations will grant substantial rate reductions in order to get business. This is probably true when a firm is in the market for a large amount of broadcasting time. The average rate charged by the stations listed herewith for advertising broadcasts is 500 milreis (at present exchange about $35 in U. S. currency) per hour. Short announcements are handled at a charge of around 10 milreis (about 70 cents) each up to 20 words. The foregoing rates apply to regular programs and advertising announcements broadcast by the station announcer.

LOCAL TALENT

Good local talent is available for broadcasting programs from stations in Rio de Janeiro and Sao Paulo. Orchestra musicians can be hired in these cities for from 30 to 50 milreis (from $2.10 to $3.50) per player for a program consisting of five or six numbers. Singers, solo musicians, and other entertainers usually charge around 50 milreis for a program of the same length. Suitable talent outside the cities just mentioned is restricted largely to orchestras, the best of which may be engaged at about the same figures as quoted above.

Despite the low cost of suitable talent, few studio programs are broadcast. For the most part, programs consist largely, if not entirely, of phonograph records of popular native and American songs and dance music.

RECORD BROADCASTING RATES

Up to the present time very few records have been employed for advertising. This is no doubt, due to the fact that local firms are the only ones, thus far, to use broadcast advertising to any extent, and they either employ announcers or have the regular station announcers handle their broadcasts. The two or three American and other foreign concerns which have recently become users of radio advertising here have also employed local announcers.

None of the stations booking advertising time has set schedules of rates for record broadcasts. However, taking an average of prices quoted by two of the stations in Rio de Janeiro, the probable cost of record broadcasting time would run around 125 milreis (about $11) per hour. This figure is based upon the actual price paid by several local phonograph-record houses, which have exclusive contracts with stations to handle the broadcasting of particular brands of records.

The above rates apply to musical selections. In all probability records containing advertising announcements would be subject to a heavier charge although stations recently interviewed here were not in a position to quote rates. However, owing to the increasing interest being shown in radio advertising by various foreign manufacturers, it is understood that stations in both Rio de Janeiro and Sao Paulo are now prepared to quote rates on specific requirements of foreign firms desiring to purchase broadcasting time.

EQUIPMENT FOR RECORD BROADCASTING

Despite the fact that phonograph records are used extensively for broadcasting in Brazil, no stations handling advertising here are equipped with turntables or other special equipment such as is found in the United States. Standard phonographs of the orthophonic type are used exclusively at the present time, although it is understood that the Radio Sociedade Mayrinck Veiga of Rio de Janeiro will install special reproducing equipment within the next two or three months, provided certain negotiations which are now pending with an American advertising agency are satisfactorily concluded.

In view of the situation above outlined, records for use by broadcasting stations in Brazil should be recorded for a speed of 78 revolutions per minute. As these stations acquire more up-to-date reproducing equipment, advertising records timed for use in the United States will, of course, be suitable for use here.

AGENCIES SELLING BROADCASTING TIME

As far as is known, no American or other agencies have contracted with stations in Brazil for the sale of broadcasting time to advertisers. However, the Radio Sociedade Mayrinck Veiga of Rio de Janerio is now in negotiation with an American firm, and it is expected that arrangements will be concluded within the near future whereby the American agency will have the exclusive rights to the sale of broadcasting time for this station in the United States. An American advertising agency is also in a position to quote rates for and arrange advertising broadcasts in Brazil, although it does not have exclusive arrangements with any of the stations here now booking time. The agency maintains two offices in Brazil.

ADVERTISERS AND PRODUCTS ADVERTISED

Only one American concern has used radio advertising to any extent here. During the past three months this firm has booked a considerable amount of time on stations in Rio de Janerio and Sao Paulo as a part of an extensive advertising campaign to introduce the new model of an American automobile. It is understood that an American food-product manufacturer is contemplating a campaign which will include a series of advertising broadcasts. Numerous local firms handling a variety of the following American and other imported products are regular users of radio for advertising phonographs, phonograph records, radio sets, proprietary medicines, toilet preparations, automobiles, and motion pictures.

The following products of domestic origin are also advertised by radio: Toilet preparations, proprietary medicines, cigarettes, lottery tickets, clothing, and furniture.

LANGUAGE REQUIREMENTS

Records sent to Brazil for broadcasting should be in the Portuguese language. English dialogue records would not be acceptable. This is true to a lesser degree with French and Spanish language records, although either would be preferable to English. The fact that radio reception in Rio de Janeiro and other coast cities in Brazil is often impaired by excessive static makes it essential that records be clear in order to avoid undue distortion in dialogue. This fact in itself would make the use of records in any language but Portuguese highly undesirable.

CONCLUSION

According to local opinion, the value of broadcast advertising in Brazil is at present definitely restricted to those products which fall into a price class within the reach of the relatively small percentage of the country's total population, making up the upper, middle, and wealthy classes. Furthermore, this advertising is effective only in certain parts of the country, where facilities for broadcasting exist and radio sets are found in sufficiently large numbers to assure the advertiser of reasonable coverage.

CHILE

By William van Dort, Office of the American Commercial Attaché, Santiago

All broadcasting stations at present operating in Chile accept commercial advertising. In fact, it is from this source that they are able to meet operating expenses.

The rates charged by station "Radio Chilena" with call letters CMAB, owned by the International Machinery Co. at Santiago, may be considered representative of the higher-powered stations in the country. Its rates by the month are shown below. Announcements as here scheduled must not exceed 50 words; advertising in excess of 50 words is charged for at the rate of 100 pesos [2] per 20 words.

Current daily advertising, one to two months, 300 pesos day, 400 pesos night, 600 pesos combined; three to five months, 250 pesos day, 350 pesos night, and 500 pesos combined; six months or longer, 200 pesos day, 300 pesos night, 450 pesos combined.

Current advertising every other day, one to two months, 300 pesos (monthly), three to five months, 250 pesos; six months or longer, 200 pesos.

For special programs the following monthly rates apply:

Exclusive half-hour daily transmission: Until 7 p. m., 800 pesos; from 8.30 to 9.30 p. m., 1,000 pesos; from 9.30 to 11.30 p. m., 1,500 pesos.

One hour exclusive daily transmission: Until 7 p. m., 1,500 pesos; from 8.30 to 9.30 p. m., 1,800 pesos; from 9.30 to 11.30 p. m., 2,750 pesos.

Noncontract transmissions: Current transmissions, 20 pesos each; combined transmissions, 30 pesos each.

For the smaller stations the rates announced by the Radio Teatro Esmeralda, station CMAQ, owned by Mr. Carlos Hueni, of Santiago, may be considered typical. These are:

From 1 to 3 p. m., 350 to 500 pesos monthly per hour; from 4 to 8 p. m., 600 to 900 pesos monthly per hour; from 9 to 12 p. m., 1,000 to 1,200 pesos monthly per hour. There is a surcharge of 20 per cent on transmission of less than an hour.

Local talent is available. The cost of an orchestra of about eight persons fluctuates between 120 and 150 pesos. A singer charges 15 pesos for three songs per evening.

All stations give record programs during the day. Records are frequently loaned free of charge by record importers; those used are of standard speed, 75 revolutions per minute. Special records now used in the United States with complete programs can not be used at present in Chile, as no motors for $33\frac{1}{3}$ revolutions per minute are employed. Efforts have been made to transmit motion-picture records, but these have also failed, owing to the lack of proper equipment in the local broadcasting stations; the equipment used did not produce a steady, clear transmission.

At present commercial broadcasting is being used to advertise the following commodities: Radio sets, batteries, tires, insecticides, tooth paste, trucks and passenger cars, electrical household appliances, and electric refrigerators.

The Spanish language is used in all Chilean broadcasting stations.

Occasionally a special program is given in English or German, but this may not exceed 15 minutes. It is the opinion of individuals very closely associated with the radio business that the public would

---

[2] A Chilean peso is equivalent to approximately 12 cents in United States currency.

not care to listen to repeated broadcasting in languages other than Spanish and that the use of such foreign languages might react unfavorably.

COLOMBIA

By Assistant Trade Commissioner James J. O'Neil, Bogota

While commercial broadcasting in Colombia is still in its infancy, it will in a short time become of wider significance in directing campaigns to popularize the use of commodities and services of various descriptions.

At present three stations have facilities for accepting commercial advertising. Stations HKC, in Bogota, and HKO, in Medellin, are both under the control and operation of the Colombia Radio & Electric Corp. S. A., of Bogota. The other station is HJN, at Bogota, and is Government controlled. The advertising concession for HJN has been granted to Antonio Puerto y Cia, of Bogota.

Stations HKC and HKO both use American equipment for records. HKC operates on approximately 48.5 meters, broadcasting between 8.30 and 11 p. m.; HKO uses a wave length of 50 meters and is on the air between 8 and 10 p. m. It is understood that these stations can be heard in Venezuela, Ecuador, and Peru, as well as in Colombia and the United States. A short-wave transmission set is used by both.

Station HJN operates on 425 meters and broadcasts from 8.30 to 11 p. m. Telefunken equipment (German) is used throughout and is believed to be somewhat obsolete. Its long-wave apparatus is said to be limited in range and quality of service for this particular climate.

There are two or three small (experimental) stations in Colombia, but these are not now authorized to accept advertising under the terms of their licenses.

Stations HKC and HKO use talking-machine speed of 78 revolutions per minute and 33 revolutions per minute for program records. HJN has talking-machine speed only.

The following broadcasting rates have been furnished by the Colombian Radio & Electric Corporation:

1 hour, station time	$25.00
1 hour, 8-piece orchestra	15.00
1 hour, 6-piece orchestra	12.00
1 hour, 7-piece jazz band	15.00
1 hour, 4-piece jazz band	10.00
Half hour, station time	15.00
Half hour, 8-piece orchestra	10.00
Half hour, 6-piece orchestra	8.00
Half hour, 7-piece jazz band	10.00
Half hour, 4-piece jazz band	7.50
Quarter hour, station time	10.00
Quarter hour, 8-piece orchestra	7.50
Quarter hour, 6-piece orchestra	5.00
Quarter hour, 7-piece jazz band	7.50
Quarter hour, 4-piece jazz band	5.00
Singers, male or female, 3 numbers per program	3.00
Singers, duets, 3 numbers per program	5.00

Monthly rates figuring one program per week, 10 per cent off.

Two programs per week for one month or one per week for three months, 20 per cent off.

Three programs per week or one per week for six months, 25 per cent off.

As far as is known, none of these stations has contracted for service with any local, American, or other agency for the sale of broadcasting time to advertisers except for the concession noted above for station HJN. Where such advertising has been used, it has been contracted for by local representatives of foreign companies. All advertising so far has been institutional, conducted by agents or representatives of foreign houses and not by the principals advertising their products. However, there are no restrictions as to who the advertiser may be.

Broadcasting is invariably carried on in Spanish. However, records of music only can be used, with local announcements of the products advertised being made in Spanish as often as desired.

PERU

By Julian D. Smith, Assistant Commercial Attaché, Lima

There is but one broadcasting station in Peru accepting commercial advertising, OAX, at Lima, with a wave length of 380 meters and power of 1,500 watts.

This station does not charge by the hour or fraction thereof, but by a fixed sum per month, half a month, or per each advertisement. Its present tariff is as follows: For 30 advertisements, at the rate of one daily each advertisement consisting of a maximum of 20 words and not lasting more than 20 seconds, 100 soles [3] per month; for 15 advertisements, at the rate of one daily, with a maximum of 20 words per advertisement, requiring 20 seconds, 60 soles for half a month; for one advertisement only, 5 soles. Most advertisements are contracted for a month or half month and very seldom for once.

However, in view of the interest shown by American concerns in commercial broadcast advertising, the station has decided to establish the following rates, which may be considered as provisional and may be changed at some future date: $60 to $70 (U. S. currency) per hour; $30 to $35 per half hour; $15 to $17.50 per quarter hour.

Local talent is available, but it is considered of a mediocre type. The local station claims, however, to be now prepared to offer excellent programs, with the enlisted cooperation of amateur elements and the two best orchestras obtainable in all Peru, organized by Professors Laghi and Matteucci, of the National Music Academy. The approximate costs for orchestras and singers are: Orchestras (five instruments), 40 to 50 soles per hour; singers, 20 soles for one presentation of three songs. This is the price charged by singers of some reputation.

Station OAX is equipped to use records. Rates do not differ from those charged for programs originating in the studio. Records should be made for a speed of 78 revolutions per minute. The station now has double electrical pick-ups for this speed, and at the time of this writing had ordered apparatus for using records at 33⅓ revolutions per minute.

The Peruvian station has not yet contracted with any local, American, or other agency for the sale of broadcasting time to advertisers,

---

[3] A sol is equivalent to 28 cents in United States currency, according to the stabilization law of Apr. 18, 1931.

but it is now negotiating with a number of American concerns which have solicited exclusive rights.

The administrator of this station states that since October 1, 1930, it has been under the control of the Minister of Government, and as it is an official institution, it has a virtual monopoly of all commercial broadcast advertising, there being no possibility of competition on the part of other organizations of its kind.

Broadcast advertising is being conducted now for the following commodities: Jewelry, electrical machinery and supplies, musical instruments, foodstuffs, canned milk, confectionery, soda water, toilet and pharmaceutical products, furniture, wall paper, carpets, wines and liquors, lumber, stoves, storage batteries, woolen goods, cable communication, department-store wares, and insurance.

Spanish is the principal language used in broadcasting. The administrator of station OAX states that records prepared in the English language could not be used effectively, since that language is understood by only a small percentage of the population.

URUGUAY

By Assistant Trade Commissioner Grant L. Thrall, Montevideo

All the more important radio broadcasting stations in Uruguay, except those owned and operated by the Government, depend to a large degree on commercial advertising for their financial support.

The original broadcasting stations were established to popularize radio and stimulate the sale of receiving sets, but later on they engaged in commercial broadcasting. As the number of listeners increased, other stations were built, primarily for entertainment and advertising purposes.

There were 27 licensed broadcasting stations and an estimated number of 60,000 installed receiving sets in Uruguay at the end of July, 1931. One of the most popular stations in the Republic is the Government's CX6, known as "Estacion Oficial," which broadcasts a program of entertainment twice daily. This official station does not accept advertising for its financial support, and maintenance is assured by revenues obtained from an import duty levied on phonographs, records, and radio apparatus.

The principal stations in the field of commercial advertising are considered to be "Radio Uruguay," CX26; "Radio Westinghouse," CX12; "Radio General Electric," CX14; "Radio Monte Carlo," CX20; and the "Difusora Colon," CX18—all located in Montevideo. However, all other stations located in Montevideo also do commercial broadcasting. Radio stations at interior points in the Republic are not important as commercial broadcasters.

Good talent for radio work is available, but its employment is limited. The fees paid to individual musicians, singers, other entertainers, and orchestras are low when judged by American standards, but they represent a heavy item of expense to the broadcasting stations in Uruguay.

One of the stations which has been employing talent to a greater extent than is generally customary states that a single singer, musician, or other entertainer of ordinary ability usually receives 4 to 5 pesos for 15 minutes' work; a 5-piece string orchestra, 10 to 15 pesos for 15 minutes' broadcast; a 5-piece orchestra, 300 pesos a week for one hour of entertainment daily; and group singers (6 persons), 27 pesos for a 30-minute broadcast. The highest price it has paid to a single entertainer was 65 pesos for a 30-minute broadcast.

Advertising rates, however, are relatively low. As advertisers are not yet accustomed to buy time and hire their own talent, phonograph records are used to a large degree.

No stations are in position at the present time to use the 33⅓ revolutions per minute records, but one station has already ordered the necessary equipment from the United States, while another is negotiating the purchase of such equipment. Other stations at some future date will undoubtedly install similar machines.

The standard 75 revolutions per minute phonograph records are in common use. Trials have been conducted with records containing advertising material with fairly satisfying results. The trial records, prepared in Spanish, were manufactured in Buenos Aires, Argentina.

Until such time as radio advertising methods in Uruguay undergo a marked improvement and advertisers show a willingness to sponsor programs, suitably prepared records of entertainment and advertising matter should prove to be effective in achieving results.

Station announcers now read a short article or repeat a sentence, prepared by the advertiser, prior to or at the conclusion of a short program of music or other entertainment furnished by the broadcasting station. Advertisers are just commencing to buy time and prepare their own programs. Consequently, the advertising rates of most commercial stations in Uruguay are still largely based on the number of words in the advertisement rather than on the length of a studio program. The rates quoted by the leading stations, their address, broadcasting hours, and authorized power are shown below. Practically all the stations operate only with a fractional part of their authorized power.

Radio Uruguay, CX26 and CX34; operated by Figueira, Canepa y Cia., Ave. Millan 2370, Montevideo. CX26: Power, 2,000 watts; broadcasting hours, 10 a. m. to 2 p. m. and 4 to 11 p. m. CX34: Power, 500 watts; broadcasting hours, 12 noon to 6 p. m. and 8 to 11 p. m. Rates are as follows:

Station and number of programs	Class A			Class B		
	1 hour	Half hour	Quarter hour	⅟ hour	Half hour	Quarter hour
STATION CX26 [1]						
Number of programs:	*Pesos*	*Pesos*	*Pesos*	*Pesos*	*Pesos*	*Pesos*
1	80. 00	48. 00	28. 80	56. 00	33. 60	20. 20
13	76. 00	45. 60	27. 40	53. 20	31. 90	19. 20
16	72. 00	43. 20	25. 90	50. 40	30. 20	18. 10
52	68. 00	40. 80	24. 50	47. 60	28. 60	17. 20
104 or more	64. 00	38. 40	23. 00	44. 80	26. 90	16. 10
STATION CX34 [2]						
Number of programs:						
1	56. 00	33. 60	20. 20	39. 20	23. 50	14. 20
13	53. 20	31. 90	19. 20	37. 30	22. 30	13. 40
26	50. 40	30. 20	18. 10	35. 30	21. 10	12. 70
52	47. 60	28. 60	17. 20	33. 30	20. 00	12. 00
104 or more	44. 80	26. 90	16. 10	31. 40	18. 80	11. 30

[1] Class A, 6 to 11 p. m.; class B, 10 a. m. to 2 p. m. and 4 to 6 p. m.
[2] Class A, 8 to 11 p. m.; class B, 12 to 6 p. m.

Radio Westinghouse, CX12; operated by Serratosa y Castells, Calle Itacabo 2620, Montevideo. Authorized power, 1,000 watts; broadcasting hours, 8 a. m. to 12 p. m. Rates in United States currency are shown in the table following. This station has a New York representative.

Hours	1 hour	Half hour	Quarter hour
8 to 11 a. m	$500	$325	$200
11 a. m. to 1 p. m	650	400	275
1 to 5 p. m	500	325	200
5 to 7 p. m	650	400	275
7 to 12 p. m	800	500	350

Radio General Electric, CX14; operated by General Electric S. A., Calle Juan Paullier Esq. Enrique Martinez, Mantevideo. Authorized power, 1,000 watts; broadcasting hours, 11 a. m. to 2 p. m. and 5 to 11.30 p. m. Rates:

Pesos per month

One short sentence of advertising per day_____ 30
One more complete sentence of advertising per day_____ 50
Two short sentences of advertising per day_____ 50
Two more complete sentences of advertising per day_____ 75
Various complete sentences of advertising per day_____ 100

Radio Monte Carlo, CX20; operated by Carlos L. Romay, Calle, Humberto No. 3, Montevideo. Authorized power, 2,000 watts. Broadcasting hours, 11 a. m. to 2.30 p. m. and 4 to 12 p. m. Rates:

Pesos per month

One advertisment per day_____ 30
Two advertisements per day_____ 40
Three advertisements per day_____ 50
 (No advertisement can exceed 30 words.)
One 15-minute broadcast interspersed with advertising_____ 150
One half-hour broadcast interspersed with advertising_____ 300

Difusora Colon, CX18; operated by Da Silva, Ravera & Bravo, Calle Rio Branco 1234, Montevideo. Authorized power, 750 watts; broadcasting hours, 8 to 9.30 a. m. and 11 a. m. to 12 p. m. Rates:

Phrases up to 5 words, 4.50 pesos per month per phrase.
Phrases from 6 to 10 words, 8 pesos per month per phrase.
Phrases from 11 to 15 words, 11.25 pesos per month per phrase.
For greater number of words up to 50, conventional rates.
From 5 to 9 announcements daily, 10 per cent discount.
15-minute broadcast interspersed with advertising, 65 pesos per month.

The stations considered of secondary importance quoting definite advertising rates are those shown below.

Radio Nacional, CX30; operated by Carlos Silva, Ave. Italia 3325, Montevideo. Authorized power, 250 watts; broadcasting hours, 12 noon to 5 p. m. and 7 to 11 p. m. Rates:

Pesos per month

1 advertisement daily_____ 15
2 advertisements daily_____ 20
3 advertisements daily_____ 25
4 advertisements daily_____ 30
5 advertisements daily_____ 35
8 advertisements daily_____ 50
16 advertisements daily_____ 75
A 15-minute broadcast daily interspersed with advert'sing_____ 65
 (Text of advertising can not exceed 35 words.)

Radio Centenario, CX36; operated by Defilippi, Walder & Cia., Calle Ignacio Nuñez 2133. Montevideo. Authorized power, 250 watts; broadcasting hours, 9.30 a. m. to 12 p. m. Rates:

Pesos per month

15-minute program daily_____ 80. 00
Phrases, per word_____ . 80
Minimum advertising rates_____ 20. 00

Stajano y Castro, Calle Misiones 1488, Montevideo, has recently developed a simultaneous radio-broadcasting scheme. This firm purchases broadcasting time from 12 different stations and in turn sells it to advertisers whose programs are put on the air simultaneously by 3 or more stations. The rates quoted, ranging from 3 to 12 stations, are as follows:

One advertisement of 20 words—	Number of stations			
	12	9	6	3
	Pesos	*Pesos*	*Pesos*	*Pesos*
1 day	15	12	9	5
3 consecutive days	40	35	26	14
4 consecutive days	50	43	32	18
7 consecutive days or in 2 separate periods	70	58	44	24
12 consecutive days or in 3 or 4 separate periods	85	70	52	30
16 consecutive days or in 3 or 4 separate periods	95	80	60	35
30 consecutive days	120	100	75	45

To date only local firms are using broadcast advertising.

The Spanish language is used exclusively. Broadcasting records prepared by individuals familiar with the Spanish terminology of the River Plate area, could be effectively used in this country. English-language records would not be satisfactory, for only a very small percentage of the radio listeners have a knowledge of English.

VENEZUELA

By Rolland Welch, Assistant Trade Commissioner, Caracas

There is only one radio broadcasting station in Venezuela, known as "Broadcasting Caracas," with call letters 1–BC and a wave length of 312.3 meters or 960 kilocycles.

This station is partially owned by a radio and phonograph distributing firm (representing an American manufacturer) and was put on the air principally to incite interest in radio and to increase sales of radio receivers. In this the station soon proved successful and has for several months been broadcasting advertising programs. It is proving a popular medium and many local firms are now using it. Of course, the phonograph and radio business is also advertised, but these are the only foreign products being exploited on the air at present.

The station is popular and reaches all of Venezuela except one or two "blind spots" in the mountains around Maracay and Malencia. Its programs are also received in Porto Rico, Colombia, and other near-by sections and have been heard as far away as New York.

It is planned to increase the power of the station. Short-wave apparatus has been ordered also, and upon its installation the programs will be broadcast simultaneously on both long and short waves.

At present, in addition to its own local features, the station occasionally picks up the programs of the Schenectady (N. Y.) short-wave station and rebroadcasts them here on long waves.

It is believed that the local station affords a fair medium for advertising calculated to reach the middle and better classes with sufficient buying power to own radio receivers. It is expected that interest in radio in this country will increase rapidly. The owners of the station are directly interested in increasing the use of radio sets and will do what they can to keep programs interesting. It is not unlikely, therefore, that this station will grow to be a favorable advertising medium.

The present regular rates are: 220 bolivars [4] per hour, 110 bolivars per half hour, and 60 bolivars per quarter hour, applicable on a six-month contract. Programs are broadcast daily from 4 to 5 p. m. and from 7.45 to 11 p. m. except Saturdays and Sundays. The afternoon programs are phonograph records. Special rates are offered for advertisers on the afternoon programs. These rates are quoted at 500 bolivars a month, with programs broadcast for one hour each afternoon except Saturday and Sunday.

Prize fights and other sporting events are sometimes broadcast Saturday and Sunday afternoons.

There seems to be ample local talent available. The talent is hardly comparable with, or rather is not of the same type as that in the larger cities of the United States, but it is reasonably satisfactory. The station has a staff of artists under yearly contract. Their salaries are not known. Some local talent can be had without cost, broadcasting being a novelty that many are willing to engage in because of personal pleasure or publicity.

Regular phonograph records are picked up from machines operated at regular speeds. The station has no connection with any advertising agency. Local cigarette and beer manufacturers and local retailers use the station for advertising purposes.

The Spanish language should be used, since the number of listeners understanding English is negligible.

---

[4] A bolivar at par equals 19.3 cents in United States currency.

NORTH AMERICA

COSTA RICA

By American Consul David J. D. Myers, San Jose

Advertising by radio has not yet become well established as a commercial activity, but there are two stations which have recently broadcast some commercial programs and are open for engagements. These are: Costa Rica Radio & Broadcasting Station, San Jose, call letters TITR, comprised of one 500-watt long-wave and one 250-watt short-wave apparatus; and an amateur station operated by Señor Gonzalo Pinto, San Jose, call letters TI1GP, 250 watts, long wave.

The Costa Rica Radio & Broadcasting Station charges $50 per hour for broadcasting advertising, and Señor Gonzalo Pinto, $10 per hour. Orchestras are available at a cost of about $2.50 per hour. Records can be used at half the regular rates, at a speed of either 75 or 33⅓ revolutions per minute.

Broadcasting must be in the Spanish language to be of real value. The results obtainable from English-language records would be practically negligible.

CUBA

By Rafael W. Bornn, Office of the American Trade Commissioner, Habana

Broadcast advertising in Cuba, although offering good prospects for the future, has not yet been developed efficiently as a whole. With few exceptions, stations are not properly equipped. Rates are low, since many stations costing as little as $1,000 or less operate in private homes with inadequate studio facilities, and they lack proper technical and artistic direction.

Thus far commercial licenses have been granted on the minimum capacity of 150 watts—based solely on the nominal capacity of the tubes. From now on, more stringent regulations will be required. A reasonable period of time is being given the plants now functioning for improving their circuits and for installing proper equipment. This will tend to make transmission plants more costly and will have its effect on the cost of advertising.

The consensus of station managers is that advertisers have not been educated to the effectiveness of broadcast advertising. They state that advertisers refuse to analyze the various features surrounding broadcasting, such as the quality of programs, the effectiveness of the stations, or the class of people to whom their advertisements appeal. To some extent this attitude has been fostered by certain isolated cases of unusual success that accompanied commercial programs over small stations when special premiums were offered to listeners.

There are in all about 60 broadcasting stations in Cuba, about 17 of which, located in Habana and its suburbs, do commercial broadcasting. A good many of these small stations work under amateurs' licenses, and one of the principal features of the proposed radio law is the regulation of this phase of broadcasting. The radio bureau of the Cuban Department of Communications has already reduced considerably this encroachment on the business of stations working under commercial licenses.

Several small-powered commercial stations occupy the same channels at different hours. On the Habana stations alone, about 60 special "hours" are known to be broadcast, with possibly two or three dozen additional. These are managed by individuals or advertising agencies which generally do their own announcing and which use mechanical music for the cheaper advertisements and local talent for the more expensive programs. Almost every kind of product, of both foreign and local manufacture, is advertised in these special "hours," and when mechanical music is used, the aggregate number of establishments or brands advertised at times is over 20 in an hour.

The following commercial stations in Habana are considered the most prominent and popular from an advertising standpoint:

Station and operator	Kilocycles	Meters	Watts
CMC, Cuban Telephone Co	840	357	500
CMK, Cuban Broadcasting Co	730	411	2,000
CMW, Diario de la Marina	600	500	1,000
CMBZ, M. & G. Salas	1,010	297	150
CMBC, El Progreso Cubano	1,000	265.3	150
CMCB, La Metropolitana	1,070	280.2	150

PROGRAMS

Very good local talent is available, but thus far this has been used by only a scattered few among the important advertisers. The majority of these artists charge from $30 to $50 per concert, although some are at present working for less, owing to the scarcity of engagements.

The personnel used by one station includes comedians from a well-known Cuban stock company specializing in theatrical representations of native color almost exclusively. Its up-to-date offerings in dialogue are as popular in Cuba as similar dialogue programs in the United States.

Some stations emphatically state that only Cuban music, or popular music, is effective. Many others rate classical music as of some importance. In general, the stations, large and small, that are most popular are the ones managed by concerns whose tastes are more refined and whose advertisements are being heard in the best households. These stations advertise high-class products like automobiles, radios, etc.

Advertisements being broadcast embrace women's wear, laundry soap, a pineapple drink, merchants of Galiano Street, merchants of Neptuno Street, cameras and photographic supplies, phonographs, radios, a weekly magazine, a sports journal, a daily newspaper, motion-picture theaters, an advertising agency, and a wide variety of other subjects.

Records are commonly used, in which cases the rates are lower than those charged when orchestral or other entertainment is furnished. All stations using records are equipped for 78 revolutions per minute only, with the exception of CMK, which is also equipped for 33⅓ revolutions per minute. Stations CMK, CMBZ, and CMCY have adequate equipment for electrical transcriptions, and it is reported that others contemplate installing it.

LANGUAGE

Spanish is used principally in Cuban broadcasting, although all the important stations have English-speaking announcers. Records prepared in the English language would not be fully effective. One small station advertises an "American hour," which is announced by a Latin American who speaks good English and uses that language about half of the time he is on the air. The "American" flavor, however, is given by a preponderance of American dance music from records, which is extremely popular.

RATES

The quoted rates of station CMC of the Cuban Telephone Co. are as follows:

For 3 months, 1 hour per week	$1, 300
For 3 months, half hour per week	780
For 6 months, 1 hour per week	2, 550
For 6 months, half hour per week	1, 550
For 9 months, 1 hour per week	3, 700
For 9 months, half hour per week	2, 225
For 1 year, 1 hour per week	4, 825
For 1 year, half hour per week	2, 900

In cases where contracts do not call for any of the above periods, the hour is charged at the rate of $100 and the half hour at the rate of $60.

The quoted rates of station CMK, Hotel Plaza, are: $50 per hour when artists are furnished; $100 per month for economic ads consisting of 3 texts at night and 3 during the day; $50 per month for economic ads consisting of 1 text at night and 3 during the day; $30 per hour for use of the station without artists

The quoted rates of station CMW, Diario de la Marina, are: $75 per hour when artists are furnished; $25 per hour for use of station without artists; $240 per month for 1 hour daily of mechanical music; $60 per month for economic ads, consisting of approximately 10 words each, 4 texts per day; combined programs of mechanical music and that furnished by artists will be contracted for on a three-months' basis at lower rates.

The quoted rates of station CMBZ, M. & G. Salas, are: $35, $40, and $50 per hour in accordance with the artists to be furnished by the station; business ads from $75 to $125 per month, according to the length of text and number of times it is mentioned; these business advertisements are broadcast each day except Sunday.

The quoted rates of station CMBC, El Progreso Cubano, are: $25 per hour, the station furnishing artists; $6.50 per hour using mechanical music; $60 per month for business ads, two texts daily, mechanical music being employed.

The quoted rates of station CMCB, La Metropolitana, are: One concert daily of one hour's duration, $20; one concert daily of one-half hour's duration, $12; one concert alternating days of one hour's duration, $22; one concert alternating days of one-half hour's duration, $13; one concert weekly of one hour's duration, $26; one concert weekly of one-half hour's duration, $14. The artists or orchestras will be selected by the station, otherwise the prices will be subject to special agreement. Under the above schedule, 10 numbers are given per hour when singers are used and 8 numbers per hour when orchestras are used, with announcements between numbers.

Station CMCB, when furnishing record music, the customer having the priviledge of selecting numbers, charges the following rates: One concert daily of one hour's duration, $200 monthly; one concert daily of one-half hour's duration, $125 monthly; one concert every other day, one hour's duration, $125 monthly; one concert every other day, one-half hour's duration, $80 monthly. Business announcements between regular programs: Three business ads daily, $75 monthly; two business ads daily, $50 monthly; one business ad daily, $25 monthly. Texts are not to be composed of more than 50 words. No contracts for a period less than three months are made. Payments are required monthly in advance.

DOMINICAN REPUBLIC

By American Vice Consul Hedley V. Cooke, jr., Santo Domingo

There is but one broadcasting station in the Dominican Republic, station HIX of the Estación Radiodifusora de Santa Domingo, at Santo Domingo.

Station HIX has, according to the most reliable estimates, about 3,000 listeners. To judge by the present sales of radio-receiving sets in the Republic, it is likely that this number will continue to increase for sometime to come. At present programs are given twice a week, on Tuesdays and Fridays, from 8 to 10 p. m. They are devoted to singing, orchestral selections, and speeches, concerning the industrial and agricultural possibilities of the Dominican Republic. The director of this station states that the number of programs will soon be increased and that in any case there is ample room for expansion to meet whatever demand for additional advertisement may be forthcoming.

At present the advertising rates of the station are quoted as follows, provided the advertising consists of music and songs: Quarter hour, $25; half hour, $35; one hour, $60.

The following prices are now being paid by the station to its performers: Orchestra (15 musicians), $30; singers (trio), $6; recitations (2 persons), $5. All rates are by the hour or fraction thereof.

Phonograph records have not yet been used for advertising. Their use is contemplated, and the director states that he will be pleased to accept advertisements in Spanish and English by this medium. It is, however, greatly doubted whether English records could be employed at all effectively.

They should be recorded for a speed of 72 revolutions per minute for use over this station. Rates for the use of phonograph records are as follows: For a program not to exceed 15 minutes in duration, $25; for one record, $5.

The Estación Radiodifusora de Santo Domingo has at present no contract with any advertising agency. The manager states that he is now negotiating with an American agency with a view to obtaining a contract.

Advertisements for the following are being broadcast: Grain products, mattresses, food products, two brands of American cigarettes, American radios, and phonograph records, hotels, theaters, and a correspondence school.

Station HIX has a wave length of 475 meters, a frequency of 625 kilocycles, and power of 1,000 watts.

GUATEMALA

By Commercial Attaché Merwin L. Bohan, Guatemala City

An American firm is endeavoring to obtain from the Government of Guatemala a concession and, if successful, will establish a broadcasting station here which will undoubtedly accept commercial advertising. Likewise a resident individual is considering the possibility of putting up a small broadcasting station, but as yet nothing definite has been arranged.

HAITI

By American Consul Donald R. Heath, Port au Prince

There is one broadcasting station in Haiti, station HHK, operating on a wave length of 325.9 meters, a frequency of 920 kilocycles, and with power of 1,000 watts. The station is owned by the Haitian Government and is operated by the department of public works under the direction of an officer of the United States Navy.

Commercial advertising is accepted and the rates are as follows for local firms: One hour, four times a month, $50; half hour, four times a month, $30. Rates for United States programs are: For a half hour, once a month $20, twice a month $35, three times a month $50, four times a month $60; for one hour once a month $35, twice a month $60, three times a month $90, and four times a month $120.

Local talent is available, but is not abundant, nor is it, with the exception of a few performers, of very good quality or popularity. Two local firms owned by Americans offered, in 1930, programs of music once each week, consisting of singing, violin, piano, etc. Later on, these programs consisted solely of record reproductions.

The rate per hour for a 10-piece orchestra is $20, and for singers $10. Performers have no fixed tariff, but in most cases would be satisfied with a few dollars per performance.

Records are used for occasional programs. However, station HHK is not equipped especially for the broadcasting of recorded music. When recorded programs are broadcast the ordinary speed of the phonograph is used.

The local station has never contracted with any firm or agency for the sale of broadcasting time. There are at present no local companies using the broadcasting facilities, nor are any firms contemplating engaging time in the near future. A reason lies in the extremely severe business depression which Haiti is undergoing.

The Haitian Government several years ago contemplated installing public address stations in 14 towns and cities throughout Haiti, through which programs of music and educational talks would be presented to the inhabitants of the Provinces. These stations were to be set up in the public markets or parks of each city and town and the programs sent via telephone to the amplifiers.

Of the 14 stations proposed, only 8 were installed and at present only 2 are in operation. It has been ascertained that the country people evince little interest in the programs offered. This fact has tended to discourage attempts on the part of the Government, which now regards the project as having been a waste of funds. The removal of the eight installed stations is proposed by the present director of radio activities.

In short, radio advertising in Haiti is dormant. There has been a steady increase in the number of radio receiving sets, but it is estimated that there are only about 200 in the hands of Haitians and non-American foreigners.

Among the 1,200 American men, women, and children here in connection with the American occupation of Haiti (mainly families of officers and enlisted men of the United States Navy and Marine Corps) radios are frequent, but they are tuned to American stations and only rarely on the infrequent programs of the local station.

The official language of Haiti is French, which is spoken by the literate 10 or 15 per cent of the population. The speech of the mass of the people, however, is "Créole." Monologues in this tongue are broadcast occasionally by a local comedian on the regular Friday night program of station HHK and are popular among the lower classes.

Phonograph records of American manufacture, consisting of dance music and classics, when broadcast, are very popular among all classes. English is understood by comparatively few Haitians, and programs in that language would be of little interest. A small number of Haitian families own receiving sets, but they tune in on those American stations offering musical programs.

HONDURAS

By American Vice Consul R. Austin Acly, Tegucigalpa

There is one commercial broadcasting station in Honduras, at Tegucigalpa, this being station HRB, which is operated by the Tropical Radio Telegraph Co., of Boston, Mass. According to the statements of the company, the station has a range covering Central America, Mexico, and parts of South America. It is also claimed that radio is an excellent form of advertising within the station's range because of the interest of the people in radio programs and the frequent custom of using loud speakers in the parks of most of the cities.

The rates for broadcasting musical programs over station HRB are quoted as follows:

Time	Cost per program			
	Once	13 times	26 times	52 times
Before 6 p. m.:				
15-minute program	$12. 50	$12. 00	$11. 50	$11. 00
30-minute program	20. 00	19. 00	18. 00	17. 00
1-hour program	35. 00	33. 50	31. 00	29. 50
After 6 p. m.:				
15-minute program	15. 00	14. 00	13. 00	12. 00
30-minute program	27. 50	26. 00	24. 50	23. 00
1-hour program	50. 00	47. 50	45. 00	42. 50

These rates include only the broadcasting facilities of the station and the services of the station announcers.

For announcements and talks, the rates for the facilities and announcers are quoted as follows:

Time	Cost per announcement			
	Once	13 times	26 times	52 times
1 minute	$3.00	$2.75	$2.20	$1.85
5 minutes	10.00	9.50	9.00	8.50
10 minutes	15.00	14.00	13.00	12.00

Announcements of 100 to 150 words are made during special musical programs after 6 p. m. at the following quoted rates, per month: Once daily, except Sunday, $50; four times per week, $40; three times per week, $30; two times per week, $20.

Local talent is available at the station. The rates charged per hour are quoted as follows: Studio ensemble (5 pieces), $25; instrumental soloists, $10; vocal soloists, $10; marimba band (12 pieces), $50; string quartet, $25; accompanists for soloists, $5.

All material and talent must be submitted for the approval of the station management, whose judgment is reported to be based on public interest, good entertainment, and accoustical characteristics. After a program has been accepted by the station management, there must be no deviation from the manuscript as approved. Contracts will not be made for any period longer than one year. They are also subject to the laws and regulations of Honduras. Contracts will be subject to cancellation unless the program starts within 60 days, and the management reserves the right to refuse to accept any advertising or to discontinue advertising programs when contrary to public order, interest, or convenience.

Programs can be arranged by the station management subject to the approval of the advertiser. In such cases talent will be engaged and paid by the station, and the cost charged to the advertiser, who may indicate in writing the type of program desired and the maximum expense to be incurred.

On broadcasts by foreign advertisers, manuscripts and programs must be submitted to the station management one month in advance of date on which they are scheduled to be given.

Records may be used in advertising programs, the rates charged being the same as those for broadcasting musical programs. Station HRB is equipped to use records of either 33⅓ or 78 revolutions per minute.

The station sells broadcasting facilities directly to advertisers. Communications on the subject of contracts should be addressed to the manager of station HRB, Tegucigalpa, Honduras. Inquiries would undoubtedly be answered by the Tropical Radio Telegraph Co., Boston, Mass.

Enterprises now patronizing the station include commission agencies, radio and phonograph dealers, local stores, automobile dealers, and local concerns offering either commodities or services.

It is recommended that the Spanish language be used. The station has a range which would reach parts of English-speaking countries, but the majority of those reached understand only Spanish. English records may be used, but it is believed that it would be worth the cost to have them prepared in Spanish. Station announcements are made in both English and Spanish.

MEXICO

By Arch F. Coleman, Assistant Trade Commissioner, Mexico City

Commercial broadcasting had its inception in Mexico in 1925, when two stations of low power were installed to advertise the interests of their owners. One of those stations was short lived, but the other, XEB, owned and operated by the Buen Tono cigarette factory of Mexico City, is still in operation. It has kept abreast of the development in radio equipment, and although its rated power is only 1,000 watts, it is considered one of the best stations in the country. As late as 1929 Mexico could boast of no more than a mere handful of commercial stations, but the last 18 months have seen the number jump with phenomenal rapidity until now no less than 30 stations are broadcasting commercial programs. In addition, 10 official and political stations are broadcasting educational and entertainment features. Within the last six months four commercial stations have ceased operation.

Mexican commercial stations range in power from 30 to 10,000 watts, and their popularity and patronage are scaled nearly parallel to their potency. Low-powered receiving sets in Mexico City find ample program range to satisfy the tastes of their owners, but more powerful sets are essential to the pleasure of the radio audience in the interior cities of the Republic. Mexican talent is concentrated in the capital city to a much greater extent than American talent is concentrated in any one city, hence the Mexico City programs are the ones most popular. Those advertisers who sell their products throughout the country, therefore, generally have given consideration to the centrally located units with sufficient power to reach the major portion of Mexico.

Remote stations of low power, however, also present artists of talent. The Mexican people are musical and romantic, and any town of sufficient prominence to have a broadcasting unit has no difficulty in providing singers and musicians. In addition, the use of records makes it possible for even the smallest station to transmit a program of real excellence. All Mexican commercial stations, and most of the official stations, are equipped with turntables and electric pickups. All can use records made for 78 revolutions per minute. Stations XEB, XEN, XETO, and XEW, at Mexico City, can handle records at a speed of $33\frac{1}{3}$ revolutions per minute. The broadcasting studios of XEW are located in the Olympia Motion-Picture Theater, and arrangements can be made to use the theater turntables. Record programs carry cheaper rates than the programs that employ living artists.

Broadcasting studios are constructed on modern principles. Materials and designs are selected to eliminate echo and foreign noises. All broadcasting equipment is of American manufacture, and the arrangement of a centrally located studio transmitting through a plant located at some distance from the city's dynamos and street cars is customary.

LOCAL TALENT

Mexico City has available musical talent of all kinds. There are police and military bands which enjoy enviable reputations; the symphony orchestra is excellent, and its members are available for solos or chamber music; certain local tenors, sopranos, and contraltos have splendid reputations by virtue of their phonograph records which have been sent to all Latin countries; native orchestras employing zithers, guitars, violins, and marimbas are numerous; and dance orchestras playing the latest jazz are available. Local artists are supplemented by visiting troupes which are usually unhampered by contract restrictions and are free to broadcast. Records of the world's best music are used in many programs, alternating with some living artist. Station XEB generally devotes Sunday mornings to the albums of well-known operas which have been recorded.

Comic dialogue is rare. English is a language which lends itself to puns, slang, and humor with great ease, but Spanish does not, and it would be extremely difficult to carry on humorous dialogue which would not, inadvertently perhaps, be offensive to good taste. Two local comedians who enjoy great popularity on the stage have tried to broadcast, but their radio dialogue, hampered by many necessary restrictions, has not met with equal success.

RECEPTION

Mexico first began to import receiving sets in quantity in 1926, and the yearly influx of such equipment has shown a rapid rise. In the United States it is estimated that four persons are served by each receiving set in use, but the number is greater in Mexico. Some dealers state that an average of seven or more persons can be reached by each receiver. It is estimated that there are 100,000 sets in use.

Two separate Mexican institutions have been responsible for placing good receiving sets in places where the general public can hear radio programs. These are the Mexican Government and the breweries. The Department of Education has placed more than 700 sets in Mexican schools in the last year, and the Department of Industry has furnished receivers for workmen's centers. The breweries are placing good equipment in the saloons which dispense their beer. In the outlying districts the cantinas always entertain a crowd listening to political talks, educational propaganda, music, and, incidentally, advertising, many of the listeners can not read or write.

EXTENT OF RADIO ADVERTISING

In the growth of radio advertising Mexican big business has borne the brunt of the burden. For a long time only those organizations which were fortunate in their control of capital could afford to experiment, and the cost was hardly worth the result. Now, however, even small retail shops are buying programs or short announcements, and the returns have been gratifying. Advertisers realize that any person of sufficient means to own a radio set is a prospective customer for all of those products customarily sold at retail. The large department stores have taken great interest in radio possibilities, and they are continually advertising their sales, bargains, and staples over this medium. The radio audience in Mexico now learns of the qualities of an American radio; that an American insecticide will free their kitchens of roaches; that the Centro Mercantil has the best bargains in ladies' hats; that a talking-machine hour is sponsored by the Mexico Music Co.; that Aguila or Buen Tono cigarettes are as good as any imported brand; that a well-known light six is the car of their dreams; and many other statements which by repetition can not fail to build up a preference in the minds of consumers.

Mexican stations maintain their own advertising staffs and do not, as a rule, contract with independent agencies. The business seems to be enjoying a steady growth, and competition between stations is becoming keen. Prices for time are on the increase, and it is usually sold on a basis which provides that the station shall furnish the artists as well as the use of the equipment. Owners are impressing the large Mexican business organizations with the importance of their service, and they are soliciting American advertising. They are trying two languages for certain products, first in Spanish and then a translation in English, and working hard to establish radio as an institution.

The table following gives important data regarding Mexican stations and the commercial use of their facilities.

COMMERCIAL RADIO STATIONS OF MEXICO, 1931

Station	Location	Power, in watts	Wave length, in kilo-cycles	Advertising rates, in Mexican pesos [1]
XEA	Guadalajara	101	1,200	1 hour, 30.
XEB	Mexico City	1,000	1,030	50 words morning, 2.50; 50 words evening, 5; 1 hour morning, 50; 1 hour evening, 100; musical program, from 50 pesos per half hour to 300 per hour.
XEC	Toluca	50	1,333	1 hour, 25 to 37.50; 50 words, 1.25.
XED	Reynosa	10,000	960.6	10 words (first), 2; each additional word, 0.20; hour rates from 200 to 300; fractions in proportion.
XEF	Oaxaca	105	1,132	100 words, 2; 200 words, 3; 1 hour, 15.
XEH	Monterrey	5,000	1,080	1 hour, 43.50 to 50; 10 words morning, 1.25; 10 words evening, 2.50.
XEI	Morelia	101	1,000	Private station for use of owners only.
XEJ	Ciudad Juarez	101	857.1	1 hour, 42.50 to 75; 50 words, 2.50.
XEK	Mexico City	101	990	1 hour, 50 to 75; 50 words, 2.50.
XEL	Saltillo	30	1,091	1 hour with artists, 25; 1 hour with records, 10; 50 words, 1.25.
XEM	Tampico	501	730	
XEN	Mexico City	1,000	711	Half hour, 90; 1 hour, 150; sliding scale for contracts; 25 words 10 times, 6 each; 25 words 100 times, 4 each.
XEO	do	5,000	940	No advertising.
XEP	Nuevo Laredo	200	1,400	1 hour, day, 30; 1 hour, night, 40; 100 words, 3; sliding scale for contracts.
XEQ	Ciudad Juarez	1,000	1,015	
XES [2]	Tampico	500	890	1 hour, night, 35; 1 hour, day, 40 per cent discount; announcement, 2.50.
XET [2]	Monterrey	500	630	Same as XES.
XEU [2]	Vera Cruz	101	800	1 hour, day, 15; 1 hour, night, 25; 25 words, 1.25.
XEV	Puebla	101	1,034.4	1 hour 50, 50 words, 2.40.
XEW [2]	Mexico City	5,000	780	1 hour, morning, 150; 1 hour, afternoon, 200; 1 hour, evening, 250; sliding scale for contracts; 10 words, daytime, 4; 50 words, daytime, 10; 100 words, day time, 16.
XEX	do	500	1,210	1 hour, daytime, 33.50; 1 hour, night, 67; 50 words, daytime, 2; 50 words, night, 4.
XEY	Merida	105	546.8	No advertising.
XEZ	Mexico City	500	588.2	
XEFB	Monterrey	50	1,280	1 hour, records, 20; announcements, day, 0.65; announcements, night, 1.25.
XEFE	Nuevo Laredo	101	980	
XETA	Mexico City	500	1,140	1 hour, morning, 33.50; 1 hour, evening, 67; 50 words, 2 and 4.
XETF	Vera Cruz	500	680	1 hour, day, 50; 1 hour, night, 66; price per word, 0.06
XETO	Mexico City	101	1,485	
XETY	do	2,000	1,300	Per hour, 100 and 150; 50 words, 5.

[1] The peso equals approximately 49 cents at par.   [2] Member of Mexican music chain.

PORTO RICO

By Darwin De Golia, Assistant Trade Commissioner, San Juan

There is only one broadcasting station in Porto Rico, that of the Porto Rico Telephone Co. at San Juan. Operating on 500 watts, station WKAQ goes on the air three nights a week.

The hourly rate for station time is $30. Half an hour costs $18 and 15 minutes $10. This charge is for the station only and includes the services of the announcer but no talent.

Local talent of a quality comparable with that in continental States is difficult to find. There are one or two dance orchestras that can perform creditably, particularly with Porto Rican dances, and there are a few vocalists of acceptable ability. There are no comedians generally acknowledged as such and no special performers. The interesting music of the native " jibaro " or mountaineer can be rendered authoritatively, and it has a fair popularity among local listeners.

For an hour's entertainment a week, an advertiser should be able to get together a program of local talent that would be interesting to Porto Rican listeners. An orchestra would cost about $30 or $35 an hour. Rates for singers vary with their estimated ability, but $5 a performance would probably attract a satisfactory one. Announcements are given in either Spanish or English or both without extra charge for announcing or translating.

The studio is equipped at present to broadcast 8 and 10 inch phonograph records at 78 revolutions per minute. It is not now prepared to broadcast records at 33⅓ revolutions per minute but will add this equipment as soon as a contract to broadcast such material makes it necessary. There is no difference in studio charges for record broadcasting.

The local station has done broadcast advertising, but heretofore only for local business houses. It has not broadcast any material received directly from the States, although American products have been advertised by local stores almost exclusively. The local station has no exclusive contract with any agent to sell time.

The station estimates that its radio audience is made up of 25 per cent English-speaking and 75 per cent Spanish-speaking listeners. For the musical or vocal program broadcast, the announcer usually makes his statements first in English, then in Spanish.

The station estimates an audience of 25,000. It can be heard clearly in all parts of Porto Rico and reasonably well in the eastern part of the Dominican Republic and the Virgin Islands. On 4 a. m. tests it has been reported from distant parts of the world, but during the evening hours it is drowned out by powerful United States stations, except within a 75-mile radius. United States stations are usually not received in Porto Rico before dark, however, so that any broadcasting over the local station in the afternoon would have a sure audience of local set owners and would probably be more effective than an evening broadcast, particularly in reaching women.

ESTIMATE OF RADIO RECEIVING SETS

The figures in the following statement are based on estimates as of July, 1931 which were secured by representatives of the Department of State and Department of Commerce from local trade sources.

North America:

Bahamas	300
Barbados	250
Bermuda	700
British Honduras	82
Canal Zone	300
Costa Rica	250
Cuba	28, 875
Dominican Republic	1, 375
French West Indies	100
Guatemala	250
Haiti	1, 000
Honduras	86
Jamaica	250
Mexico	100, 000
Netherland West Indies	50
Nicaragua	50
Panama	300
Porto Rico	5, 000

North America—Continued.

Salvador	1, 000
Trinidad and Tobago	40
Virgin Islands	50

South America:

Argentina	400, 000
Bolivia	100
Brazil	190, 000
British Guiana	25
Chile	35, 000
Colombia	5, 000
Ecuador	150
Falkland Islands	16
French Guiana	8
Paraguay	150
Peru	70, 000
Surinam	18
Uruguay	60, 000
Venezuela	2, 500

(30)

HISTORY OF BROADCASTING:
Radio To Television
An Arno Press/New York Times Collection

Archer, Gleason L.
Big Business and Radio. 1939.

Archer, Gleason L.
History of Radio to 1926. 1938.

Arnheim, Rudolf.
Radio. 1936.

Blacklisting: Two Key Documents. 1952–1956.

Cantril, Hadley and Gordon W. Allport.
The Psychology of Radio. 1935.

Codel, Martin, editor.
Radio and Its Future. 1930.

Cooper, Isabella M.
Bibliography on Educational Broadcasting. 1942.

Dinsdale, Alfred.
First Principles of Television. 1932.

Dunlap, Orrin E., Jr.
Marconi: The Man and His Wireless. 1938.

Dunlap, Orrin E., Jr.
The Outlook for Television. 1932.

Fahie, J. J.
A History of Wireless Telegraphy. 1901.

Federal Communications Commission.
Annual Reports of the Federal Communications Commission.
1934/1935–1955.

Federal Radio Commission.
Annual Reports of the Federal Radio Commission. 1927–1933.

Frost, S. E., Jr.
Education's Own Stations. 1937.

Grandin, Thomas.
The Political Use of the Radio. 1939.

Harlow, Alvin.
Old Wires and New Waves. 1936.

Hettinger, Herman S.
A Decade of Radio Advertising. 1933.

Huth, Arno.
Radio Today: The Present State of Broadcasting. 1942.

Jome, Hiram L.
Economics of the Radio Industry. 1925.

Lazarsfeld, Paul F.
Radio and the Printed Page. 1940.

Lumley, Frederick H.
Measurement in Radio. 1934.

Maclaurin, W. Rupert.
Invention and Innovation in the Radio Industry. 1949.

Radio: Selected A.A.P.S.S. Surveys. 1929–1941.

Rose, Cornelia B., Jr.
National Policy for Radio Broadcasting. 1940.

Rothafel, Samuel L. and Raymond Francis Yates.
Broadcasting: Its New Day. 1925.

Schubert, Paul.
The Electric Word: The Rise of Radio. 1928.

Studies in the Control of Radio: Nos. 1–6. 1940–1948.

Summers, Harrison B., editor.
Radio Censorship. 1939.

Summers, Harrison B., editor.
**A Thirty-Year History of Programs Carried on
National Radio Networks in the United States, 1926–1956.** 1958.

Waldrop, Frank C. and Joseph Borkin.
Television: A Struggle for Power. 1938.

White, Llewellyn.
The American Radio. 1947.

World Broadcast Advertising: Four Reports. 1930–1932.